HITLER'S ROUTE
TO BAGDAD

HITLER'S ROUTE TO BAGDAD

PREPARED FOR THE INTERNATIONAL
RESEARCH SECTION OF THE
FABIAN SOCIETY

BY

BARBARA WARD

THE HON.
BARBARA BUCKMASTER
CLARE HOLLINGWORTH
VANDELEUR ROBINSON
LILO LINKE

Introduction by
LEONARD WOOLF

Maps by
J. F. HORRABIN

Essay Index Reprint Series

BOOKS FOR LIBRARIES PRESS
FREEPORT, NEW YORK

First Published 1939
Reprinted 1971

INTERNATIONAL STANDARD BOOK NUMBER:
0-8369-2046-5

LIBRARY OF CONGRESS CATALOG CARD NUMBER:
70-142624

PRINTED IN THE UNITED STATES OF AMERICA

CONTENTS

INTRODUCTION

By Leonard Woolf

THIS book, the work of five authors, is the result of a scheme of research initiated some time ago—not indeed so very long ago—by the International Research Section of the Fabian Society. Nothing could bring home to one more alarmingly the instability of Europe than the fact that in the course of months rather than years events themselves have more than once changed the face of Europe and therefore compelled us to revise our plan. Those who have read the documents relating to the official negotiations in July 1914 will remember that diplomatists or statesmen, desperately attempting to stop themselves slithering down the slope which was obviously leading them into war, from time to time helplessly remarked to one another that such and such a proposal had 'already been outstripped by events'. The kaleidoscope of 1939 is more alarmingly kaleidoscopic even than that of 1914. We must go back to the first decade of the nineteenth century to find a time at which the social, political, and territorial instability of Europe was as great as it is today. There are inhabitants of a good many states, with a long history behind them, who, when they go to bed at night, cannot be certain that their nationality will be the same when they wake up next morning. And the writer of a book on any nation of South-Eastern Europe knows that the whole of his work may be outstripped by events, that the nation about which he has written may have ceased to exist in the short interval between the correction of his proofs and the binding of his book.

At the time of the International Section's original scheme, we still thought of 'the Balkans', the Little Entente, and the

Balkan Pact. Our idea was to provide for the growing number of ordinary persons who desire some background of knowledge in international affairs a series of short studies of the Balkan countries. These studies were to give the facts regarding the history and the political and social structure of each country without which an intelligent understanding of the problems of its foreign policy and its position in the international kaleidoscope is impossible. The first product of this scheme was a study of Czechoslovakia by S. Grant Duff, which was published in pamphlet form, under the title *German and Czech: A Threat to European Peace*, at the end of 1937. That we had chosen rightly and that there was a need for the kind of information which it was our object to provide was shown by the reception of the pamphlet and by the events of the next twelve months. Czechoslovakia became the storm centre of Europe in 1938 and brought us all within a hair's breadth of war.

But the sequel showed the difficulty of carrying out our original scheme. Czechoslovakia has ceased to exist; Albania has practically disappeared; the Little Entente, the pivot of Balkan policy, is now nothing but the memory of a name; every Balkan state is politically and economically unstable. The reason for this is obvious. South-Eastern Europe has reverted to a system of sheer, unmitigated power politics. The independence, the existence of every state which lies between Nazi Germany and Bagdad is threatened; it is the ancient menace of Mittel-Europa or the *Drang nach Osten* revived in its most brutal form. That is what now gives a unity to these studies and an appropriate title to the book. The five countries dealt with here are Yugoslavia, Rumania, Bulgaria, Greece, and Turkey. If you look at Mr. Horrabin's maps, you will see at once that geography imposes upon them a unity. On the south-east they lie across Hitler's path to world empire; they form a bastion which must be taken by assault or induced to surrender if the fascist domination of Europe is to be completed.

This situation makes the need for a book of this kind all the greater. In international questions propaganda is so universal and so subtle that accurate facts about the political and economic contemporary situation in the various states of Europe are by no means easy to come by; yet without a knowledge of such facts it is impossible to understand what is happening or to come to an intelligent decision regarding policy. The object of the authors of these studies has been to provide such facts as accurately and impartially as possible.

The thanks of the Society are due to them for working on these studies and endeavouring by constant revision to outpace Hitler's progress. Also to J. F. Horrabin for the excellent series of original maps which illustrates this book, and to Dr. A. E. Mende for assisting with the Turkish chapter.

August, 1939   Fabian Society
                                                  11 Dartmouth St.
                                                  S.W.1

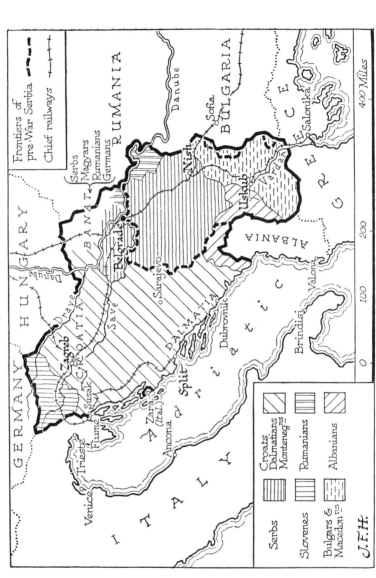

DISTRIBUTION OF RACES AND FRONTIER CHANGES IN YUGOSLAVIA

YUGOSLAVIA

BARBARA WARD

1. INTRODUCTION

IT is sometimes said that Yugoslavia is an artificial creation, a cardboard state brought into being by the arbitrary fiat of the victors of Versailles. This is quite untrue. The movement of South Slav nationalism which brought Serbs, Croats and Slovenes together in 1918 was a perfectly spontaneous one, and far from the victory of the Entente bringing about the union, the desire for this union was one of the preliminary causes of the war itself. The Allied victory created Yugoslavia only in so far as it brought about a necessary pre-condition of union, the collapse of the old Austro-Hungarian Empire under whose rule 8 out of the 14 million South Slavs were living up to 1918. And here again Allied responsibility is not absolute, for the internal decay and disintegration of Austria-Hungary (largely due to the South Slav movement) was one of the causes of the Allies' success.

The movement towards union was certainly spontaneous, but the fusion of Serb, Croat and Slovene into one state did not come about without friction, and the whole structure of the state has shown signs of strain ever since. That this is so is largely due to the history of the three South Slav peoples. Originally of the same Slav race, their historical development created certain definite lines of cleavage which could not be overcome in a day. All three had in the past sustained the loss of national independence, but here the resemblance ended, for whereas Serbia was absorbed as a vassal 'Roumili' province into the Ottoman Empire and Slovenia was reduced to serfdom in the German feudal economy, Croatia retained

13

a certain measure of autonomy and in 1918, although she had been subject to Hungary for some five hundred years, she had a separate form of state with jealously-safeguarded rights and privileges.

All three peoples were stirred by the nationalist awakening of the late 18th century. In all three, poets, historians and men of letters were the first apostles of their race and often the first revolutionaries. But Serbia began to free herself as early as 1804 and her independent national sovereignty was virtually complete by 1829 whereas Croatia and Slovenia were still dependent in 1917—a disparity due to the fact that the 19th century saw the collapse of the Ottoman Empire in Europe whereas Austria-Hungary's power in the Balkans tended to flow as the century advanced and reached its high water mark in the annexation of Bosnia-Herzegovina in 1908.

Since Serbia was the first to achieve that national independence which was the goal of all political striving in the 19th century, it followed that she began to exercise a powerful attraction upon her South Slav neighbours, for the Croats still lived beneath the yoke of Hungary, the Slovenes of Austria. Now the two main preoccupations of the Habsburg Emperor lay on the one hand in holding what he had, on the other, in adding to it. Serbia was an obstacle on both scores. As a rallying point for South Slav (or Yugoslav) irredentism in Croatia and Slovenia she threatened the territorial integrity of the Empire. As a fiercely race-conscious and independent state on the Empire's Balkan frontier she blocked all Austria's attempts to expand down into the peninsula. And she did not stand alone, for backing her resistance to Austrian imperialism stood Russia, self-appointed protector of all the Slavs, whose desire to keep Austria out of the Balkans and away from the Bosphorus was a function of her determination to push down to the Dardanelles herself. With the addition of Germany, who after

1890 stood behind Austria, the stage was set for the Great War.

The murder at Sarajevo on 28 June 1914 was the signal for European conflict just because Austria and Germany were determined to wipe out Serbia and Russia was determined that they should not. The murder of the Archduke was perpetrated by South Slav irredentists. It took place in Bosnia-Herzegovina, the last South Slav province to be added to Austria-Hungary. Thus it was just another confirmation of a fact which the Empire could no longer ignore —that dependent and independent South Slav lands could not permanently exist beside each other, for the dependent would move to the independent just as separate grains of quicksilver fuse together. Therefore in the opinion of Austria-Hungary the time had come to destroy Serbia, the rallying point for South Slav irredentism, and at the same stride extend the Empire to the frontiers of Greece. Russia could not allow such an increase in Austrian influence and her mobilisation followed Austria's declaration of war on Serbia, then Germany followed Russia, France Germany, and Europe was at war.

After four years' bitter struggle, the Empire of the Habsburgs collapsed and on what had once been its southern frontier, a South Slav state was established. Two factors influenced above all the actual circumstances of its birth, the secret Treaty of London which in 1915 brought Italy into the war on the side of the Allies, and the special position of Serbia which alone among the South Slav peoples was fighting for the Entente. For the Croats and the Slovenes were an integral part of the armed might of the Central Powers. It is true that there existed abroad a Yugoslav committee under the presidency of Trumbić, representing Croat and Slovene irredentism. This committee did achieve a certain recognition, for Lord Northcliffe espoused its cause in 1918, and it was due to its influence that the Allies included 'the liberation of the Serbs *and Slavs*' in their peace terms of 1917. But Italy's territorial ambitions in the Adriatic prevented any specific recognition of Croat and Slovene belligerency, such as was accorded to the Czechs.

The secret Treaty of London satisfied Italy in the Adriatic by conceding Trieste, Istria, Gorizia and Dalmatia, territories which the Croats and Slovenes looked on as fundamentally Slav. (Except for Trieste and parts of Istria and Gorizia they had every justification.) When things were going badly with Italy early in 1918 she made a show of moderating her claims but the triumphant advance of November (against an utterly defeated foe) swept into the disputed territory and soon Italian battalions were threatening Laibach and the Slovene plain.

This sudden thrust on the part of Italy right into the heart of their territory drove Croats and Slovenes with undue speed into the arms of Serbia, whose Premier, Pasić, representing the only South Slav belligerent, had the ear of the Entente. It was not that the South Slavs hesitated about independence or even about an ultimate union. At Zagreb between 6 and 19 October, Croat-Slovene (or Yugoslav) independence was proclaimed and a government elected which claimed to represent the new state. But its leaders wanted no precipitate union with Serbia. Pasić's 'Great Serbian' ambitions were suspect. The Croats' cherished independence was at stake and they were as ready to fight a unified centralised Serb state as they had been to oppose all Magyar attempts at centralisation. In fact, however, the Croats and Slovenes had no choice. The Italians were at the door. Dalmatia and Fiume—'arch-Slav' territory—seemed as good as lost. Serbia alone could save the South Slavs, so they turned to Serbia. A delegation went from Zagreb to Belgrad and on 1 December accepted the fusion of the 'independent state of the South Slavs' and the kingdom of Serbia into a 'unified' Serb-Croat-Slovene state.

Thus Yugoslavia came into being independently of the Allies and in direct opposition to one of them—Italy. The Peace Treaties did not create Yugoslavia, they only initiated the troubled negotiations which finally fixed her frontiers. The most difficult to draw were naturally those along the Adriatic and it was not until 1924 that a final agreement was reached whereby Dalmatia remained with the Slavs but all the rest (including Fiume) came under Italian rule.

2. THE ECONOMIC STRUCTURE

AGRICULTURE

The new Yugoslavia covered an area of 248,987 square miles inhabited, according to the 1931 census, by just under 14 million people. At the close of the war the state was almost purely agricultural and today, when some 76 % of the inhabitants get their living from the land, the peasantry, with its virtues and limitations, is still the basis of Yugoslav society.

The special character of the land system in Yugoslavia is the universality of small holdings and peasant ownership. Pre-war Serbia almost alone in Europe never passed through the stage of feudal economy, and the departure of the Turk in the 19th century left a community of independent peasants, of whom 96 % possessed their own land. Immediately after the war agrarian reform laws were introduced to bring the new provinces into line with Serbia. The first step was a proclamation by the Prince Regent in January 1919, followed a month later by enactments which outlined the general principles of reform. After ten years' activity on the part of the Ministry for Agrarian Reform, another law was introduced in June 1931 to liquidate 'the Agrarian Reform on

Large Estates', supplemented by two other laws, one of 1931, the other of 1933.

Properties of over 300 hectares[1] of cultivated land or of over 500 hectares in total area were—with certain qualifications such as the exemption of artificially drained land—to be expropriated, whether the owners were individuals, corporations, communes or religious bodies. The number of estates affected in the new provinces amounted to 850 of which 367 lay in the Voivodina.

At first the expropriated land was rented to the beneficiaries, but after 1925 direct purchasing began. In spite of some compensation the land reform led to the ruin of the old landlord class, and that this was partly the aim of the law sprang from the fact that a majority of the expropriated owners were of foreign origin, Magyar in the Voivodina for example, or German in Slovenia. Thus agrarian reform in Yugoslavia cannot be regarded as purely a social act. It was as much a nationalist measure, designed to increase the preponderance of the Yugoslav element inside the new frontiers of Yugoslavia.

The type of peasant benefiting by the reform confirmed its national character. In the Voivodina, colonists from the Yugoslav interior and war-time deserters from the armies of the Central Powers to the Serb forces (or *Dobrovoljci*), although far fewer in numbers, received almost as much land as the local inhabitants and received it on far more favourable terms. Local feeling was particularly exasperated when the expropriated land handed over to the new Yugoslav colonists had belonged originally to a commune. In most cases these communes were Magyar and the Reform Act amounted to the expropriation of the local non-Yugoslav peasantry in the interests of the nationals of the new state. One of the tragic results of this national policy is the continued existence in

[1] A hectare = 3·9 acres.

the Voivodina of a class of landless agricultural labourers who must number some 100,000 souls of whom three-quarters are Magyar.[1]

In the south, in Serbian Macedonia, the population was so scanty that it was possible to settle Serbian smallholders on the land. The greatest obstacles to agrarian reform were met with in Bosnia. Here the large landowners were Moslems and used their political party to block expropriation, and it was not until after the abolition of party government that a final settlement was reached in 1929.

Thus the agrarian problem in Yugoslavia is not to give the land to the peasants. They have it already. It is to secure them a living on their land. Family farms and self-sufficient village communities run on patriarchal lines give a secure, if modest, living to a large percentage of the population, but such an economy is inelastic and cannot cope either with a large increase in population or with the needs of a modern state. Small mixed farms designed to cover the needs of one family do not produce a big agricultural surplus for export, nor do they lead to an accumulation of capital. And with the population increasing by 200,000 a year, the subdivision of small family farms among numerous children tends to create units which are not even equal to supporting one family. For example, in Serbia every peasant has land but a percentage have no house. Such low standards carry with them an inevitable load of debt. Indebtedness is endemic in an economy where the farmer produces no surplus to cover the costs of fertilisers and machinery, but in Yugoslavia the peasants' indebtedness has been aggravated by the special circumstances under which many of them obtained their land. Immediately after the war financial chaos reigned in Yugoslavia, the dinar lost value and the peasants borrowed

[1] I am indebted for this account of agrarian reform to Mr. C. A. Macartney's book, *Hungary and her Successors.*

money at this low level to buy their land. Then the value of the dinar rose and with it the interest which the farmers were expected to pay on the original loan. Long before the world economic crisis of 1930 it was recognised that the debts of the peasant were a millstone round the neck of the agricultural community. After 1930 these debts were a really catastrophic factor in the country's economic distress.

To support a growing population and meet the needs of a modernised nation—including a large military establishment —the government could adopt two courses, increase the productivity of agriculture and push forward the process of industrialisation. Actually, the two are interdependent.

Agriculture has been encouraged in a variety of ways. It was realised that so long as the farmer had no capital and was paralysed by debt, hopes of increasing the output of agriculture were vain. One of the government's first steps was to encourage the co-operative movement. Peasant co-operatives played a large part in the liberation of the Slovenes and Croats and the movement had a strong foothold in pre-war Serbia. Co-operatives for agricultural credits predominated and in Slovenia a habit of saving was definitely growing up among the peasantry. In 1925 and 1927 the government passed Acts in favour of further co-operation and the economic crisis gave the movement a new impetus. Between 1929 and 1932 the number of co-operative societies increased by 24, co-operative membership by 46 %. Today roughly one peasant in fourteen is a member of some co-operative. An interesting development has been the creation of a number of new co-operatives for the collective use of agricultural machinery and for co-operative animal husbandry. A loose federal structure now unites the various co-operatives and in the north they are linked with agricultural schools and centres for research and instruction. In 1936 the movement gained new strength in Croatia and Slovenia where the peasants began to co-operate to regulate prices and production in the so-called *gospodorska sloga*.

At the height of the crisis the peasants' debts fell little short of 7,000 million dinars. The state of the market had wiped out the small surplus formerly earned by the farmers, and to meet the service on the debt they would have been obliged to borrow more. The government declared a moratorium in 1932 which lasted until 1936 when new legislation was introduced to liquidate the debt over a period of years. In 1929 a privileged Agrarian Bank had been set up to provide state credits for the farming community and now in 1936 the farmers' debts to banks and credit co-operatives were reduced by 25 %, the state took over a further 25 % and the remainder was transferred to the Agrarian Bank. Debts to private individuals (about 45 % of the total) were reduced by 50 %. For the outstanding debt the rate of interest was fixed at 3 %, and it was calculated that in 20 years the debt would be liquidated.

Although this settlement of the debt problem was an inevitable preliminary in the process of restoring agricultural prosperity, it was and is negative. The government by various laws has taken positive steps to improve standards of production, to clear and irrigate the land, to institute official inspections in the various provinces. In this work the co-operatives give their assistance but much remains to be done. For example nearly 13 % of the cultivable land is untouched and the percentage of forest (30 %) is probably too high in an agricultural country. One problem, however, lies beyond the competence of the government, the problem of overseas trade. The exports of Yugoslavia are all of primary raw materials and foodstuffs, with grain predominating. Whatever steps the government may take to encourage the co-operatives and to increase the country's output, Yugoslavia is dependent upon the willingness of other countries to take her supplies, and between 1929 and 1931 her export trade fell by 50 %. In the world economic crisis the greatest fall in price was registered by such primary products as wheat and maize, and what little surplus the Yugoslav farmers may have earned before 1929 was brutally cut off by the breakdown of international trade. Thus the agricultural debt problem came to a head during the crisis and, further, the two fundamental weaknesses of the Yugoslav economy were laid bare, its lack of capital and its dependence upon markets overseas.

INDUSTRY

Recent geological surveys have shown that for mineral wealth Yugoslavia is the richest country in Europe, not only in coal and iron, lead and copper (of which she heads the list of European producers) but in the rarer ores, magnesite, bauxite, chrome and zinc. She is known to possess gold and silver, petrol is a possibility, her forests are far from being fully exploited and her mountainous well-watered territory promises a great future to the development of electricity.

Yet the intensive industrialisation of the country has barely begun. For example in 1937 agriculture and forestry together accounted for over 13,000 million dinars in the national income, whereas the share of industry proper (apart from cottage crafts and the like) was only 6,000 million dinars. And these figures are misleading for they do not include all the agricultural produce (a big percentage) which is directly consumed by the peasant.

This backwardness is due in part to the policy of Austria-Hungary, which regarded its Slav provinces and especially Bosnia-Herzegovina as areas of exploitation for Austrian and Hungarian capital, but the root of the matter is a difficulty which faces every agricultural community in the early stages of industrialisation, how to raise sufficient capital to meet the outlay on plant, transport, power, etc., which must precede industrial development. As we have seen, the peasants live to cover their own needs and to produce only a small surplus. There is no feudal class of large landowners with an accumulated reserve, and although the co-operatives are beginning to create a habit of saving among the farmers (deposits increased by 1,099 million dinars in 1937), their capital is not even sufficient to modernise agriculture, let alone to finance industrialisation. And the primitive standards of agriculture react unfavourably upon industry in yet another way. The family farm, producing just enough to cover its simple needs, is a poor market for industrial goods.

To cope with her difficulties Yugoslavia has resorted to three of the usual expedients, state intervention, foreign loans and foreign trade. The state has given the initiative in most of the industries, owns the mineral rights, exploits many large industrial ventures such as the Zenitza iron plant, runs the production of silk and cellulose, and works part of the forestry and timber trade. Since the crisis, exchange control has been introduced with all the added powers it bestows on the state to regulate the character, bulk and direction of foreign trade. In the worst years of the crisis, 1932 and 1933, the state bought up the entire wheat supply at a fixed price, arranged for its export in the desperately restricted world market and pocketed the heavy loss. On the other hand, although the constitution enshrines the principle of expropriation with indemnity in the interests of the common good, private property is recognised and private enterprise is encouraged within limits such as the 1936 decree which placed all cartels under state control. Yugoslavia's most successful industry—textiles—is in private hands. (Between 1920 and 1930 the share of local industry in the textile market rose from 34 to 61 %.)

In short, the industrial economy of Yugoslavia is one common to many countries which have approached the problem of industrialisation in the post-war world. It is a mixed economy in which the state plays a leading part not only as director but also as producer, in which lack of capital hands over most large-scale developments (such as railways or civil aviation) to the public purse, but in which there is no systematic socialisation of the means of production. However, the state's role will probably increase rather than decrease as the industrial economy develops.

FOREIGN CAPITAL

Until recently, Yugoslavia's exceptional wealth in minerals had not been properly surveyed, and as a small agrarian country she did not offer many attractions to the foreign investor. France headed the list of creditors, but her loans were to a large extent political, a financial underpinning of her 'status quo' policy in East Europe. She financed Serbia's campaigns in the Great War to the extent of some 1,000 million gold francs, in 1924 there followed 300 million more to rescue the régime from the financial chaos which followed the war, and in 1931 France played a leading part in securing Yugoslavia an international loan of over 2,000 million dinars to stabilise the dinar (at 276 dinars to the £). France's commercial loans are not so heavy. A certain amount is invested in mining, but Germany is beginning to oust her here. The United States have mining concessions in Bosnia; Italy has an interest in Yugoslav timber and Great Britain exploits a variety of important mineral concessions. The lead and zinc Trepča mines have recently merged with three other concerns to form a single company which, since 1937, has acquired 15 more mineral concessions. Germany is, however, for reasons we shall discuss later, the coming Power. At present with over 400 million dinars at stake in the country she stands seventh on the list of foreign investors but is rapidly overtaking her competitors. New German firms are being formed and since the Anschluss Austria's important investments have fallen in to the Reich.

Yet Yugoslavia—in common with many other small countries—probably realises that in the long run no amount of foreign capital invested indiscriminately in her rich mineral reserves will raise her standards or modernise her industrial structure. A foreign capitalist, shipping valuable ore away from Yugoslavia to cover the investments of shareholders at home, directly benefits Yugoslavia only to the amount paid out in royalties to the government and in wages to local labour (and even so foreign firms usually bring out their own better-paid technicians). True, where the foreign capital is invested in roads or railways or capital improvements the community gains by them, but the price can be too heavy. In 1931 Yugoslavia's budget had fallen by 2,000 million dinars but service on her foreign debt was as high as ever and accounted for one seventh of the total expenditure. However, under the stress of the crisis, the government ceased payment and in 1937 a very favourable settlement was reached with certain foreign creditors, among them France, whereby a debt of nominally 22 million dollars was liquidated for just over 4 million.

The root of the difficulty is that the principal creditors—France, Great Britain, the United States—are none of them markets for Yugoslavia's goods. Foreign capital serves a country's purpose when in return for foodstuffs and raw materials the industrialised creditor state equips its debtor with a modernised transport system and a basis for its own industrialisation. This was the typical exchange of the 19th century. But Yugoslavia's creditors (Appendix I brings this out clearly) are not her principal markets. Payment has to be made in currency or gold, which Yugoslavia cannot afford, or else the foreign investors are 'concessionaries', occupied in stripping Yugoslavia of the minerals which later she will need in her own industrialisation, in other words in exploiting, not in developing her. These factors help to explain Germany's success. When Dr. Funk visited Yugoslavia in October 1938 he offered to absorb a large proportion of her output at guaranteed and stable prices and in return to equip her industrially for the better exploitation of her own ores.

The final absorption of Czechoslovakia into the German Reich in March 1939 had serious consequences in the sphere of the investments of foreign capital in Yugoslavia. Czechoslovakia had invested more capital in Yugoslavia than in any other country, and in 1939 it amounted to 741,200,000 dinars. By swallowing up this capital—just a year after absorbing Austria's share (336,200,000 dinars)—Germany, in spite of her own comparatively small investments (54,600,000 dinars), has sprung to the head of the list of foreign investors with 1,132,000,000 dinars as against the 1,056,100,000 dinars of France and 873,600,000 of Great Britain. The inevitable consequence of such a position is a crippling increase in the extent of Yugoslavia's economic dependence.

The precise nature of German economic policy in Yugoslavia following on the territorial changes was not made clear all at once, but Dr. Funk's speeches in October 1938 outlined a scheme of commercial co-operation very much on the lines of the German-Rumanian Economic Agreement; and since this mode of co-operation best suits a country which, like Germany, is very short of foreign capital, there is every reason to suppose that she will propose to supply Yugoslavia with capital goods, machinery, equipment, etc., in return for a large share of the ores which her co-operation will make it possible to exploit. There is nothing in itself unacceptable in this kind of help. It will expedite the industrialization of Yugoslavia and thus relieve the growing pressure of population. The penalties are political rather than economic, a growing dependence on the German Leviathan, a vanishing hope of preserving a truly independent national existence.

FOREIGN TRADE

Yugoslavia's foreign trade is that of a rich but undeveloped country. She exchanges raw materials, grain, livestock, ore, timber, for manufactured goods. So little processing has been done on the spot until recently that for many years Yugoslav cattle were exported live to Italy, where the hides were made into leather and sold back to Yugoslavia at a handsome profit.

Before the war, Slovenia, Croatia and the Voivodina, Bosnia-Herzegovina and Dalmatia were all part of the free trade unit formed by the Austro-Hungarian Empire. Within this great unified market a balance had been established between the industrial west—Austria and Bohemia—and the agricultural east in which the grain lands of the future Yugoslav provinces were included. Although after 1906 Serbia was cut off from this unit by her trade war with the Empire, she had a close economic understanding with Bulgaria. The war shattered the economic balance of Danubia. Nine national barriers cut across the old unified market and the exchange of east with west was destroyed. Economics became an instrument of political nationalism, and the Successor States, behind higher and higher tariff walls, sought to double their political independence with economic self-sufficiency. Hungary, Rumania and Yugoslavia (whose tariff barriers were the fourth highest in Europe) encouraged industrialisation at home. Czechoslovakia replied by becoming self-supporting in grain and after 1930 Austria embarked on a programme of agricultural self-sufficiency. The agrarian states had to look for markets elsewhere, but in the post-war years the chances of their primitive farming systems competing with the vast 'grain factories' of the New World grew steadily slighter. The culmination of the process was the world crisis of 1929 in which the bottom dropped out of the prices for primary products and the agrarian states suffered earlier and more severely than any others.

In Yugoslavia the end of ten years' desperate struggle against the tide of economic dislocation in Danubia and of contracting markets in the outside world was a fall in foreign trade of 3,000 million dinars, wholesale bankruptcy among the peasants, the collapse of the small internal market, a resulting check on industry and a severe internal and external debt crisis. Import, export and currency controls were imposed and various 'clearing' agreements initiated a system of barter with a number of countries.

This period of crisis lasted until about 1935 when the gradual recovery of the world market brought about a measure of improvement in Yugoslavia. The really striking outcome of the crisis was a reorientation of her foreign trade. Up to 1931 Austria and Czechoslovakia usually occupied first place in Yugoslav trade, a direct inheritance from pre-war days when Austria and Bohemia had been industrial suppliers for Danubia. Italy was usually a good second, while Germany with a certain amount of fluctuation steadily grew in importance as an exporter of industrial goods. After the crisis, Germany forged ahead to become by 1936 easily the largest importing and exporting country in Yugoslav foreign trade. From sharing a fairly balanced proportion of 13 to 14 % of Yugoslavia's imports and exports, Germany increased her share to 32 % of Yugoslavia's imports and 21 % of her exports in 1937. After the absorption of Austria (whose share in 1937 was 10·2 % of the imports and 13·5 % of the exports) and Czechoslovakia the proportion is still higher.

This phenomenal increase was due partly to old pre-war trading connections with German firms, partly to the goods with which Germany flooded Yugoslavia to the extent of 80 million marks a year in payment of war reparations, partly to the lucky accident which during the Sanctions period handed over to Germany part of Italy's trade with Yugoslavia, but mainly to the new German trading methods elaborated by Dr. Schacht. In 1934 Yugoslavia was importing from Germany about 100 million dinars more than she exported. An agreement was reached in the hopes of establishing a balance. On the strength of it Germany began to buy, until by December 1935 the balance in favour of Yugoslavia was 400 million dinars. But Germany's technique was designed to corner not only the export trade but imports as well. When Yugoslav traders asked for a settlement of the debt they learnt that the alternative before them was to leave their money frozen in Germany in the shape of non-convertible blocked marks (with the possibility of devaluation) or to accept German goods in exchange. The latter course presented less risk and between 1933 and 1937 Germany's share in Yugoslavia's imports rose from 13 to 32 %.

Yugoslavia was undoubtedly disturbed at Germany's inroads on her economy. In 1937 a booming world market offered her all the inducements of trade with free-currency countries as against the controlled exchanges and arbitrary imports of Germany (aspirin, mouth-organs, microscopes in return for wheat and maize!) and she increased her purchases from Great Britain and from Czechoslovakia, while France offered very favourable terms for Yugoslav grain. But the old difficulty had not been overcome. The free-currency countries did not need Yugoslavia's exports. They would sell her their goods but take only a small share of her supplies in return. Thus, while in 1937 Great Britain's share of Yugoslavia's imports increased slightly, Yugoslav exports to Great Britain actually fell away. Until the free-currency countries are prepared to buy more from East Europe, Germany has little to fear from their competition.[1]

The absorption of Czechoslovakia affected the balance of Yugoslavia's foreign trade, for her already dangerous dependence upon Germany was increased still further. Now 50 per cent of both her import and export trade are with the Greater Reich, and Germany was presented with a particularly appetising morsel in Czechoslovakia in the shape of the Czechs' active trade balance with Yugoslavia amounting to 76 million dinars. This stranglehold is not likely to relax for, in spite of the efforts of Yugoslavia during 1938 to increase her trade with France and Great Britain, her trade with the former remained at the same low level, and with the latter actually decreased. It is true that France and Yugoslavia signed a new Trade Pact on April 1 with the object of facilitating an exchange, but there was nothing in it to suggest an effective counterweight to Germany's predominance. As for Great Britain, the British Trade Mission did not go to Belgrad, and confined its attentions to the countries to whom the Government had given a political guarantee.

As a virtually self-supporting agricultural country, Yugoslavia's foreign policy may well depend less on foreign trade than that of other countries who have to rely more upon outside markets. But the fact remains that economic co-operation gives a stable basis to any political rapprochement. Now Yugoslavia has been ill served in this connection. Her political interests all lie in the direction of a close understanding with the small states of Danubia and the Balkans.

---

[1] Trade negotiations between Germany and Yugoslavia during 1938 and Dr. Funk's visit to Belgrad in October 1938 are discussed on pp. 84 ff.

Only thus can she resist imperialist pressure from her great neighbours. But with the exception of Czechoslovakia, her trade until 1938 with those of her neighbours who could be counted on to support the status quo and the process of East European consolidation has been negligible. Austria is an intermediate case, for her policy was never actively revisionist, but her instability drew her first into the camp of Hungary and Italy and finally led to her union with Germany. And now with the absorption of Czechoslovakia into the economy of the Reich, Yugoslavia's last important independent trading partner has disappeared. The attempts made in 1933 and 1934 to increase inter-Danubian and inter-Balkan trade (an Economic Council of the Little Entente and a Balkan Economic Council were set up) achieved little practical success and there was no regional consolidation to withstand the onslaught of the German trade drive which began a year later. Yugoslavia's relations with the Great Powers follow the same unfortunate lines. The two status quo Powers are France and Great Britain, but they have never provided markets for Yugoslav goods. Italy and Germany, the protagonists of revision, are Yugoslavia's most important buyers and sellers. These Powers are, as a corollary of their revisionism, actively opposed to any movement towards consolidation in East Europe and can put an economic spoke into the wheels of the smaller Powers when they show signs of independence.

3. SOCIAL CONDITIONS

It is difficult to give a unified picture of social conditions in a country in which the whole range of cultural, social and economic development varies from province to province. The standardising steam roller of western industrialism has not yet passed over the surface of the country, undeveloped communications help to preserve regional differences and the rural economy is on the whole at so simple a level that it faithfully reflects the geographical peculiarities of each region. For example, the rhythm of life in the peasant communities of Croatia and Slovenia, where the light but fertile soil which can be worked by the family unit is divided into small holdings on an average of 2 to 5 hectares, differs from the Voivodina whose rich, heavy earth, requiring for its cultivation teams of horses or agricultural machinery, tends to produce a large landowning peasantry and, as a corollary, a class of landless labourers.

One general observation is, however, possible. Yugoslavia has entered upon a dynamic period of change. The old peasant economy of individual holdings and subsistence farming must give way to modern methods of agriculture (there is at least a chance that this change will be carried through by a healthy development of the existing co-operative movement) for, with a population increasing by 200,000 a year and destined, once the industrialisation of the country begins in good earnest, to increase by thousands more, pressure on the land must modify the existing rural structure.

The undeveloped state of industry is shown by the employment figures. In a population of over 14 millions, insured workers accounted in 1937 for only 680,000. The number actually engaged is larger, for insurance does not cover all the working class, nor do the figures indicate how many peasants supplement the low yield of their land by part-time employment in local factories, but even so, the figure is not high. Yet the signs of modernising activity are present. Belgrad for example is typical of the 'boom' town, the small country capital which has thrown off its provincialdom in a decade and blossomed out into reinforced concrete and chromium-plate and functional building. The city's face has been transformed and its transformation—which is partly inspiring in its youth and vigour and partly distressing in its uncouth modernism and its ruthless sweeping away of an honourable past—is typical of the community in general. The post-war government with its 'get-rich-quick' politicians, its financial scandals, its passion for construction, was typical of a peasant community taking its first plunge into a modernised commercial world. In Belgrad a real analogy can be drawn between the bankers, deputies and industrialists of the new age whose parents were farmers on the Serbian plain, and the new boulevards of the city, from whose broad paved side-walks cobbled streets branch off into the tumbled alleys of the old town.

The emergence of a new bourgeoisie out of an undifferentiated peasant community has been accompanied by the creation of a small but growing urban working class. The beginnings of industrialisation are as usual imposing a heavy burden on the mass of workers and the standard of living is extremely low. The trade union movement is not strong and unemployment figures fluctuate round a high average. Nevertheless there is evidence that the fearful abuses which accompanied, for example, the opening up of South America by foreign capital are being mitigated by government action. The state has a positive conception of its prerogatives in the industrial field[1] and there has been a steady development of social legislation, particularly in 1937 when the principle of collective agreements between employers and workers and arbitration for disputes was established by decree, coupled with the introduction of a fixed minimum wage of 2 dinars an hour for the whole country. Later in the year the insurance of workers against disability, old age and death became obligatory (compulsory health insurance had been in existence some time). In 1938 compulsory contributions towards

[1] Cf. page 23 on the extent of government enterprise.

a pension fund for private employees was extended to the whole country and the internal loan floated in 1938 of 4,000 million dinars which is to be spent on public works[1] will help to counteract unemployment. To what extent the good legislative intentions of the government are carried out in practice, it is impossible to say, but after a series of strikes at the time of the depression, 1937 and 1938 are reported to have been years of industrial peace.

One aspect of unemployment presents a particular problem—that of the intellectual unemployed. The three universities (at Belgrad, Zagreb and Ljubljana) are turning out engineers, technicians, and professional men more rapidly than the national economy (which is still little more than one step removed from that of a purely peasant community) can absorb them. The university fees are astonishingly cheap (at Zagreb about £7 covers the academic year) and the students who profit by them are in the majority peasants' sons and extremely poor. This combination of poverty with the danger of unemployment lies at the root of the radicalism of the Yugoslav student body, a radicalism which is always referred to as 'Communist' by the authorities. The difference, however, which frequently causes astonishment, between the 'Rightism' of the student body in Poland and Rumania and the 'Leftism' of the students in Yugoslavia and Bulgaria is in part due to the absence of any large Jewish commercial class in the latter two countries. The students do not find Jews established in the jobs they want and thus do not turn to Right-wing anti-Semitism.

---

[1] The money is to be spent thus:

				Million dinars
National Defence	..	..	..	1,000
Railway construction	..	..	..	1,500
Road buildings ..	..	..	..	500
Public buildings ..	..	..	..	500
Land Reclamation	..	..	..	500

The fact of radicalism is obvious, but the extent to which
it is in any orthodox sense Marxist is more difficult to assess.
In 1918 the Serbian Socialist Party opted for communism
and fought the first general election in Yugoslavia as a
communist party. It had an immediate and surprising
success with the conquest of 54 seats in the Skuptšina. But
the success was short-lived and misleading. Much of the
regional anti-Serb discontent of the various nationalities
found expression by voting for the only regular party in
opposition to the Serb government. By 1923 this discontent
had found its true voice in the establishment of parties on
a specifically regional basis (the Bosnian Moslems or Slovene
Clericals for example). The Communist Party had, moreover,
been banned after a communist attempt on the Regent in
1921. Thereafter it disappeared from the public scene. The
radicalism of the students is thus unconnected with an
organised political party and it represents different aspects
of communism varying from orthodox Russian Marxism or
unorthodox 'Trotskyism' to a more vague sympathy with the
workers and peasants and a desire to free the Balkans from
foreign political influence and foreign capitalism. 'The
Balkans for the Balkan people' takes the form of a federation
on Russian lines of Balkan republics, particularly of all the
South Slavs including the Bulgars, in which the various
racial groups would enjoy cultural autonomy within a wider
political frame. This aspect of the students' 'radicalism'
touches on the most difficult problem of the whole peninsula
—that of the various national groups and minorities.

4. NATIONAL MINORITIES

OVER and above the three racial groups—Serbs, Croats and
Slovenes—whose union formed the kingdom of Yugoslavia,
the state includes a number of national minorities. The

largest minority is German, some 500,000 to 600,000 strong,[1] of which the Swabian Germans living in the Voivodina are the biggest regional concentration. The Voivodina also includes a vast majority of the next most numerous racial group. Of the 370,000 Magyars[1] in Yugoslavia 300,000 live in the Voivodina, the remainder in Croatia. The Rumanian minority (about 200,000) is also to be found in the Voivodina. Thus, with the exception of certain groups of Turks and Albanians and the inhabitants of Serbian Macedonia, who constitute a special problem,[2] the minority question in Yugoslavia is largely confined to the Voivodina.

All minorities suffer the general disadvantages of Serb minority rule and Yugoslavia's record in this respect is very bad. Her signature of the Minorities Treaty has not been followed by any serious attempt to put its provisions into practice. The various groups complain of the terrorism and espionage which have accompanied an administration which, since local elections have only been held once (in 1927) and then only for the results to be swept away again two years later, is arbitrary and dictatorial. Economic grievances include the expropriation of non-Serb peasants, the unfair incidence of taxation (until the economic crisis the land tax was 320 dinars a yoke in the Voivodina compared with 70 dinars in Serbia[3]) and the equally unfair redistribution of public funds, of which a lion's share, it is claimed, goes to Serbia. These and similar grievances leave the minorities with the conviction that they are politically tyrannised and economically exploited. And behind these political and economic grievances is the fundamental national difficulty from which in part they spring—the determination of the Serbs to impose

[1] The difficulty in giving exact figures lies in the big difference between official statistics and those collected by the minorities themselves.   [2] See page 38.

[3] It is also true that the Voivodina possesses the richest land in Yugoslavia.

themselves as the dominant race. Measures of Serbisation are the rule, Serb is the only language of administration, local names are transformed, German villages receive the names of Serb statesmen and letters are not delivered if addressed in the old way. One important result of such measures is virtually to exclude all non-Yugoslavs from official careers.

Within this general framework the various minorities have fared differently, their fortunes varying with the degree to which, in Serb opinion, they constitute a menace to the integrity of the state. Variations on the general theme of repression are brought about by the practice of playing off irredentist against non-irredentist minorities. Since the Voivodina formerly belonged to Hungary, the Magyars have suffered most, are most heavily penalised in the matter of schools and cultural rights, and least able to put any kind of pressure upon the government. Yugoslav policy has the success it deserved. Of all the minorities, the Magyars would return to their mother country with the lightest heart. The Rumanians are rather better off while the German minority has at times been positively courted. In the Voivodina the S.D.K.B. (or *Schwäbisch-Deutsche Kultur-Bund*) and in Croatia the K.W.D.D. (*Kultur und Wohlfahrtsvereinigung der Deutschen*) are able to provide the German minority with a great variety of cultural activities (singing clubs, sports associations, literary evenings, excursions) which are now run on emphatically Nazi lines. Nevertheless even here Yugoslav policy is quick to react to any potential danger. The small German minority in Slovenia, since it marches with the German frontier, is in a much less favourable position and finds its activities curtailed. For example, no central cultural organisation exists. As might be expected, the result has been to breed a strong Nazi spirit which goes further than the official *staatstreu und volkstreu*[1] attitude of the other groups.

[1] True to the state and true to the race.

37

But these variations do not really modify the fact that all the Yugoslav minorities are fighting an uphill fight against the repressive policy of the régime. In the absolutely crucial question of the schools, Yugoslavia is completely illiberal. The government has interpreted its Minorities Treaty guarantee as applying to elementary education only. It denies that the minorities possess any right to secondary education in their own language and the 1929 Act provides for 'the language of the state' only in secondary schools.

These disabilities help to account for the movement for self-government in the Voivodina within the framework of a Yugoslav federated state which has started to make some headway in recent years.

The problem of Serbian Macedonia has its roots in history. Until 1878 the province of Macedonia formed part of the Ottoman Empire. During the Russo-Turkish war of that year Bulgaria was freed from the Turk and both the Bulgarians and the Macedonians took it for granted that Macedonia, whose inhabitants looked on themselves as of Bulgar blood would become part of the newly independent Bulgar state. The intervention of Germany, Austria and Great Britain at the Congress of Berlin was disastrous from the Macedonian standpoint. Perturbed by the size of the new Bulgaria (which entailed a corresponding growth in the scope of Russian influence in the Balkans) they restored the unfortunate Macedonians to the Turks. The incredible misrule which the decadent Ottoman Empire inflicted upon its subject peoples led to the formation of a revolutionary movement inside Macedonia, the Internal Macedonian Revolutionary Organisation or I.M.R.O. which countered the Turks' terrorism with its own and was responsible for the revolt, bloodily suppressed, of the Elindin in 1903.

I.M.R.O. wanted autonomy inside Bulgaria or else complete independence. Until 1912 it was a matter between them and the Turks, but in 1912 the land of Macedonia was used as bait to draw the Balkan Powers together and when the Balkan League was formed to drive out the Turk, Macedonia was divided up between Serbia, Greece and Bulgaria. The division agreed to in 1912 was the basis of the post-war frontiers and in 1919 the Macedonians found that far from achieving autonomy or independence, they had been wiped out of existence as a separate entity.

Two men, Alexandroff and his successor Michailoff, were responsible for restoring I.M.R.O. after the war. Their base was that part of Macedonia now in Bulgaria. This they ruled practically as a separate province and carried on from it irredentist propaganda in Serbian and Greek Macedonia. The brutality of the Serbian rule under the Serb Governor Lazić played into I.M.R.O.'s hands. Serbian officials and officers were shot, bridges destroyed, railways dynamited in the pre-war Balkan tradition. So long as I.M.R.O. could operate from its Bulgarian base it was safe from Yugoslavia and Greece. Inevitably it became a major cause of strife between the Bulgarian, Yugoslav and Greek governments. Yugoslavia was constantly bringing pressure to bear on Bulgaria to clear up I.M.R.O. and on the same issue Greece and Bulgaria nearly went to war in 1925. But the Bulgarians who sympathised with I.M.R.O., had never reconciled themselves to the loss of Macedonia and they gave I.M.R.O.'s irredentism covert encouragement. Yugoslavia's uneasiness was increased by rumours that Italy, too, gave tacit support to I.M.R.O., with the idea of a possible dismemberment of Yugoslavia. Thus, although the Serbs resolutely refused to recognise Macedonia as a 'Minority' problem (for them Serb Macedonians were 'South Serbs'), nevertheless for ten years after the war the Macedonians were a more serious threat to Yugoslavia's peace and integrity than any of the properly so-called national minorities.

There remains one more question. From this account of Yugoslavia's minorities one fact emerges vividly. The dominant race has never been a trinity of Serb, Croat and Slovene. The Serbs alone took the initiative and their policy has been pan-Serb rather than pan-Yugoslav. What then is the position of the Croats and Slovenes? Are they, too, dominant racial groups? Or are they little better than national minorities? Here we come upon the fundamental problem of the nascent Yugoslav state and it can best be studied in relation to the domestic politics of the post-war period since, from the state's first hour down to the present day, the struggle between Serb and Croat has been the pivot upon which internal politics have turned.

5. DOMESTIC POLITICS

THE PARLIAMENTARY RÉGIME, 1918–29

One glance at a pre-war map of the territories now included within Yugoslavia helps to explain the problems which faced the new country in 1918. The chief difficulty was not racial. Serbs, Croats and Slovenes all spring from the same stock. The provincial divisions do not follow clear ethnic lines and mixed populations of Serbs and Croats are common in the north-eastern provinces. The religious difference between Croat and Slovene Catholics and the Orthodox Serb is probably not as great as the Concordat riots of 1937 suggest. In most districts Orthodox, Catholic and Moslem groups manage to live side by side in peace and, as we shall see, it was the national rather than the religious status of Orthodoxy which was defended with such bitterness in 1937. Economic cleavages are not decisive in a community of independent village units. The root of the problem lies in the clash of culture produced by the sudden crowding together in one state of a number of provinces culturally and politically at a different stage of evolution—Serbia and Montenegro, small independent peasant kingdoms; Serbian Macedonia until 1912 under the heel of the Turk; the Voivodina, an integral part of Hungary; Slovenia and Dalmatia, Austrian crown lands; Bosnia-Herzegovina under dual Austro-Hungarian control; and finally Croatia, part of Hungary yet enjoying a measure of autonomy and possessing an independent tradition which could be traced back a thousand years.

The greatest gulf of all divided Croatia from the other South Slav provinces. Ever since her emergence as a national entity she had belonged to the sphere of western thought and culture.[1] Her territory was converted by Catholic missionaries, all her historical and political links lay northwards and westwards, her tongue though differing little from Serb was written in Latin characters, for hundreds of years she had formed part of Hungary and of the economic system based on the Danube and linked to the political structure of the Habsburg Empire. Thus her economic life was more developed, her culture, centring in the middle class of Zagreb, more sophisticated and self-conscious than those of the provinces of rough peasants and soldiers lying to the south, and the Croat believed himself with some justification to be superior in civilisation and education to the Serb. The only other province which could compare economically and culturally with Croatia was her neighbour Slovenia. Here, too, Slav national life expressed itself in western forms, in Catholicism, in the Latin alphabet, and Slovenia, also linked economically with the old Empire, possessed a higher standard of living and a stronger peasant co-operative movement than could be found further south. But there was this crucial difference between Croatia and Slovenia. Slovenia had never been anything but a crownland of the Austrian

[1] In contrast to Serbia which was converted to Greek Christianity and uses the Greek or Cyrillic alphabet.

Empire. The Slovenes passed straight from a subordinate position under the Romans to a state of feudal servitude in the Holy Roman Empire. Up to 1918 Slovenia had always been a province among provinces, and the Slovenes alone among South Slav peoples had not one hour of national independence in their past history. The Croats on the contrary looked back to a brief but brilliant period of independent nationhood when in the 11th century, under King Tomislav, Croatia commanded the Adriatic, and under King Demetrius was recognised by the Holy See. The following century saw the incorporation of Croatia into Hungary but the process was not one of complete absorption (*Gleichschaltung*). Croatia retained certain rights including a measure of local autonomy, a local legislature (the Sbor) and the recognition of her status as a *corpus separatum* under the Hungarian Crown. With few modifications this position, part dependent and part autonomous, was still hers in 1918.

These centuries of semi-independent existence within an alien state left deep marks upon the national psychosis of the Croats. They had not retained their prized autonomy without a severe struggle against the centralising tendencies of the Magyars. The long years of opposition gave their politics a negative flavour and the bitterness of their fight with a would-be dominant Magyar race made them deeply suspicious of political relations with national groups other than their own and prone to see hints at domination where none was intended, or to resent as encroachments perfectly reasonable suggestions for co-operation. The Serbs would have needed an almost miraculous measure of collective tact in order to smooth over the first shock of union, and tact can hardly be said to be a characteristic of the Serb nation. In Slovenia the only difficulty was cultural, a real but bridgeable cleavage. Croatia doubled the cultural division with a fierce spirit of political particularism and it was on this reef that the political experiments of the first twenty years invariably came to grief.

But it must not be thought that Croatia bore sole responsibility. The Serb tradition of independent national existence was immortalised by Tomislav's contemporary, the Emperor Dušan, preserved through centuries of oppression under the Turks, restored in the 19th century to become the rallying point of South Slav nationalism and a thorn in the flesh of the Austrian Empire, wiped out of existence for two years during the Great War to re-emerge triumphantly in 1918 under the aegis of the Allied Powers. Its upholders were in no mood to compromise about the new state which they felt to be primarily the product of Serb fortitude and Serb arms. They were ready to receive their South Slav brothers (although until the last months of the war Croats and Slovenes had been fighting against Serbia in the armies of the Central Powers) but on their own terms, which envisaged the new state in the form, not of a South Slav federation, but of a 'Great Serbia'. This Serb nationalism was as 'totalitarian' and centralising *vis-à-vis* the Croats as had been the Magyar nationalism which it was to replace. The Croats' weapon against the Magyars had lain in their statute of autonomy. It was the most precious expression of their national independence. Thus when under pressure of external invasion and internal collapse they hurried to join the Serbs, the real crux turned out to be their status. Slovenes, Moslems, Magyars, Germans had nothing to lose by entering a unified Serb state. They knew no other condition. But the Croats *had* something to lose—their autonomy. When in the first constitution they lost it, they became the centre of an intransigent opposition which has lasted ever since.

That they lost it was largely due to the 'Great Serbia' policy of the Serb leaders. The dominant Serb party was Pasić's Radicals, who had evolved from their early days of socialism and pan-Slavism to support of an ultra-conservative and fanatically pan-Serb programme. The rival Serb party, the Democrats, led at the end of the war by a Serb from Croatia, Pribitcevic, were no less pan-Serb. Serbia had borne the heat and burden of the day, had survived the war and had gained the omnipotent Entente as ally. As a French journalist wrote in 1918: 'Here in Belgrad the Serb idea has conquered Yugoslavism. The only differences are in degrees of pan-Serbism'. Now pan-Serb policy forecast a South Slav community in which the Serbs would play as dominant a part as they had played in the old purely Serb state. By centralising all administration in Belgrad, initiative and control would remain in the hands of the Serbs. Thus the issue between Serbism and Yugoslavism was narrowed to the struggle between a central and a federal state, a Great Serbia and a confederation of South Slav peoples.

Some compromise would undoubtedly have been achieved had there been time for properly prepared and patiently pursued negotiations between the various peoples, but we have seen the state of stress under which they came together in 1918. Italian ambitions in the Adriatic, in Croatia and Dalmatia threw the Slovenes and Croats on to the mercy of the Serbs who were alone in a position to plead their cause at the Peace Conference. The crucial formative years between 1918 and 1924 were spent under the shadow of Italy's expansive threat and ended in the loss of Fiume. Yugoslavia had to come together at all possible speed in order to offer a united front to Italy. But many of her problems could not be settled speedily, with the result that they were not solved at all.

In 1918 only a fraction of the Croat deputies opposed union with Serbia. But the elections for the constituent assembly were not held until 1920 and during the unsatisfactory interregnum the pan-Serb tendencies at Belgrad and the experience of various districts when occupied by Serb troops were enough to make the Croats hesitate. The defeat at the Peace Conference was largely at the expense of the non-Serb peoples, and the chaotic social and economic conditions prevailing in the north—local terrorism from the 'Green Corps', war on the Carinthian frontier, food shortage, the appalling economic dislocation brought about by the collapse of the vast unified market of the Old Empire— produced a ferment of unrest among the Croat peasants who were ready to listen to any programme provided it was sufficiently radical. Thus when Stefan Radić formed his Croat People's Party—with the slogans of no more war, no taxation, home rule and republicanism—he swept the country and obtained 50 out of the 419 seats at the Constituent Assembly.

Radić was an extraordinary character, eloquent, impassioned, a fierce upholder of his Croat peasants, a born leader, of dynamic personality. But his eloquence was marred by demagogy, his leadership by the wildness of the schemes he was prepared to support, his whole personality by a streak of instability. Moreover his past training unfitted him for parliamentary leadership. A disciple of Starcević,[1] for a certain time in the Frank party, his experiences in pre-war Croatia had given him a type of mind incapable of compromise and permanently opposed to the government whatever the government might be.

Radić's first error in tactics—he made many—was to refuse to co-operate in the work of the Constituent Assembly, and his *bloc* of 50 stayed away from Belgrad. Thus the most important political group who would have opposed the Serb

---

[1] In pre-war Croatia, Starcević led a Croat party which was bitterly hostile to the Serb element in Croatia. The Magyars of course played upon this hostility with the principle of 'Divide et Impera' in mind. Frank was Starcević's successor.

tendency towards complete centralisation voluntarily destroyed their chances of influencing the structure of the new state. The Assembly's deliberations lasted through the winter of 1920–21 and on 28 June 1921 the new constitution became law.

It was passed by 223 votes to 35, apparently an imposing majority, but 161 deputies did not vote at all and must be counted with the opposition. Thus the government obtained a majority of only 27 for the country's constitution, surely an insufficient majority for the laws which were to determine the whole structure of the new state.

The three most important non-voting groups were the Croats, the Slovene Clericals and the communists. The Slovene Clericals led by Father Korosetz represented Slovenia's desire for autonomy. As a well defined, well integrated people, with a separate speech and cultural tradition and a prosperous economy based on peasant co-operatives and on a few successful industries, the Slovenes disliked Serb centralism as much as the Croats. On the other hand, they had no tradition of autonomy. They did not feel, like the Croats, that they were being deprived of an old status, merely that they were failing to obtain a new one. Thus their opposition was never so intransigent as that of the Croats. The group of 54 Communists was a temporary phenomenon, bred of post-war conditions. People voted communist to express their economic discontent or dislike of the Serb government. But with independent peasant proprietors accounting for 80 % of the population, communism had no prospects of success. At the 1923 elections, not a single communist was returned. Crisis conditions were passing, communism had been defeated in Hungary and Bulgaria, the Yugoslav government vetoed the party and resorted to pressure after a communist attempt on King Alexander's life in 1921, and finally the dissident voters now found their spiritual home among the nationalist party groups—the Slovenes or Croats or Bosnian Moslems. Communism as an organised political party became negligible and remained so. (Its lasting influence upon young intellectual circles has already been discussed.)

The parliamentary régime inaugurated in 1921 lasted eight troubled years. From 1921 to 1926 Pasić was in control and for the first three years Radić continued his intransigent opposition. His attacks upon the government and upon the Royal House grew in vigour and venom and in 1924 he made a series of much advertised journeys abroad to Paris and to London to gain diplomatic support for the Croat cause. He followed these visits by a journey to Moscow, during the course of which he affiliated his Croats to the communists' Peasant International. In fact this step was nothing more than another attempt to frighten Belgrad, this time with the bogy of social revolution (to which it was sensitive). On his return he was arrested, but within a month or so of his imprisonment there occurred another of those *voltes-faces* for which Radić's career was remarkable. He sent his Croats to the Skuptšina (the Yugoslav parliament) and offered the Serbs his collaboration. On 18 July 1925 four Croats entered the Cabinet whither they were followed in November by Radić himself.

However, it was not the beginning of a new era. Within a few months Radić was back at his old speech-making and in October 1926 he provoked a ministerial crisis which put an end to Serb-Croat collaboration. A month later, Pasić died and the Radicals split into two wings. Thereafter the position in parliament became more and more confused. The Croats were in bitter opposition, the split in the Radical Party placed the Cabinet at the mercy of an unstable coalition, legislation ceased, an atmosphere of corruption and intrigue undermined the prestige of the whole system. To add to the

47

tension came external difficulties with Italy over the status of Albania. Finally, on 20 June 1928 the political tension culminated in a wild crime in the Skupština. A Montenegrin deputy, Račić, killed two Opposition members and wounded three others. One of the wounded was Radić who died shortly after. With his death, the Croat cause had a martyr.

Father Korosetz, leader of the Slovene Clericals, formed a Cabinet which lasted some six months. In the meantime rioting broke out in the north and by December the Croats were calling for a 'free Croatia'. On 30 December 1928, Korosetz resigned. The King spent a week sounding the various political leaders, then on the night between 5 and 6 January 1929 he declared his dictatorship.

Why were these years of parliamentary government so unsuccessful? The fault lay, first, in the centralising tendencies of the 1921 constitution. In place of the old provinces were substituted 30 departments which did not coincide with the former frontiers and whose autonomy was nothing more than a certain administrative independence. The irritation provoked by these new divisions was intensified by the filling of most important administrative posts by Serbs, and there were other sources of friction. Little attempt was made to unify the legal system which differed from province to province, and these differences often led to gross miscarriages of justice. Until 1927 taxation, too, varied according to the various provinces. Slovenia and Croatia had been part of a modern, highly-developed and efficient Empire. Their taxation laws reflected the needs of a Great Power whereas Serbia's taxation was based upon the simple needs of a small peasant community—with the result that the northern provinces found themselves providing a disproportionate share of the country's budget. All these maladjustments increased the friction between Serbs and Croats to the point where co-operation—parliamentary or otherwise—became impossible.

The parliamentary system itself must bear some part of the blame, or rather, the leaders who controlled it. Radić's dynamic but unstable personality unfitted him for the unsensational work of day-to-day legislation. Pasić's methods of personal influence and intrigue opened the door to corruption which the financial chaos of the post-war years made all too simple. But the leader who carried the heaviest single responsibility for the breakdown of democracy was King Alexander himself.

On declaring the dictatorship, he let it be understood that he intended only a temporary measure which would give place to democracy once the country's political health had been restored. In fact, this *coup d'état* sprang from a conviction which had been growing since the war that personal authoritarian government was to be preferred to any other. King Alexander had been educated at the Court of the Czar, his early manhood was spent in the army and he was at home with the military type of mind. At first his attitude towards the constitution had been irreproachable but after 1926 there was a change. He began to influence party government by backing weak leaders who would be subservient to his own policy. For example when Pasić died in 1926, a nonentity, Vukičević, was chosen by the King to follow him. The weakness and corruption of parliament certainly played into the King's hands but the outcome would have been different had he wished to reform, not destroy it.

THE DICTATORSHIP, 1929–34

The setting up of Alexander's dictatorship practically coincided with the first onslaught of the economic crisis. Thus he was faced with three problems, to raise prices and restore the purchasing power and prosperity of the farmers;

to return to a democratic system (in accordance with the wishes of a vast majority of his subjects) and finally, to bridge the widening gulf between Serbs and Croats. It cannot be said that he was successful.

Various measures (already described) were taken to restore the health of agriculture, such as the wheat monopoly of 1932 and 1933, the peasant debt moratorium, and various decrees promulgated to encourage the co-operative movement, but the restoration of prosperity when it came was due to the recovered prosperity of the world market rather than to governmental action. As for the return to democracy, it was soon obvious that it had no place in the King's programme. For the first two years, Yugoslavia remained without a constitution and the country changed overnight into a 'police state'. All the normal democratic liberties—of speech, of the press, of public meeting—were suppressed, the police were given a free hand with political suspects, arrests were arbitrary, the prisoners dealt with by secret political tribunals and the citizen had no redress against such unlawful prosecution. In 1930 by Royal Proclamation the old political parties were dissolved for ever. The tone of the régime was clearly indicated by the presence of General Zhivković at the head of the government, for he was a 'political' soldier with a reputation for time-serving who made no secret of his contempt for democratic forms and stood for the pan-Serb ideals of certain sections of the army.

By 1931 the bankruptcy of the new régime was only too apparent. Alexander had energy and courage but neither the knowledge nor the imagination necessary for benevolent despotism. Discontent was rife not only in perpetually dissident districts such as Macedonia and Croatia but in Serbia itself where the peasants saw the democratic liberties of fifty years destroyed. Foreign public opinion became active and Léon Blum began a campaign in the *Populaire* against the support by French democracy of a Balkan dictatorship just at a time when Yugoslavia needed French help in a loan to stabilise the dinar. In September 1931 Alexander as a sop to opinion both at home and abroad promulgated a new constitution which was to preface the much-advertised return to democracy. It did nothing of the kind, but finally slammed the door on Yugoslavia's democratic past. Under it, the King's constitutional powers were dictatorial, the new Second Chamber (or Senate) would be nothing but an assembly of royal nominees, an electoral law for the lower house was introduced which has been described as farcical. Among other provisions—in a country where all interests tend to be on a regional, racial or religious basis—regional, racial or religious parties were specifically banned. When elections were held, the opposition abstained, and the result was the inevitable assembly of subservient deputies.

The King's most signal failure lay in the sphere of national reconciliation. It was the cleavage between Serbs and Croats which had produced the parliamentary deadlock. Thus it was Alexander's most urgent duty to restore unity. But people quickly realised that Alexander's solution was merely to pursue with greater vigour the policy of centralisation which had produced the breach in the first place. In 1929 the name 'Kingdom of the Serbs, Croats and Slovenes' gave way to 'Yugoslavia', a change which was interpreted as a blow to federalism. In 1930 the proclamation which abolished the old parties abolished the old provinces too, and substituted nine 'Banovinas' based upon the various river basins and cutting across the old historical and traditional boundaries. The old policy of administrative centralism was carried through even more rigidly than before with the result that all the non-Serb nationalities went into intransigent opposition. The government countered their opposition with further repression and police terrorism became the rule

51

particularly in Croatia and Macedonia, the two centres of most violent discontent. Resentment reached fever pitch when Radić's successor, the Croat leader Dr. Matćek was arrested, tried, and, in defiance of the evidence, flung into prison.

Macedonia had been a source of anxiety to the Yugoslav government ever since the peace settlement,[1] but now the activities of I.M.R.O. took on a more serious character, for they began to link up with other centres of disaffection inside Yugoslavia and were apparently seeking support across the frontiers in countries such as Hungary and Italy which had a direct interest in a possible dismemberment of the Yugoslav state. Up to the time of Alexander's dictatorship, terrorism was largely confined to the activities of I.M.R.O. in Serbian Macedonia, but the growing tension between the Serbs and the Croats led, after 1929, to the emergence of a new group in Croatia, the Ustasi, who under the leadership of the wild and irresponsible Dr. Ante Pavelić, modelled themselves directly on I.M.R.O. and began to co-operate with the Macedonian revolutionaries in various centres abroad. The Italian government connived at, or at least tolerated, the presence of Croat and Macedonian irredentists at Ancona and Brescia, and Hungary set up a camp at Janka Puzta on the Hungarian-Yugoslav frontier designed apparently for the recruitment and training of young terrorists. From this and other centres (including Vienna) during 1932 and 1933 Ustasi and I.M.R.O. carried out a series of outrages with bomb and dynamite on Yugoslav territory.

That Alexander's régime was able to withstand the bitterness and discontent which his dictatorial and centralising policy aroused on every side was partly due to the action of I.M.R.O. and the Ustasi. The fact that terrorists were

[1] Cf. page 38.

receiving foreign support suggested to Serb and Croat alike that however bitter their internal hostility, they could unite in a common opposition to the policy of Yugoslav disintegration pursued by Italy and Hungary. Here the King's obvious determination to consolidate his country won him back a measure of the support which his internal tactics had lost him. In 1933 the Little Entente was reinforced, in 1934 the Balkan Pact came into being. Bulgaria was not a partner to the Pact and Alexander realised that so long as his neighbour held aloof there could be no true Balkan consolidation. He it was who took the initiative in creating more friendly relations and in September 1934 he paid a state visit to Bulgaria. In the meantime bloody internecine struggles inside I.M.R.O. coupled with some disgraceful crimes in the Bulgarian capital had discredited the Macedonian movement among the Bulgarians themselves. Yugoslavia's 'friendly representations' no longer fell on deaf ears, Bulgaria cleaned up Bulgarian Macedonia and the I.M.R.O. leaders dispersed, Michailoff to Turkey, one of his lieutenants, Georgiev, to Janka Puzta.

Alexander's reconciliation with Bulgaria, although it was probably his finest service to his country, sealed his fate. This same Georgiev went from Hungary to France and on 9 October 1934 he murdered Alexander in the streets of Marseilles.

YUGOSLAVIA UNDER STOYADINOVIĆ

1935–1937.—A council of three under the leadership of Prince Paul, the late King's cousin, took over the Regency for Alexander's young son, Peter II. The whole nation's horror and indignation over the Marseilles crime undoubtedly created a favourable opportunity for some conciliatory gesture to the Croats on the part of the government, but it was allowed to pass. Yet Prince Paul was a more moderate and tolerant statesman than King Alexander. The Serb extremists—now formed into a semi-fascist 'Yugoslav National Party'—became uneasy at the government's more liberal tendencies and challenged it in January 1935 to declare itself unequivocally for the principles of 1929 and the Constitution of 1931, whereupon the prime minister, Yevtić, dissolved the Skuptšina and fixed new elections for 5 May.

The Opposition, which had long accounted for a majority of the population, was concentrated on two different fronts. In Serbia three parties—the Democrat, the Agrarian and the Radical People's party—formed the so-called Belgrad Opposition. They represented the tough democratic tradition of old Serbia and the chief plank of their platform was a return to the fully democratic system with which Yugoslavia had set out. They were not in principle federalists but when they offered the Croat People's Party an electoral alliance, Dr. Matćek accepted it eagerly. Matćek's party, which included Croats, Serbs, Dalmatians and many of the discontented minorities of the Banat, made up the other wing of the Opposition. Both wings had in common their desire for democracy, free elections and a new constitution. On the issue of federalism there was no unanimity, but common opposition to the government had brought Serbs and Croats together and the Belgrad Opposition were ready to reconsider the issue. Two other groups formed part of the electoral alliance, Father Korosetz's Slovene clericals and Dr. Spaho's Bosnian Moslems, but their position was not so well defined with regard either to federalism or democracy.

The May elections were carried through under the 1931 electoral law with the almost unlimited powers of pressure and intimidation — including the open ballot — which it bestowed upon the government. In face of such restrictions the result was a virtual victory for the Opposition, for they obtained 1,063,000 votes again the government's 1,738,000.

However, according to the provisions of the electoral law, this voting gave the government 305 seats in the Skuptšina against the Opposition's 67. Dr. Matćek's *bloc* decided therefore to continue to boycott parliament, but this time not without an official protest. A delegation headed by the Catholic Archbishop of Zagreb, Mgr. Bauer, visited Prince Paul and denounced the corruption and intimidation with which the government had conducted the electoral campaign. Prince Paul withdrew his confidence from Yevtić and shortly afterwards a cabinet reshuffie took place out of which Stoyadinović emerged as prime minister, a post he was to fill for over two years.

His régime was rather more liberal than the King's dictatorship. His approach seemed to be that of the banker or the technician rather than of the soldier. He was not less convinced of the necessity of a rigidly centralised state, for Pasić schooled him in political life and his government's attitude was unyielding on this point, but the political bankruptcy of the earlier system led Stoyadinović to modify the police régime, to relax the censorship and to liberalise the press laws. He was prepared for co-operation with non-Serb groups (within the centralised limits laid down by Belgrad, and he was successful when forming his cabinet in winning over two dissident parties from the Opposition, the Slovene Clericals led by Father Korosetz (who became Minister of the Interior) and Spaho's Bosnian Moslems. With them he formed a new government party, the Yugoslav Radical Union.

Towards the Croat opposition, the attitude of the Regent and the Premier was one of readiness to co-operate provided they, not the Opposition, laid down the terms. Some conciliatory gestures were made. One of the government's first acts was to amnesty some 10,000 political prisoners; later on dissident Croats such as Dr. Kosutić were permitted

55

to return from exile and Stoyadinović's ill-fated attempt in 1937 to ratify the Concordat with the Vatican was to some extent an attempt to conciliate the Catholic Croats. Although the outburst of Serb Orthodox opinion against the Concordat, which in July 1937 reached the point of rioting in the streets of Belgrad, falls into the sphere of foreign rather than domestic politics, the excuse for the demonstrations rose from the status of the various churches in Yugoslavia.

In 1919 the three most important bodies of religious opinion, the Orthodox predominating in Serbia and the Voivodina, the Catholics in Slovenia, Croatia and Dalmatia, the Moslems in Bosnia together with smaller groups such as the Uniates, the Protestants and the Jews, were promised full equality of status within the new state. Actually the position of the Serb Orthodox church, intimately bound up as it was with the heroic national struggle of the Serbs against the Turks, tended to become dominant in a state wherein Serb centralism had won the day. It followed that in 1929 the legal position of the Orthodox church, together with its attendant rights and certain definite privileges, received statutory definition earlier than those of any other body. The Moslems' legal position was not defined until 1936 and in 1937 Stoyadinović pointed out that in satisfying the Concordat he was only giving the Catholics the equality of recognition which had been accepted in principle in 1919. The Orthodox leaders replied that certain provisions went far beyond equality and bestowed exclusive privileges on the Catholics—such as the benefit 'of the clergy', whereby clerics, for certain offences, were amenable to ecclesiastical authority only, or various clauses concerning property, or the freedom guaranteed to 'Catholic Action' which the Serbs maintained placed a sinister instrument of propaganda in the hands of an extra-Serb power.

The political use made of these grievances throws interesting light on the political situation under Stoyadinović. While his semi-dictatorial régime had done nothing to conciliate the two wings of the Opposition at Belgrad and at Zagreb, it had proved to be too liberal for the extremists. Between 1935 and 1937 the fascist Yugoslav National Party received distinguished recruits in the persons of two ex-Premiers, Yevtić and later, General Zhivković. Their following was limited to Serbia and small at that, for the large majority of the Yugoslav populace remained un-compromisingly democratic. They had little hold even in the usual stronghold of fascism, the universities, for here the general trend of opinion was radical—a radicalism which the government readily called communist although the influence of orthodox Marxism was and is slight (it could hardly be otherwise in a predominantly rural and intensely democratic society). In July 1937 this Yugoslav National Party tried to mobilise the outburst of religious feeling against Stoyadinović by representing the Concordat as a betrayal of the Serbs to the Italians. The result was hardly what they expected. The Serb peasants swallowed the bait and joined in the demonstrations against Stoyadinović, but they demanded not a dictator but a complete return to democratic institutions. In Croatia where the Premier had hoped for a favourable reaction profound indifference pre-vailed. Some interpreted the Concordat as a genuine gesture to the Croats, but others looked upon it as an attempt to drive a wedge between the peasant masses and their clerical leaders, in other words, a means of breaking the unity of the Croat opposition just as the disaffection of Korosetz had divided opinion in Slovenia. If this was the meaning of the manœuvre, it failed. Dr. Matćek declared that the Croats only demanded the revision of the constitution and were interested in political not religious reform. The lack of interest in Croatia, combined with the fury of resentment in Serbia led Stoyadinović at the beginning of 1938 to announce that he had given up all intention of negotiating a Concordat. The Catholic hierarchy met the announcement with a dignified protest and there the matter dropped.

Apart from the Concordat disturbances the first two years of the Stoyadinović régime brought little change in the domestic policy of Yugoslavia. The government, based upon the 'Yugoslav Radical Union', was undisputedly in control. Periodic rioting in the universities and discontent among the peasants testified to the unwillingness of the people to be governed quasi-dictatorially, but the relative quiescence of the Opposition showed the difficulty of crystallising and canalising the general discontent. It is one thing to oppose a government, quite another to have an alternative ready. Moreover, once the return of world prosperity began to solve many of the old agrarian problems and the relative liberality of the Stoyadinović régime took some of the bitterness out of Croat and Slovene public opinion, the Opposition had to concentrate its criticism more and more upon the foreign policy of the government. And it is here that an opposition is least likely to exercise any decisive influence.

The rapprochement between the two wings of the Opposition which had begun with the electoral alliance of 1935 was taken a step further in October 1937, when the Belgrad and Zagreb Opposition signed a manifesto which laid down the basis of their collaboration and the fundamental points upon which agreement had been reached. The document is interesting for it also outlines the means whereby the Opposition hoped to bring about their reforms. They were agreed that the Constitutions of 1921 and 1931 had no validity, since they were made without the full consent of the sovereign people. Thus the present government was without legal status and the Opposition parties had now to co-operate in order to establish a legal (i.e. democratically elected) government which would substitute for the 1931 Constitution a Fundamental Law guaranteeing a liberal democratic parliamentary and constitutional monarchy, at the same time draw up a new and fully democratic electoral law and then decree free elections for a Constituent Assembly. This assembly would seize the nettle of federalism versus centralism and determine the final organisation of the state.

YUGOSLAVIA SINCE THE ANSCHLUSS

1938 was spent under the shadow of events abroad—of the Anschluss in March and the Czech crisis in September. The sweeping changes wrought by the Germans in Central Europe transformed the whole aspect of Yugoslavia's domestic problems by striking at their root—the Croat Opposition. At the beginning of 1938 there were still three groups among the Croats, the nationalists of General Sarkotić, the terrorists or Ustasi (in exile, naturally) and the political opposition of Dr. Matćek. Since the first group pinned their faith to a Habsburg restoration which would unite Austria, Hungary and Croatia, the Anschluss deprived them of their programme. The Austrian Legitimists were in prison and Hitler in Vienna. General Sarković let it be understood that he and his followers would welcome a rapprochement with Belgrad and would be prepared to accept autonomy for Croatia and Dalmatia within the limits of the present constitution. The Ustasi had lost one sanctuary when Italy and Yugoslavia buried the hatchet in 1937. In March 1938 Vienna was closed to them while throughout 1937 Hungary had been steadily improving her relations with Yugoslavia and Janka Puzta was a thing of the past. They had now no base beyond the frontiers of Yugoslavia and this fact, combined with the relative liberality of Stoyadinović's régime, put an end to terrorism.

As to Stoyadinović's relations with the official Opposition

(Matćek's Croat party and the Belgrad Opposition), the external situation played straight into his hands. By the agreement of November 1937, the two main planks of the Opposition were, first of all the abolition of the present constitution coupled with elections for a new Constituent Assembly and then the drawing up of a new constitution which would satisfy the democratic and federal aspirations of the people. The Opposition linked their demand for democratic institutions with the question of expediency in foreign politics. The great western democracies had no desire to expand at the expense of smaller states whereas the Axis Powers were bent on imperialist aggression. Surely in the interests of Yugoslavia's very integrity, the time had come to make a stand for democracy, the West and the *status quo* against the permeation, the propaganda, the politicised economics and power politics of Germany and her junior partner, Italy.

The answer given by Stoyadinović to the Opposition programme did not vary. He maintained that new constituent elections and a new constitution would throw the country into an uproar and possibly create a deep cleavage just at a time when a united front and internal stability were most necessary to meet the possibility of foreign aggression. The stabilising work of twenty years could not be overturned in this manner. Moreover he resolutely turned his face against any modification of the constitution until young King Peter II should come of age. The work of his father must be handed on to him intact. Actually these appeals to dynastic sentiment were quite secondary. Stoyadinović's main line of argument was the need for internal stability in face of the possibility of an international crisis.

The second plank of the Opposition programme—the return to democracy and some measure of federalism—fared no better. Stoyadinović denied that his régime was dictatorial. He had restored many liberties, Croats were free to come and go and criticise as they pleased, in the first few months of 1938 alone over seventy *emigrés* had returned to Croatia. If Matćek had in mind an unleashing of the more radical elements in the towns and universities (which the government were determined to classify as communist) then let him consider the melancholy example of Spain. Yugoslavia, argued Stoyadinović, could not permit herself the luxury of a civil war and the foreign intervention which would inevitably accompany it. To which the Opposition could only reply that the denial of democratic rights to the people might bring about a revolution more rapidly than a properly organised general election with the promise of democracy to follow.

This is roughly how government and Opposition martialled their arguments in March 1938. Thereafter the arrival of German divisions in Carinthia gave Yugoslavia a common frontier with the Nazi Reich. The whole country—especially Slovenia and Croatia in the north—were profoundly disturbed. Stoyadinović assured them that Germany desired a strong united Yugoslavia and had guaranteed to treat the Slovene minority in Carinthia fairly. The arrival—almost simultaneously with this assurance—of a Slovene delegation to complain of their ill-treatment by the Nazis led the Yugoslavs to wonder whether Germany meant equally little by her 'desire' for a 'strong Yugoslavia.'

The Opposition reacted immediately to the new danger. As the leading personality of the whole Opposition, Dr. Matćek could not follow General Sarković's right-about turn and accept the hitherto unacceptable constitution, but he gave signs of a more conciliatory attitude. His speeches began to stress the need of unity and of settling the Serb-Croat split while there was yet time. At the beginning of August it was announced that he would go to Belgrad for the first time since 1935. He arrived on 14 August and was greeted by large crowds. People noticed that his first speeches made no reference to federalism and seemed milder in tone; however any hope of conciliation was immediately dashed. Dr. Matćek conferred only with the leaders of the Belgrad Opposition. He saw neither Stoyadinović, nor Korosetz, nor the Regent, and on the 15th the joint Opposition issued a strongly worded manifesto condemning the government and calling for democracy and constituent elections. The warmth of Matćek's reception in Belgrad was in part due to the clouds gathering on the Czech horizon. The youth of the country, led by the Sokols and the students, were already demonstrating for their 'fellow Slavs' against Nazi tyranny and for the return of Yugoslavia to her 'traditional friendship with France. This was, of course, the line taken by the Opposition, and Matćek warned the government repeatedly that its pro-Axis policy would finally entail the enslavement of Yugoslavia.

Stoyadinović's reply was first to ban all public demonstrations, then on 27 August to reconstruct his Cabinet. The significance of the change lay in the fact that two ministers, Croat by birth, were dropped and Dr. Buitsch, the Minister for Physical Culture, lost his portfolio. Now Dr. Buitsch, as official leader of the whole Sokol movement, had endorsed their anti-Axis, pro-west policy. His dismissal was thus a rebuff to public opinion and an indication of Stoyadinović's determination to continue his balancing act between the Axis and the democracies.

After the September crisis, the Munich agreement and later the Vienna Award the government could argue that its policy had been triumphantly vindicated. Czechoslovakia's democratic institutions had not brought her the support of the western democracies. Hungary, the semi-authoritarian state, gained people and territory through her friendship with the dominant Axis Powers. Yugoslavia could not have been given a more striking example of where her real interests lay. Stoyadinović realised that the psychological moment for new elections had come, and on 10 October they were announced for 11 December.

The Government's Radical Union, consisting of Stoyadinović's followers in Serbia and in official positions all over the country, the Slovene Clericals and the Bosnian Moslems, gained a new recruit at the beginning of the electoral campaign in the form of M. Hodjera's Yugoslav People's Party, a group to the extreme right which a year before had helped to instigate the Concordat rioting against the government. Now Hodjera received a portfolio. The electoral campaign which covered six weeks was noticeably less repressive to the Opposition than any previous elections since 1929. The government founded their case partly upon their foreign policy, but mainly upon the process of internal consolidation which had been going on since 1935. The régime was now so liberal that Dr. Matćek could come to Belgrad and make violent public attacks on the government. This compared favourably, declared Father Korosetz, with Croatia, where Matćek's Peasant Guard made short work of any criticism of the Croat leaders. Stoyadinović let it be understood that he considered the Croat problem to be one which time and patience and restored prosperity would settle without the need for big constitutional changes which he would continue to oppose. He preferred to deal with the problem—as a banker and an economist well might—not from the point of view of frayed nerves and nationalist sensibilities, but from the 'business' aspect, the increased prosperity of the peasants since their debts had been taken over by his government, the new stability given to the workers by the 1937 Social Insurance Acts, the benefits which would accrue to the whole people by the new Six Year Plan of development

63

and public works, financed by a 4,500 million dinar internal loan, which in itself was a sure sign of returning prosperity. Thus the government's campaign touched far more on economic than on constitutional topics and Stoyadinović's appeal to the country was based on work achieved and the prospect of further construction. One other aspect of Stoyadinović's campaign deserves comment—his adoption, tentative but sufficiently obvious, of a semi-fascist technique of 'leadership'. On a number of electoral tours he was accompanied by uniformed green-shirted youths for whom the populace coined the name 'the Milan[1] guard'. This guard performed the function of a claque, to which they added the rather more significant practice of greeting Stoyadinović with cries of 'Vojda, Vojda' (Leader, Leader) and an ostentatious display of saluting. Among the democratic peasantry and urban working class these tactics aroused deep suspicion and certain districts in the heart of old Serbia voted the Opposition list. Among them—significantly—was Topola, the home of the Karageorgević dynasty.

In October the Opposition were in a far less advantageous position than they had been in August. Their main argument —foreign policy—had been turned against them and with it their chance of invading the government's stronghold, Serbia, and of securing a majority which would sweep them to a dominant position in the new Skuptšina. They, like the government, had their ranks swelled by new recruits at the beginning of the campaign but their addition was really an added embarrassment. According to the 1931 electoral law, any party offering candidates had to be able to get a nomination in every constituency. Croats standing alone could not find the necessary supporters in Serbia. The Serb Opposition was handicapped in the same way when it came to Croatia. This purely strategic difficulty had partly

[1] After Milan Stoyadinović.

determined their electoral alliance in 1935. Now in 1938 another group—the extreme right wing semi-fascist Yugoslav Nationalists of Yevtić and Zhivković—were similarly handicapped. There were many constituencies in which they could not secure a nomination, in which case they would be debarred from presenting candidates at all. They approached the Croat and Serb Opposition and it was agreed that a united anti-governmental *bloc* with a single Opposition list should be formed. And it was on this basis that the Opposition 'went to the country'.

It is difficult to imagine why Dr. Matćek consented to such a singular *mésalliance*. Up to October 1938 it was perfectly clear that the Opposition stood for democratic institutions, a new constitution and a settlement of the federal issue. The inclusion of Yevtić and Zhivković meant that the Opposition list now included opponents of democracy more thorough-going than Stoyadinović's fairly liberal Radical Union, opponents of federalism so uncompromising that Matćek had in the past suffered imprisonment at their hands, and centralists as rigid at least as the late King Alexander. The ordinary elector could be pardoned a certain bewilderment at the choice of candidates set before him. He was no longer being asked to vote for a specific programme but merely against the government and he might well ask, if the Opposition were successful, to what kind of team he would be entrusting the coach of state. Everything in their past history suggested that the horses would pull in diametrically opposite directions.

The elections passed off in relative quiet, but in some districts demonstrations ended in violence and rioting, during which four people were killed and some fourteen injured. The uncertainty introduced by the joint Opposition list has been carried over into any analysis of the results. The government list obtained 1,636,000 votes or 58·9 % of the electorate. The Opposition list received 1,336,000 votes or 40·9 %. The government figures were 52,000 less than in 1935, the Opposition 250,000 more. Must this be interpreted as a striking defeat for the government and a vindication of the general desire for democracy, a new constitution and a reorientation in foreign policy? It is difficult to give a definite reply. Compared with the 98 and 99 percentages of Germany or Russia, the Stoyadinović régime made a poor showing. But it is just this poor showing which goes to prove that Yugoslavia is far from being a complete dictatorship. A government which admits that over 40 % of the electorate have voted against it cannot by any stretch of the imagination be called totalitarian. The issue between dictatorship and democracy is thus far from being a clear one. To a certain extent the choice lies between degrees of democracy and it must be remembered that the government list got 70 % of the votes in Slovenia whose collective peasant economy is infinitely more democratic than the economies of many fully democratic states. The question was further complicated by the extent to which the 250,000 increase in the Opposition list was due to added votes from the semi-fascist Yugoslav Nationalists and the government's lower vote due to the transference of Nationalist support to the Opposition. It is true that both Yevtić and Zhivković were defeated in their Serb constituencies, but it has been estimated that over 500,000 Nationalists voted the Matćek list. If this was the case, the strength of the Opposition proper (based not on vote catching but on fidelity to full democratic principles) had fallen by 250,000 and the government (which presumably in 1935 had the advantage of these 500,000 extremists) increased its voting strength in other and possibly more moderate circles.

The regional division of the voting is more instructive. Stoyadinović received 70 % of the votes in Serbia and

Slovenia; Matćek 80 % in Croatia and Dalmatia. Here was obvious statistical evidence of the deep gulf between Serb and Croat which the last three years of semi-liberal government and all Stoyadinović's optimism had done nothing to bridge. If Stoyadinović's aim in holding elections had really been to make use of the September crisis and the German danger in order to rally the whole country into a national front behind him (as 'Vojda' perhaps!) then he failed lamentably. The old divisions reappeared, reinforced by three years' waiting and disappointment. When (under the electoral law by which the majority—however small—obtains three-fifths of the seats and a share of the rest) the government secured 306 seats to the Opposition's 68, the Croats announced that they would boycott Belgrad and thus the elections ended in a tragi-comedy similar to those of 1921, 1931 or 1935. As a record of progress towards national unity it was not impressive.

The new year opened in an atmosphere of uncertainty. Some observers saw signs of impending change in the transference on 21 December of Dr. Korosetz from the Ministry of the Interior to the Presidency of the Senate. His change of office gave rise to speculation, for Matćek was known to dislike him and some suggested that Korosetz had been moved from the ministry in order to open the way to Serb-Croat negotiations. Another theory was that Korosetz had proposed a National Unity cabinet including Opposition Croats to Stoyadinović and had resigned on his refusal to consider it. In the light of the much greater changes which were to follow early in the new year, this second view seems more plausible.

On 15 January the Opposition formally announced their non-co-operation with the Skuptšina and when on 3 February parliament assembled to examine the validity of the deputies' mandates, only the 19 members of the Belgrad

67

Opposition put in an appearance. And they came with a specific purpose, to bring to light the grave electoral abuses —pressure, intimidation, use of the police force, of armed youths, terrorism in country districts—of which the Stoyadinović régime had been guilty in the previous December. The indictment was impressive and its effect heightened by the behaviour of two of Stoyadinović's followers who denounced the Croats from the tribune and made on them what virtually amounted to a declaration of war. The fact that one of these men, Atćimović, was the ex-Prefect of Police and present Minister of the Interior added a sinister tone to the outburst.

In the night five ministers resigned from Stoyadinović's cabinet. This faction forced his hand and Belgrad woke up on 4 February to find that his long 'reign' had come to an end. The Regent asked another member of the Radical Union, the Minister of Social Policy, M. Tsetković, to form a ministry. The choice seemed significant, for Tsetković was one of the ministers whose resignation had brought the issue to a head. Stoyadinović had no post in the new cabinet, but after a few days' uncertainty it became clear that he was not likely to make an attempt to split the Radical Union by seceding and taking as many followers as he could with him. He announced his support of Tsetković and (perhaps as a *quid pro quo*) retained the Presidency of the Union.

The passing of Stoyadinović—sensational in its unexpectedness and speed—gave rise to much speculation. The foreign political issues are discussed on another page[1] and although it is probable that the February crisis was not primarily concerned with foreign politics, they may have played a contributory part. On the home front the semi-official explanation was the Regent's determination to find some solution to the endless problem of Serbs and Croats. The

[1] Cf. page 88.

elections made it clear that Stoyadinović had failed. Reports of Nazi activity among the dissident Croats and general discontent over the government's electoral campaign combined to stir the Regent to activity. Some circles even suggested that, unknown to Stoyadinović, an approach had been made to Matćek through Tsetković and that Matćek had drawn the line at negotiating with a cabinet which included Stoyadinović. The Regent therefore decided to deprive Stoyadinović of office and set up a cabinet whose task it would be to pass the budget and open negotiations with Matćek. Thereafter a 'unity' cabinet including Croat ministers would work out a final settlement and possibly prepare for new elections.

Support for this interpretation of the change can be drawn from the presence of M. Rujić, a Croat and a popular ex-Ban of Croatia, in the Cabinet as Minister of Justice, from the statements made by M. Tsetković in the Skuptšina urging the necessity of a rapid settlement, from the passing of a law to increase the scope of local autonomy and to relax the decrees dealing with freedom of the press, speech and public meeting. But for some months after the formation of the Tsetković government no move was made to open negotiations with Matćek in spite of his repeated warnings that the Croats were impatient, Nazi propaganda busy and the time short. This dilatoriness on the part of the government led certain critics to take an entirely different view of Stoyadinović's downfall.

Ever since the formation of the Yugoslav state, through its internal and external crises, behind a screen of changing statesmen and short-lived ministries, stable, unyielding, conscious of its prerogatives and of its secular connection with the nation's history, the dynasty of the Karageorgević has stood apart from the flux of political change and served as a principle of identity underlying the vicissitudes of Yugoslav politics. Since the death of Pasić in 1926 the political power of the reigning monarch has been very nearly absolute, not only during the period of royal dictatorship but before it, when Alexander chose puppet leaders for parliament (Vukičević for example) and ruled through them, or after it, under the Regency, when the influence exercised by Prince Paul was no less important for being eclipsed in the public eye by Stoyadinović. Of the two methods, government through a ministry has perhaps proved more successful, for so long as there has been a ministerial scapegoat the sovereign has been able to avoid the odium incurred by governing a country of independent peasants and dissident minorities quasi-dictatorially. Alexander's experience of undisguised autocracy was not a happy one.

The ministerial scapegoat has also acted as a species of safety valve. When some particular manifestation of governmental policy became too unpopular, it was possible to sacrifice the minister and not the policy and thus to draw off the pressure of indignant public opinion. In 1935 Yevtić's electioneering roused such protest that, after representations from the Croats, Prince Paul dismissed Yevtić and substituted Stoyadinović—to carry on exactly the same policy. Recent happenings offer an almost direct parallel with 1935. Stoyadinović was responsible for the electoral campaign. When the Belgrad Opposition made representations, Stoyadinović was deprived of office as quietly and easily as his predecessor, Yevtić, and the next Premier, Tsetković, was Prince Paul's choice to carry on an old policy under a new name.

Prince Paul was perhaps influenced by one other factor. A dictator in Yugoslavia can hardly be anything but a Karageorgević. The green-shirts, the saluting, the 'leadership' tactics of Stoyadinović probably helped Prince Paul to his decision. The Serb conception of kingship is not compatible with a non-royal centre of absolute power. Now Tsetković is a less remarkable personality than Stoyadinović. He is said to be more malleable. He does not hanker for shirted youths and organised acclamation and he is certainly the Regent's man. The absorption of Czechoslovakia frightened the government and on April 2 M. Tsetković opened negotiations with Dr. Maček in order to settle the twenty-year quarrel between Serb and Croat. Both had learnt from the fate of the Czechs and the Slovaks what small divided and uncertain nations must expect if they happened to have the misfortune to live within the German *Lebensraum*. Nazi propaganda was known to be increasing in Croatia. Maček had given a solemn warning that, if there were further delay, he could not answer for the patience of the Croats. So it was in an atmosphere of urgency, and to some extent of enthusiasm, that negotiations opened.

The first *élan* was sufficient to skirt two serious difficulties. The Croats abandoned their demand for an immediate abolition of the Constitution, new elections and a new Constituent Assembly while the Serbs abandoned their opposition to a federal solution. This principle once established, it was possible to go forward to a more detailed examination of the country's future status, but here the information yet available is so scanty that it is not possible to do more than indicate over which points the greatest difficulties arose. The scheme of division of powers between the local and the federal government has not been published but undoubtedly the question of the army must have aroused heated debate. It is known that Maček meant to demand a separate army for the Croats (the exclusion of Croat officers from advancement in an army predominantly Serb, had long been a serious grievance). If he did so, he must certainly have come up against the united opposition of the Serb General Staff.

Other administrative points were probably less thorny since a measure of bureaucratic decentralization has been gradually introduced in the last few years. Serious difficulties however arose over the question of the boundaries of the future Federal State of Croatia. Bosnia has been the bone of contention. This district contains a mixed population of about 48 % Orthodox Serbs, 20 % Catholic Croats and 30 % Moslem Bosnians. Its Serbs naturally want to go to Serbia, its Croats to Croatia. The Bosnians, threatened with the status of a minority in either state, have demanded a fourth—Bosnian—federal state to which the Croats say they are ready to accede provided the Croats in western Bosnia are allowed a plebiscite to say whether or no they wish to join Croatia. No agreement was reached, and within a short time questions of foreign policy engaged the Regent's attention.

It is hard to say whether Yugoslavia has lost her last chance of settling the internal problem. The Regent is undoubtedly in a difficult position. Behind him in Belgrad are the Serb oligarchs who have profited by their twenty years' ascendency, the Serb army which regards itself as the backbone of the state, the politicians who fear the consequences of granting autonomy to a people with such a strongly democratic temper as the Croats. In Zagreb, the discontented majority grow impatient, the more so now that agreement has been dangled before them and snatched away. Foreign propaganda is strong. The young men are not altogether deaf to those who suggest to the Croats the parallel of the Slovaks who now "freed from the yoke of the Czechs" enjoy a (nominally) independent existence as a Reich protectorate. Before either party makes a decision it may be too late.

6. FOREIGN POLICY

THE post-war history of Yugoslavia's foreign relations falls into two clearly distinct periods, the first opening with the Peace Treaties, the second with the Nazi Revolution. Roughly coinciding in time with this division was the change in Yugoslavia's internal structure from a democratic to an authoritarian régime. But though the periods are distinct, in reality the same struggle has been going on throughout the post-war years, the struggle between regional consolidation—on the lines of 'the Balkans for the Balkan peoples'— and the external pressure of the great Powers. The break marks a change not in the plot but in the dramatis personæ.

1919–1933

Consolidation.—Yugoslavia's geographical position gave her a footing in Danubia and the Balkans. The Balkans enjoyed a century-old reputation for violence and unrest; the Peace Treaties had just confirmed the disintegration of Austria-Hungary into five Danubian states whose economic nationalism and frontier disputes threatened to 'Balkanise' Central Europe. It followed that a policy of consolidation might be easier to postulate than to pursue.

The chief obstacle lay in the fact that both in Danubia and the Balkans the war left a legacy of victorious and defeated Powers, and the Peace Treaties satisfied the former and drove the latter into resentful isolation. In the heart of Danubia there was Hungary with her territory reduced by two-thirds, and over three million of her people living as minorities in the surrounding states. Revision of the Peace Treaties was the permanent refrain of her foreign policy, and territorial revision could only be at the expense of Czechoslovakia, Rumania and Yugoslavia. They, having

73

profited by the Treaties, rejected revision and supported the *status quo*.

This was the first deadlock. The second concerned Yugoslavia more urgently than either Rumania or Czechoslovakia, because it was connected with the Croat problem. The collapse of the Habsburg Empire had made possible the passing of the South Slav provinces of Austria-Hungary to Serbia. Once united with their Serb brethren, Slovenes and Croats found themselves on the defensive against the centralism of Belgrad. Certain groups—the Croat Nationalists of General Sarković for example—went further than the demand for Croat autonomy and played with the idea of a Habsburg restoration which should unite the two rump states of Austria and Hungary and draw back to their former allegiance the old South Slav provinces. The greater the tension between Serbia and Croatia, the more the Yugoslav government had to fear from any attempt to restore the Habsburgs.

From the first, Yugoslavia made it clear that she regarded such a restoration as a *casus belli*. In 1921 the ex-Emperor Charles made two abortive attempts to regain the throne of Hungary. Yugoslavia, Rumania and Czechoslovakia replied by forming the Little Entente, which was virtually a pact of mutual assistance against Hungary. This Entente may be called the first step towards Danubian consolidation. Unfortunately it had several radical defects: it was purely negative (designed only to prevent something), it was directed against another Danubian country and it crystallised the revisionist-*status quo* split while producing no machinery to overcome it.

Austria was also no partner to the Little Entente. Her objection to the *status quo* took the form of a keen desire to join her six million Germans to Germany's sixty-six. But Czechoslovakia felt as strongly about the Anschluss as did Yugoslavia about a Habsburg restoration. Thus the Little

Entente turned its face against either change (and indeed against every other) and Danubia remained unconsolidated.

In the Balkans, Bulgaria and her revisionist claims prevented close collaboration of all the Balkan Powers. As we have seen, Bulgaria's territorial grievance lay in Macedonia, where she disputed the right of Greece and Yugoslavia to share a territory which she held to be inhabited by Bulgars. Her encouragement of I.M.R.O. added fuel to the flames and the heavily guarded frontier between Bulgaria and Yugoslavia with its fence of barbed wire offered an unhappy commentary on Balkan peace. Bulgaria's other grievance was her state of unilateral disarmament.

External pressure.—Pre-war Serbian history was dominated by Austro-German pressure eastwards and the protective counter-action of the great Slav Power, Russia. At the end of the war, Yugoslavia found herself without her traditional guarantor. The Czarist régime had disappeared in a violent revolution; the communist dictatorship of the Russian proletariat which stood in its place was no ally for King Alexander, who had been brought up at the Court of the Czar and later, in 1921, was threatened by a communist attentat. A very marked anti-communist feeling has dominated governing circles in Yugoslavia ever since the creation of the state, so much so that to this day the Yugoslav government almost alone in Europe has never officially recognised Soviet Russia. Thus the old make-weight against Germany (and the only state which by its geographical position and sheer weight of numbers could ever hope to act as a make-weight in Eastern Europe) was excluded from the Balkans.

During these years France tended to take Russia's old place. French armies had made possible Serbia's success, French money had tided the state over its first financial difficulties. They were sister democracies united in a keen dislike of Italy. France counted on Yugoslavia in her Eastern

75

scheme of reinsurance treaties, although a definite pact was not signed until 1927. Above all, France as the great *status quo* Power could be relied upon to preserve the *status quo* for Yugoslavia. France gave her blessing to the Little Entente which in its turn supported France's policy on the League of Nations.

Thus the pre-war mantle of Russia fell upon France's shoulders. And Italy's expansive threat took the place of the old Austro-German *Drang nach Osten*. For the first ten or twelve years after the Peace Treaties a constant state of tension existed between Italy and Yugoslavia. It began of course with Italy's attempt to detach not only Trieste, Gorizia and Istria from Yugoslavia (here she was successful) but Dalmatia too. Then came the struggle for Fiume which after five years was also taken from the Yugoslavs. In 1924 the two countries attempted to make the best of their long bickering and signed a Treaty of Friendship. It was given a very lukewarm reception in Yugoslavia, for the people remained convinced that Italy's final schemes included the total exclusion of Yugoslavia from the Adriatic. The Treaty of Tirana between Italy and Albania in 1926 and a further agreement in 1927 which virtually gave Italy a mandate over Albania and closed the narrows of Otranto at the entrance to the Adriatic led to a fresh outburst of hostility. With Venezia, Giulia, Trieste and Fiume gone and Albania pocketed, how long would it be before Dalmatia, Yugoslavia's only outlet into any sea, would go the same way? In 1929 the Treaty of Friendship was not renewed, a violent press campaign kept feeling at fever pitch which exploded in anti-Italian rioting when in 1932 Mussolini's intervention to preserve the Venetian lions in Troguir lent colour to the rumours of Italy's schemes in Dalmatia.

The Adriatic offensive was accompanied by other manœuvres which seemed to threaten not only Yugoslavia's Adriatic seaboard but the very integrity of her territory. We have seen how her internal stability was disturbed by Croat and Macedonian opposition. Italy appeared to be giving tacit support and sanction to terrorists from both regions. I.M.R.O. and Ustasi agents came and went through Italy and there were camps for them in various Italian towns. Finally Italy seemed ready to back any foreign Power with designs upon Yugoslavia. After 1926 Mussolini began to give open encouragement to Hungarian revisionism; in 1933 he was caught smuggling arms into that country[1] and there were rumours that he was toying with a Habsburg restoration backed by Austrian, Hungarian and Croat Legitimists. In the south, Greece was egged on to block Yugoslavia's attempts to negotiate a free zone in the port of Salonika, and any conciliatory move by Yugoslavia was countered by some Italian *démarche* (for example her treaties with Greece and Turkey). Needless to say, Italy's tactics were especially suited to blocking all attempt at independent consolidation in Danubia or the Balkans.

1933–1937

Consolidation.—The first Nazi onslaught upon Austria in 1933–34 was the earliest intimation to the eastern states that the Nazi revolution had restored a great Power of ruthless ambition and restless dynamism to the European scene. The reaction in Danubia and the Balkans was a definite move towards closer co-operation. The Little Entente revised its statute and arranged for a collaboration so close as to amount to a practical fusing of their three foreign policies into one. But consolidation remained incomplete. Austria and Hungary did not move into the orbit of France, the League and the Little Entente, but drew closer to Italy, signing the Rome Protocols with her in 1934, a policy which might be

[1] The Szent Gothard affair.

directed against Germany but equally well threatened the interests of Yugoslavia, especially since the Schuschnigg government in Austria was openly legitimist (that is, in favour of a Habsburg restoration). All Czechoslovakia's attempts in 1935 and 1936 to establish more friendly relations with Austria and Hungary and achieve a measure of co-operation between the two rival *blocs* came to grief on the issue of the Habsburgs, whom the Austrians would not give up nor the Yugoslavs accept.

In the Balkans, however, the policy of consolidation made tremendous strides. The new Nazi danger hastened the *pourparlers* which had been going on for some time between Rumania, Yugoslavia, Greece and Turkey, and in February 1934 a Balkan pact was signed in Athens providing for concerted action against external aggression and for a measure of consolidation on foreign political issues. Bulgaria and Albania stood out of the agreement, Bulgaria because of her still unsatisfied claims to a revision of the Peace Treaties (covering Macedonia and her unilateral disarmament), Albania because she was not a free agent.

Yugoslavia was not content to let the matter rest. In 1933 King Alexander had already embarked on a policy of rapprochement with Bulgaria; in 1934 the troublesome Macedonian problem was shelved—perhaps permanently—by Bulgaria's vigorous dissolution of I.M.R.O. The disarmament provisions remained, but they were not sufficient to check the growth of cordiality and in January 1937 Yugoslavia and Bulgaria signed a Treaty of Friendship. As Stoyadinović took this step without consulting the council of the Balkan Entente, the agreement was given a malicious welcome in Italy and Germany as a blow at the Balkan Pact. Events proved their rejoicing to be premature. The work of consolidation went on.

External pressure.—Germany's return to power soon dominated every other political interest. Italy was quickly ousted from her place of principal disturber of the peace in Eastern Europe, but direct pressure on Yugoslavia was at first slight. General Goering began to holiday on the Adriatic coast and a few official visits were exchanged; the German offensive —as we saw in Section 2—lay in the sphere of trade and the visits of Dr. Schacht were for the time being more important than those of General Goering. Nevertheless an intensive propaganda campaign began to disseminate Nazi views and advertise Nazi efficiency. The organisation of the German minorities in Slovenia and the Banat went forward along the usual lines. Slovenia soon had its S.S. and its S.A., which by 1937 were conducting field days and manœuvres in the Karst. A subtle form of economic penetration accompanied this activity. In the crisis years 1931 and 1932 Slovenia went through a period of agricultural bankruptcy. This opened the door to a system of land purchase by Germans which obviously had political and strategic motives, for land was acquired all along the main lines of communication. Wilhelm I used to dream of a German corridor to the Adriatic and had encouraged German settlement in Slovenia. The new policy seemed uncomfortably like an echo of the old scheme and in 1937 the Yugoslav government set up a Slovene commission to regulate the sale of Slovene land. However, the Germans were able to evade the restrictions by setting up Slovene strawmen to do the buying for them. The reaction of the Slav peasantry was unanimously opposed to German permeation, but the increasingly pro-German policy of the government tied the hands of Father Korosetz (the Slovene Minister of the Interior).

Once the expansion of Germany's trade with Yugoslavia had reached important proportions, political overtures began to accompany the commercial drive. In 1936 Dr. Schacht spoke of the political understanding which closer economic relations must bring and in 1937 the German Foreign Minister, Von Neurath, paid an official visit to Belgrad. Foreign journalists began to speculate whether Yugoslavia was not by now firmly on the Axis, and it is significant that, after a visit paid to Italy in December 1937, Stoyadinović had specifically to deny that he intended either to leave the League, join the anti-Comintern Pact or recognise General Franco. The significance, of course, lay not in his denials but in the fact that the questions were ever raised at all.

The growing influence of Germany at least did one good turn to Yugoslavia. Italy's enmity and contempt changed into an almost frantic desire to make friends. By 1937 it was obvious that Italy could no longer hope to keep Germany out of Austria. She sought a counterweight to Germany's hegemony in Central Europe by signing a Pact of Friendship with Yugoslavia in March 1937. The secrecy and suddenness of the negotiations were a serious blow to the Little Entente, whose 1933 statute arranged for common consultation. As with Bulgaria and the Balkan Pact, Yugoslavia's independent treaty was greeted by the Axis Powers as a weakening of the Little Entente. In this case, their delight had more foundation.

The new friendships with Germany and Italy brought with them an obvious decline in cordiality towards France. Since 1932 the world crisis had so crippled France's economy that she ceased to be the universal provider of East European loans. Herself an agricultural country, she had never been a great purchaser of Danubian foodstuffs. Now she bought even less. Moreover, the authoritarian and anti-communist régime of Stoyadinović felt little warmth towards France's Popular Front government. Stoyadinović had probably not forgiven M. Blum's anti-Yugoslav and anti-dictator campaign in 1931. When the French Foreign Minister, Delbos, visited Belgrad in the course of a goodwill tour in December 1937 he received little response from the government, in spite of offering extraordinarily favourable terms for the import of Yugoslav grain. But it was France's external policy rather than her home front which was responsible for the alienation. French policy identified itself with the League and the *status quo*. Since 1933 two events of major importance had occurred. Russia had been admitted to the League and by her pacts with France and Czechoslovakia now joined the defenders of the *status quo* in Eastern Europe. The other event was the failure of Sanctions against Italy which destroyed the prestige of the League. Yugoslavia's reaction was inevitable. The government preferred German to Russian intervention in the Balkans. Soviet Russia remained the unrecognised Bolshevik state. And the failure of Sanctions (whose application incidentally handed over about 60 % of Yugoslavia's Italian trade to Germany) convinced Stoyadinović that the League system and the power of the western democracies was not what the smaller states had supposed. But if the collective guarantee had failed, a small state had only one alternative policy—to make friends with the potential aggressor and hope for the best; this in so many words was what Stoyadinović proceeded to do.

It need not be supposed that people liked the policy. It was a cabinet, not a popular programme. As early as 1936 the Serb Opposition raised their voices to protest against a policy of 'abandoning old alliances, weakening bonds of tried friendship and committing' Yugoslavia 'to exactly contrary combinations'. The youth movement of the Sokols was strongly pro-French, pro-Czech and pro-Russian. So were the students. So—naturally—were the democratic Opposition. When President Benes paid Yugoslavia a state visit in 1937 the populace made use of the occasion to stage a huge demonstration for democracy. Later in the same year, the rioting in Belgrad over the Concordat was directed as much against the Italians as against the government. The

Serbs protested that the 'selling' of Yugoslavia to the Vatican was the latest step in the enslavement of their country to the fascist Axis. The Premier was unmoved. His policy, he said, was one of keeping old friends and making new ones. The Opposition retorted that in a crisis everybody's friend is nobody's friend and that might be Yugoslavia's fate.

YUGOSLAV FOREIGN POLICY SINCE THE ANSCHLUSS

Consolidation.—When with the Anschluss of March 1938 the Nazi battering ram hurtled its first tremendous blow against the territorial system of the Peace Treaties, it was not only the walls of Austria which crashed to the ground. Every straining beam, every weak point in the masonry, every crumbling brick felt the impact. Old grievances took on a new urgency, territorial ambitions which had been put by reappeared on the scene, revisionism received a new lease of life. The old cleavage between 'revisionist' and *status quo* Powers ploughed its way once more across the face of Europe, much in the same way as the seismic disturbances of an earthquake, however distant, can fissure the ground at points where the crust is permanently weak. It follows that the process of consolidation since the Anschluss has gone forward very fitfully. Even such results as can be registered are of doubtful validity. When all the old bitter issues are suddenly reopened, new groupings can very well represent attempts to snatch a passing advantage from the general disintegration, rather than a serious attempt to bring it to an end. Moreover, some old revisionist claim or some new vista of revision (opened up by Herr Hitler's high-handed actions), cuts across almost every conceivable combination of states in Eastern Europe. Thus it is difficult to register as an act of pacification the agreement reached at Bled in August 1938 wherein the Little Entente Powers jointly recognised Hungary's right to re-arm, and all four states promised better treatment to

82

their respective minorities. Under normal circumstances such an agreement—the first formal act of consolidation on the part of Hungary and her neighbours since 1918—might have been called epoch-making. In fact, within two months Hungary was transferring the territory occupied by the Magyar minority in Slovakia to her own rule and pushing her claim to bring the whole of Ruthenia under St. Stephen's Crown, and there were rumours that the new contacts between Hungary and Yugoslavia might be used to press Hungarian claims on Rumania.

Similarly, the agreement reached on 28 July between Bulgaria and the State members of the Balkan Pact (Rumania, Yugoslavia, Greece and Turkey), wherein recourse to force was renounced and the Balkan Powers recognised Bulgaria's right to re-arm, could also—given a normal situation—be described as a milestone along the road of Balkan consolidation. But here again rumours that the break up of the Versailles system was tempting Bulgaria to toy with the idea of recovering the Dobruja from Rumania or of making a break through to the Aegean by annexing Greek Macedonia—with the help of anyone, great Power or Balkan neighbour, who might care to back the claim—suggests that the sweets of aggrandisement are likely to outweigh the virtues of co-operation so long as the European order continues to be regularly and violently convulsed.

The Balkan Powers cannot of themselves put an end to this succession of earthquakes. Only the intervention of extra-Balkan great Powers can restore stability. While there is a chance of fishing in the troubled waters churned up by the Axis Powers, Hitler will continue to find clients. The small states will swallow baits of their neighbours' territory even at the risk of finding themselves, together with their victim, firmly hooked to the Nazi line.

Thus the only consolidation worth speaking of lies in

signs of active intervention on the part of the important *status quo* Powers, of France and Great Britain to the west, of Russia to the east. Of these three, a guarantee from the western democracies would be more welcome for the simple reason of their geographical position. Russia is too near and too powerful and, as we have seen, inspires the Yugoslav Regency with profound distrust. But in spite of Prince Paul's visit to London in November 1938, in spite of rumours that England had a hand in Stoyadinović's downfall, in spite even of British talk (after the final rape of Czechoslovakia) of collective security against German aggression, the definite binding offer of support and co-operation which alone would commit Yugoslavia to a policy of resistance to the German advance, has not been forthcoming. Until it does, there will be no consolidation in the Balkans.

External pressure.—Since the Anschluss, Yugoslavia's external relations—like those of any other East European Power—have been dominated by Herr Hitler's succession of violent coups in Central Europe. Until 1938 the promise of future Nazi activity was everywhere, but after the first check in Austria in 1934 in no country had Hitler's offensive been actually launched. In Yugoslavia there was talk of the *Drang nach Osten*, the activities of local Nazi groups roused interest, the state of the country's trade balance with Germany caused a little uneasiness, but no one realized how fragile in fact was the structure of the Peace Treaties, nor how dynamic and irresistible the forces in Germany which were massing for the attack. March and the Anschluss brought a Reich, seventy millions strong, to the frontiers of Yugoslavia; September saw the dismemberment of a sister Slav state, like Yugoslavia a *status quo* Power; October brought the German Minister of Economics, Dr. Funk, to Belgrad with a grandiose scheme for undertaking the industrial development of Yugoslavia; March 1939 completed the process of annihilation in Czechoslovakia and established a German protectorate over nine million Slavs, and in the wake of the German Leviathan, smaller fish snapped up what they could in the prevailing chaos. Poland entered Teschen in September, Hungary secured parts of Slovakia and Ruthenia in October, to which she added the remainder of Ruthenia and a line of strategic Slovak towns in the following March.

It is against this background of disintegration and violent change that Yugoslav foreign policy has been played out. Situated at one remove from the heart of the disturbance, the Yugoslav government has endeavoured to keep up the appearance of a scrupulously detached observer, an understandable policy but not one which appealed either to the Opposition or—if demonstrations and rioting are any indication—to the people in general. In March 1938 the appearance of the German divisions on the frontiers of Slovenia shook the country to the core, and Matćek used the crisis to attack the whole basis of Stoyadinović's policy. A new force was at work in Europe which the Yugoslavs would find themselves powerless to resist. Offers of friendship made to the invading hosts resembled the behaviour of the young lady of Riga. Only firm action could put a stop to a process which would bring Hitler to Slovenia tomorrow, Belgrad next week, the Bosphorus in a year's time. And firm action could mean one thing only, collaboration with the great western democracies for the preservation of the European equilibrium. This became the rallying cry of the Opposition generally and was taken up by the more radical elements in the population. As the crisis deepened in Czechoslovakia, the protest grew more passionate. Students rioted and demonstrated and a tremendous welcome was accorded to Matćek when he came to Belgrad in August. Stoyadinović, however, kept up his attitude of complete reserve. In August demonstrations were banned and a supposedly pro-Czech minister dropped from the Cabinet. Otherwise the government's attitude was one of masterly inactivity. Even at the height of the September crisis, Stoyadinović refused to order either general or partial mobilisation—a fact which seems to contradict the rumour that he had agreed to honour his obligations under the Little Entente Pact should Hungary invade Slovakia.

The outcome of the September crisis appeared to justify Stoyadinović. Czechoslovakia had thought it safe to ignore Germany and to rely upon the West and Russia—a policy which the Opposition in Yugoslavia contrasted favourably with Stoyadinović's practice of being on friendly terms with all the great Powers, but especially with his Axis neighbours. Now, argued Stoyadinović, the nemesis of relying on France and Great Britain had fallen upon the head of the Czech nation. Stripped, dismembered, defenceless, this 'friend' of the West was an adequate commentary upon the proposed change of policy, whereas Hungary, by courting the Axis, had obtained an important increase of territory and population. Stoyadinović's decision to hold elections reflected the degree to which he felt his foreign policy had been justified. The voting, however, showed that the Opposition was entirely unconvinced. The visit of Prince Paul to London in November also suggested that the Regent had his doubts about the wisdom of leading Yugoslavia into the dictators' camp.

Was this Stoyadinović's intention? It is certainly true that in his two years of office he broke away from the 'traditional' friendship with France, weakened the Little Entente and established cordial relations with Germany and Italy, but he could argue that his policy was dictated, not by a specific preference for the ideology of the Axis, but by a realist appreciation of the fact that the rise of Hitler had created

86

an entirely new problem for the East European states, and one which the old methods were quite inadequate to meet. To give one example, reliance on France had point so long as the League system still functioned and the Rhineland was demilitarized. To rely on France when both factors had disappeared would have meant placing Yugoslavia in much the same position as that which caused the downfall of the Czechs.

If this interpretation of Stoyadinović's policy is correct, it follows that he was as anxious as the Opposition to preserve the independence of Yugoslavia, but differed on the question of means. Speaking in the Skuptšina in 1937 he had declared, 'I am neither Germanophil nor Francophil but simply Serb,' and certainly his activity in bringing Bulgaria into closer contact with the Balkan Pact states, his consultations, following Munich, with his neighbours Rumania and Bulgaria and, above all, his reactions to Dr. Funk's economic proposals, suggest that he was sincere, for the sequel of Funk's much advertised offer to Yugoslavia to develop her territory and resources in return for a monopoly of her exports[1] was Yugoslavia's decision to sell no more to Germany than Germany could sell to her in order to avoid a dangerous onesidedness in the Yugoslav export trade.

On the other hand, certain manœuvres at the Mediterranean end of the Axis seemed to suggest that Stoyadinović was not wholeheartedly behind a common Balkan front, and even toyed with the idea of snapping up some trifle for Yugoslavia. After the Bled agreement with Hungary (of August 1938) there were rumours that Hungary's old patron, Italy, had been encouraging Yugoslavia to get into closer touch with her protégée. What the aim of such a move might be remained obscure, but after the visit of Count Ciano to Yugoslavia in January 1939, rumours circulated

[1] Cf. the German-Rumanian trade agreement of March 1939.

that the proposed rapprochement would be at the expense of Rumania. Hungary's claims on Transylvania would be pushed with Yugoslav support in return for Hungarian support should Yugoslavia re-open the question of the Banat and demand the cessation of Temesvar. Besides illustrating the extent to which Hitler's success at Munich re-opened every territorial issue in Central Europe, the proposal was significant in that it cut across another possibility of rapprochement, that of the 'Cordon Sanitaire', a linked line of neutral states from Baltic to Balkans, isolating Russia from Europe and blocking Germany's advance eastwards, a line which so far existed only in an embryonic form in the Polish-Rumanian Pact and to which it had been suggested that Yugoslavia might adhere. When the Rumanian Foreign Minister, M. Gafencu, visited Belgrad at the beginning of February 1939 some such Rumano-Yugoslav collaboration may have been suggested[1] and some observers linked Stoyadinović's fall (which occurred immediately after Gafencu's visit) with the possibility that he and the Regent were at cross purposes in the Rumanian problem, the Regent supporting Gafencu, Stoyadinović preferring Italy and 'Danubian co-operation' which would be 'within the framework of the Rome-Berlin Axis' (as Count Ciano expressed it on 23 January). Certain pressmen went so far as to suggest that Prince Paul during his November visit to London had been given the hint to draw closer to Rumania (in which country Great Britain had begun to show a certain positive interest). If this interpretation is correct, the fall of Stoyadinović must be counted as a setback to the Axis policy of disintegration in Eastern Europe.

One difficulty of interpretation lies in the fact that Italy's behaviour was decidedly ambiguous. Since the disappearance

[1] In a press *communiqué*, M. Gafencu said that the political action of the two countries made a closer alliance necessary.

of Austria, Yugoslavia had become the weak point of the Axis. The hastily patched up Italo-Yugoslav friendship of March 1937 was accompanied by a trade agreement which made a bid to salvage some of Yugoslavia's trade with Italy which Sanctions had delivered up to Germany. When Ciano visited Stoyadinović in January 1939 their conversations covered commercial relations, and Italy was said to have offered very advantageous terms to Yugoslavia in order to increase the volume of trade between them. These facts are reminders that before Dr. Schacht began his brilliant series of trade drives into Eastern Europe, Italy had slowly and painfully been building up for herself a sphere of economic and political influence there, and that on the Adriatic at least, the interests of the two ends of the Axis came into direct collision. It follows that when, during his January visit, Ciano spoke of collaboration for peace and order 'in that constructive spirit which characterises the Rome-Berlin Axis', he may have been urging Yugoslavia to follow Hungary's example of 12 January and join the anti-Comintern Pact; on the other hand he may have been discussing ways and means of constructing an East European *bloc*, tacitly backed by Italy, to keep Germany out of the Balkans.

Out of this maze of move and counter-move there emerged one unmistakable and unescapable fact, that Germany's expansion must sooner or later come into collision with the integrity of the Yugoslav state. In this context the annexation of Czechoslovakia was doubly significant, both with regard to the technique of aggression and to the aims pursued. One of the chief instruments of disintegration which Hitler found ready to hand in Czechoslovakia, was the existence in Slovakia of a deep-rooted desire for autonomy which, fed by Nazi money and propaganda, grew into a separatist movement, strong enough (with outside help) to disrupt the state. In Yugoslavia the same political lever existed. For twenty years the Croats had demanded autonomy and had instead been submitted to the centralising régime of Belgrad. To some extent the position was more serious in Yugoslavia, for here the dominant Serb majority is in many ways culturally inferior to the Croat minority. The Croat leaders lost no opportunity of declaring their fidelity to the dynasty and to the integrity of the state within its present frontiers, but after the annexation of Czechoslovakia Dr. Matćek issued a statement in which he appealed to the government to expedite negotiations with the Croats, for the eleventh hour had struck. A few days later it was officially denied in Zagreb that the Croats had appealed to Hitler to help them achieve 'autonomy', and the fact that such a denial should be necessary confirmed the rumour that among the younger and more violent autonomists (the Ustasi groups, for example, who have been receiving German money for some time) the idea of drawing Hitler into the dispute was at least under consideration.

Even more disturbing, from the Yugoslav point of view, was the sudden enlarging of the horizon of German expansion which the March crisis brought to light. It was no longer a question of the union of all Germans into one Reich. The former safeguard—that Hitler did not wish to annex foreign racial elements for fear of weakening his own— vanished overnight, and a new principle appeared in the speeches of the Nazi leaders, not a racial but an historic principle. Bohemia and Moravia were returning to their historic position of subordination within a great Germanic Empire. And the Yugoslavs remembered that Croatia and Slovenia and Dalmatia emerged from a similar position at exactly the same time under almost identical conditions. Why should the new historic claims cease on the frontiers of Carinthia? Or at the foot of the Julian Alps? Trieste was

once an Austrian port serving a German hinterland. Mussolini's speech on 26 March 1939—coinciding with the second
anniversary of the new Italo-Yugoslav friendship—included
the significant statement that in the Adriatic Italy's interests
were pre-eminent but not exclusive of those of the Slavs.
Did Mussolini add the mental reservation, 'But quite exclusive of those of the Germans'?

The new 'historic' principle
when applied to the Adriatic might strain the Axis to
cracking point, and Mussolini's pointed reference to Italo-
Yugoslav friendship and the interests of the Slavs suggested
that in this area Italy would be prepared for collaboration,
possibly 'inspired by the constructive spirit of the Axis' but
definitely directed against its other end.

The absorption of Czechoslovakia initiated three months
of unparalleled activity and confusion in the Balkans. The
already unstable framework was given another hearty shake
and long before it had recovered some kind of equilibrium,
however unsteady, Italy's invasion of Albania set the building
once more rocking on its foundations. Against these repercussions may perhaps be set Great Britain's departure
from her policy of passivity in Eastern Europe, her guarantees to Rumania and Greece, her pact with Turkey, but the
outcome of these British initiatives as far as Yugoslavia is
concerned remains obscure.

Yugoslavia is now reaping the dangerous fruits of Stoyadinović's policy of 'accommodation' with the Axis. The
independent basis of Danubian and Balkan co-operation has
almost disappeared. The Little Entente has vanished, the
Balkan Pact owing to the ambiguity of Yugoslavia's position
is showing signs of strain. Revisionism has reappeared in
Bulgaria, Greece and Rumania are guaranteed by the west.
Turkey, without consulting her Balkan co-signatories, has
come to an agreement with Great Britain. A reorientation
of the Balkan states into the old and fatal division of *status quo*

and revisionist Powers is thus clearly visible. How does Yugoslavia stand *vis-à-vis* this regrouping?

Everything depends upon her relations with the Axis Powers. Her economic dependence on one at least of the partners is immense, but need not necessarily be decisive. (Rumania for example has her economic pact with Germany and her British guarantee.) The real problem lies in the relations between Italy and Germany, thus in a matter *external* to Yugoslavia herself (the penalty of a policy of 'accommodation'). So long as Italy could hope to play an independent role in the Mediterranean and south-eastern Europe, Yugoslavia could hope, too, for independence in playing off Italy against Germany. Italy regarded German encroachments in Slovenia and German propaganda in Croatia with little less disfavour than the Yugoslavs and her anxiety for a strong Yugoslavia was shown by the sympathetic interest with which she followed the Serb-Croat negotiations and by the tenor of the visit paid by the Yugoslav Foreign Minister to Venice at the end of April. This community of interest in keeping Germany out of the Adriatic *may* have been at the bottom of the quiescence with which Yugoslavia greeted the occupation of Albania. The Germans are less likely to push down through Slovenia to Fiume, once Italy is in a position to close the straits of Otranto.

But Italy is ceasing to be a free agent. Even in March and April her policy was ambiguous. Since the signature of the Italo-German Alliance, her independence has in all probability been, practically extinguished—and with it goes Yugoslavia's only chance of independence, that of balancing herself between each end of the Axis. Prophecy is dangerous; but in all probability it will be her melancholy fate first to act as a lever to prise open Balkan solidarity and, that once accomplished, to be thrown away as of no further use.

The first steps of such a policy are already apparent. The Axis is bringing all its economic and diplomatic battery to bear upon Yugoslavia in order to persuade her to form a *bloc* with Hungary and Bulgaria. These three—opposed to the states guaranteed by or allied to the West (Rumania, Greece and Turkey)—would reopen the old territorial issues at the expense of the *'status quo'* (guaranteed) Powers. Bulgaria might demand the Dobruja, Hungary Transylvania, Yugoslavia the Banat from Rumania; Bulgaria and Yugoslavia could divide Greek Macedonia. Acquiescence in such a role would however virtually transform all three countries into Reich protectorates, for without the backing of the Axis, they could not hope to obtain either 'peaceful' or violent revision. Once they were committed to German help, they would have no defensive weapons left to stem the inevitable advance of German economic and political penetration.

If Yugoslavia were to resist, the outlook would be even more desperate. With Balkan solidarity destroyed, totally isolated from the West, at the mercy of her great neighbours, Yugoslavia may see a Nazi-sponsored movement for Croat independence deprive her of Croatia, a revolt among the German minority in Slovenia hand that province to the Reich while Italy may stage a 'protective' landing in Dalmatia to complete the claims of 1919. The Serbs, reduced to their pre-war status, will be lucky if they get as much independence as the Slovaks.

This is the unhappy position in which the Yugoslavs find themselves in 1939. Their internal disruption plays into the hands of the Axis. The decay of Italian independence hands over the country almost without hope of respite to Germany. In 1938 it could be said that the independence and integrity of Yugoslavia depended ultimately upon two things; her ability to solve her internal problem, to reconcile Serb

93

and Croat and to deprive Hitler of a weapon of disruption compared with which the organisation of the German minority in Slovenia and the Voivodina was insignificant; and the possibility of Yugoslavia taking part in some system of collective resistance to Hitler's advance. On both points the outlook was uncertain after the March crisis. The inactivity of the Tsetković government, however much it might be attributed to the necessity of passing the budget first, suggested a dangerous blindness to the urgency of conciliating the Croats and the need for positive action now. As for the possibility of collective resistance, the answer lay in the attitude of the British government. If a lead were once given, there could be little doubt that the Yugoslavs would follow eagerly. They have no desire to crown their centuries-old achievement of independence with final extinction. But they cannot take a stand alone. They cannot give a lead. They cannot risk the anger of Germany without a concrete assurance of Great-Power support. Like Poland, like Rumania, like Turkey, perhaps even like Hungary, Yugoslavia is waiting for the West and only a firm stand on their part can rally the small, frightened, desperate but mutually suspicious Eastern states into a collective *bloc*, pledged to the defence of their integrity and their independence. In the absence of such a firm stand, Yugoslavia will be fortunate if she survives the next two years.

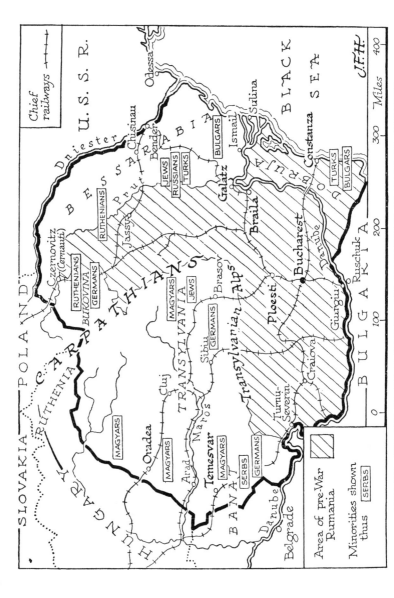

RUMANIA, SHOWING FRONTIER CHANGES AND DISTRIBUTION OF PRINCIPAL MINORITIES

RUMANIA

BARBARA BUCKMASTER

1. INTRODUCTION

THE Rumanians are proud of being an outpost of Latin civilisation in the East. The Slav circle that encloses them is complete, save where the Magyar wedge breaks through in the west, dividing the Serbs and Bulgars from their northern kinsmen. Though the Romans only occupied Dacia for 163 years, the impress they left on the original inhabitants was permanent. The Rumanian language, in spite of later Slav and Turkish additions, is Latin in structure and vocabulary, and the appearance and temperament of the people today is obviously Latin. Rumanians would like to think that the ready adoption of Latinity by their ancestors, who later resisted much more prolonged attempts at assimilation on the part of Slavs and Magyars, argues a natural affinity with Rome. It was isolation as well as the vigour of the national type that made it possible for the Daco-Roman people to preserve their identity through successive invasions. When once Aurelian's legions had left Dacia in 271 A.D. the country was undefended, and the inhabitants were forced up into the Carpathian ranges before the advancing Serbs and Bulgars. It is from these mountain shepherds that the modern Rumanians are descended, and they thus claim the Carpathians as the cradle of their race.

This point is of importance for an understanding of the Magyar-Rumanian controversy over Transylvania. The Hungarians argue that it was a desolate and empty country into which their armies swept in the 11th century. Proof is impossible, but the very name Transylvania 'beyond the forest' (a literal translation of the Hungarian *Erdely*) suggests, as Dr. Seton Watson points out, a medieval Hungarian *Drang nach Osten*. The Rumanian contention is supported by the undoubted fact that it was in the Carpathians that the Daco-Romans, or Vlachs as they came to be called, took refuge from the Slav advance.

It was not until the decay of Serbia and Bulgaria in the 14th century that the Principalities of Moldavia and Wallachia, from which Rumania was to grow, make their appearance in history. But other powers were arising and in the 16th century the new states fell under Turkish domination, which they were never wholly to escape until the 19th century. It was to prove only too true that *les Principautés roumaines se trouvent sur la route de tous les maux*. Situated on the point of intersection of the Austrian, Russian and Ottoman Empires, and controlling the mouth of the Danube, they had no chance of keeping out of war or preserving independence. Whenever Russia felt strong enough to defy Turkey she assumed a virtual protectorate over the Principalities, which lay across her path to the Straits, and it was not until her defeat in the Crimean War that Moldavia and Wallachia were allowed to unite under one prince in 1859. Tribute still had to be paid to Turkey even after the union, and final independence was not achieved until 1881, when Charles of Hohenzollern, who had been opposed by the powers as Prince of the United Principalities in 1867, was crowned Carol I, King of Rumania.

Once the Principalities were united in an independent kingdom they provided a rallying point for all the other Rumanians still left under the rule of Austria-Hungary and Russia, but the goal of complete national unity was not realised until after the Great War. The choice before Rumania in 1914 was difficult. Her geographical position made permanent neutrality impossible, and with so much at stake it was natural that she should weigh her decision carefully.

Both sides made glowing promises; Germany offering Bessarabia, the Allies Transylvania and the Banat. Gratitude to France for the part she had played in securing national unity and independence and the close cultural ties between the two countries, recent co-operation with Serbia in the Balkan war and general sympathy with the ideals of the Allies, inclined Rumania to the Entente. On the other hand, the personal sympathies of King Carol I, the secret treaty with Austria and Germany which he had signed in 1883, and traditional Rumanian fear of Russia worked in Germany's favour.

With the death of King Carol the balance changed. His nephew and successor King Ferdinand still had German sympathies, but Queen Marie, half English and half Russian, was openly on the side of the Allies and had a more vigorous personality than her husband. In 1916 the uneasy neutrality ended.

The course of the war might have gone very differently for Rumania if it had not been for Bulgarian enmity, which made it possible for the Germans to push through across the Danube and occupy Bucharest. In spite of initial reverses, the army made a fine stand at Maraşesti, and it was not until the collapse of the Russian front that surrender became inevitable, and a separate peace with Germany had to be signed at Bucharest in May 1918.

2. THE PEOPLE OF RUMANIA

THE RUMANIANS

The victory of the Western Powers in the autumn of 1918 quickly reversed the position, and as a result of the Peace Treaties not only was the Treaty of Bucharest cancelled but

Rumania doubled her territory and population. She has now a total of 19 million people in a country the size of Great Britain and Ireland. Seventy-four per cent of this total speaks Rumanian as its mother tongue. The provinces of Moldavia and Wallachia, which formed the original Rumanian kingdom, possess an overwhelming Rumanian population, but in those which were added later the minorities form a very considerable part of the population, and the problems they create have a profound influence upon the country's present and future.

There are, however, nearly a million Rumanians still left outside the present frontiers. In Hungary there are 23,760 on the western frontier of Rumania, and in Ruthenia between 20,000 and 40,000, also on the frontier. Yugoslavia has nearly 250,000; 70,000 are in scattered villages in the Banat, in the Timok valley there are 150,000 who were almost without national consciousness until the Serbs tried to assimilate them, and in Serbian Macedonia there are 10,000 to 20,000 of the Ruman-speaking Kutzo-Vlachs; 19,700 more of these people are in Greek Macedonia, and one estimate suggests that there may be nearly 140,000 of them in the Balkans as a whole. In Bulgaria there are about 70,000 Rumanians living round Vidin along the Danube. The numbers across the Dniester are difficult to estimate (the Soviet Union Year Book, 1928, gives 300,000 as the figure, and the Rumanians say 800,000), but there were enough for the Soviets to set up a Moldavian autonomous republic opposite Bessarabia as an example to those over the water.

THE MAGYARS

The most important of the minority groups is the Hungarian. There are nearly a million and a half Magyars in Transylvania and the Banat. Apart from the compact body of 540,000 Szeklers settled in Eastern Transylvania (in the

exact centre of Greater Rumania) these are mostly concentrated on the western frontier, or scattered in the towns,
where they often form a majority of the population. Hungary
never ceases to voice her grievances over Trianon, and it is
natural that her fellow countrymen over the border should
listen. Have they real cause for complaint, or is it all a matter
of historical feeling and racial sentiment?

The position can best be understood if it is compared with
that in Eire. Like the native Irish, the Rumanians of Transylvania had mostly been kept down to the status of peasants
and labourers, and like the immigrant Protestant gentry, the
Magyar landowners were of a different religion from the
mass of the people. The Rumanians remained faithful to the
Orthodox Church and were never converted to Calvinism
or Catholicism by their masters. Both the Irish Protestant
gentry and the Magyar landowners found themselves after
the war handed over to the rule of their former subjects, and
both had their lands taken away in favour of the local
peasantry.

This loss of their estates is one of the main complaints of
Transylvanian Magyars. The reform was, it is true, slightly
more severe in Transylvania than in the Regat, or Old
Kingdom, but the Regat landowners (the boyars) also
suffered heavily and the Hungarian peasants in Transylvania
gained. An Hungarian estimate gives 36,481 as the number
of Magyars endowed with small holdings. In any case, had
Transylvania remained Hungarian, the landowners could
not have permanently escaped expropriation; Hungary herself is now being obliged to work out a land reform policy.

The question of the expropriation is closely linked with
that of education. Before the war, the Magyar schools in
Transylvania were owned partly by the state, and partly by
the different churches. Such Rumanian schools as existed
were all denominational. In the Regat, elementary schools

had been, and still are, exclusively state owned. After the union, the minorities were allowed, as a great concession, to keep their denominational schools, but the churches suffered so severely in the expropriation (practically all their revenue was derived from the land) that it became increasingly difficult to maintain the schools. The Orthodox Church, of course, also lost its land, but it had never owned large estates in Transylvania, and the closing of denominational schools did not much affect Rumanian children, who had the new state schools which were as good or better to fall back on. There are indeed state minority schools where some of the teaching is given in the minority languages, but they are usually staffed by teachers from the Regat who know little or no Hungarian, and the children do not learn much. Even in the minority Church schools, Rumanian history and geography must be taught in Rumanian. This is not unreasonable, though it often defeats its own object; in any case the amount of compulsory instruction in Rumanian is less than that in Magyar under the Apponyi Law of 1907.

The compulsory examination in Rumanian for teachers and candidates for the university and administrative posts is often criticised. It sounds fair enough on paper (a Welshman would not be admitted to Oxford or even Bangor if he knew no English) but it may be that in practice candidates are sometimes failed for political reasons.

The third main grievance of the Magyar minority is the decline of administrative standards. This was only to be expected. The Magyars had had a thousand years' experience of administration, while Rumania did not obtain full independence until 1881, and had the habits ingrained by long experience of corrupt Phanariot[1] methods to eradicate. Meanwhile, the petty tyrannies of subordinate officials must necessarily be galling. Hungarian landowners whose estates

[1] The Greeks appointed by Turkey to govern the Principalities.

have been divided by the new boundaries are sometimes kept waiting six weeks for a three days' permit to cross the frontier; nor do they like to see grapes from their vineyards requisitioned in large quantities by Rumanian road contractors. The Rumanians are a genial people, and do not yet regard themselves as a *Herrenvolk*, but it is natural, particularly in outlying districts, that the smaller men should sometimes try and get their own back on their former masters.

THE GERMANS

The Germans are in a different position. In Transylvania there are about 250,000 Lutheran Saxons. These have never been big landowners like the Magyars, but form solid middle-class communities. It was their churches and cultural institutions rather than private individuals which were affected by the land reform. Still the Saxons have as many schools in Transylvania as they had in 1914 and the Catholic Swabians of the Banat have more. These latter are about as numerous as the Saxons, and have a fairly prosperous life, for the Banat industries mostly deal with armaments and are humming. The Saxons, too, are doing well, for some of the industries of the north have been moved to Braşov for strategic reasons. Both in Transylvania and the Banat the German minority Press flourishes, though it is subject to the same censorship as all Rumanian papers.

The 80,000 Germans of Bukovina have memories of an efficient Austrian administration and have suffered somewhat from the Rumanisation of the University of Czernowitz, but those who have more title to feel aggrieved are the 80,000 German colonists of Bessarabia. They were invited to settle there by Russia in the early 19th century, along with some French and Swiss communities, and were given many privileges. Today they are victims of the general economic depression of Bessarabia; in addition the frost of 1929 killed most of their vines and they have no capital with which to replace them. No German newspapers are now allowed in the Province, and there are practically no German Church schools. Last year even Christmas trees were forbidden. Germany is not likely to be unmindful of these unfortunate lost brothers so opportunely placed on the Black Sea. Since the rise of Nazism, the scattered Germans in Rumania have gradually been acquiring a sense of unity, which they never had before. Their new N.E.D.R. organisation (National Union of Germans in Rumania) was disbanded after M. Barthou's visit to Bucharest in 1934, but in 1935 a new association, *Volksgemeinschaft der Deutschen in Rumänien*, was founded. Herr Fabricius and Herr Hendrich are the leaders, and the party is increasingly subject to Nazi influence. Their scattered geographical position prevents these Rumanian Germans from playing the role of Sudetens, but they can exercise a fairly powerful influence on Rumanian internal politics, and could provide a disruptive force in outlying minority districts if orders to that effect were given from Berlin. There is, however, no solidarity between them and the Magyars. They realise that they are in many ways better off under Rumania than they were under Hungary, and also better off than their fellow Germans in Hungary today. To that extent they may be a help to Rumania, by providing an additional argument in Berlin against German support of Hungarian revisionism.

THE UKRAINIANS

The Ukrainians also suffer from the trade depression and loss of markets. There are about 225,000 Ukrainians in Bukovina and a similar number in Bessarabia who form a continuous *bloc* with their fellows in Ruthenia, Galicia and the Ukraine proper. They are mostly peasants, at a lower cultural and economic level than the other minorities in Rumania. They are considered by Ukrainian organisations to be the most unfortunate of all European minorities, but this is exaggeration; it is more from neglect than repression that they suffer in Rumania. It is true that their language and national culture is not encouraged; there are now no schools where Ukrainian is the medium of instruction. In the early days after the war the Ukrainians took part in communist risings. The Russian cars and bicycles in Tiraspol can be clearly seen from the Rumanian bank and so can the theatre and the smart new factory. But communism is not popular among peasant proprietors, however impoverished; it is more possible that discontent might incite them to listen to German propaganda. German villages are conveniently interspersed among the Ukrainian settlements in southern Bessarabia.

THE RUSSIANS

The Russians of Bessarabia are not regarded as a minority by the government, and therefore can expect no relief from the new statute. Their position is full of difficulty. They are mostly landowners and officials who enjoyed a rich social and intellectual life under the Czarist government. They have no sympathy with Soviet Russia, but are cold-shouldered by the Rumanians. No Russian newspaper or book, however classical and respectable, can be bought in Chişinau (the second largest town in Rumania), and Russian must not be spoken in streets or shops or learnt in schools. The land reform in Bessarabia was more severe than anywhere else, and the loss of markets and dislocation of trade on the closing of the Dniester hit the landowners in their own degree harder than the peasants. The Rumanians argue that had Bessarabia remained with Russia, the landowners would have lost everything, but the justice of this argument does not lessen their sense of grievance at being less well treated than their neighbours across the Pruth. A town of 160,000 inhabitants like Chişinau cannot provide adequate intellectual and social life and there is comparatively little intercourse with Bucharest, which is a long and expensive journey away. It used to take only four hours or less to get to Odessa, which is now inaccessible, and the community is thus stranded.

THE BULGARS

In southern Bessarabia there are from 150,000 to 350,000 Bulgars, about 70,000 in northern Dobruja and 150,000 in southern Dobruja. It is the latter who have most grievances to voice, though the former, along with the other Slavs of Bessarabia, complain of the discouragement of their language, and the forbidding of the use of Slavonic in Church services.

The Bulgars of the Dobruja have real grounds for complaint over the compulsory colonisation of their territory by Kutzo-Vlachs from Macedonia. When Greece after the war filled her newly acquired portion of Macedonia with expelled Greeks from Smyrna, she made room for the newcomers by turning out these uncouth semi-Rumanian shepherds. The Rumanian government, embarrassed by the arrival of these doubtful co-nationals, planted them in the Dobruja to give the province a more Rumanian complexion. The local Bulgars were steady gardeners and agriculturists who were naturally dismayed at having to give up their land to wild newcomers, who, to make matters worse, were often billeted in their houses. Turkish rules of land tenure which had been in abeyance during the 35 years of independent Bulgarian control, were called on to justify the partition.

The Rumanians had to plant these Kutzo-Vlachs somewhere, and nowhere would it have been convenient. They cannot therefore be blamed for choosing the Dobruja, which was the land nearest to the former home of the immigrants; it may, however, have been an unwise move, for any discontent among the Bulgars of the Dobruja is taken advantage of by the irredentists over the border and the province might become a danger zone if any outside power chose to back Bulgarian claims.

THE JEWS

Before the union there were about 250,000 Jews in Rumania. Today there are more than three times as many. A large proportion of the population of the new provinces was Jewish, and the numbers have been still further swollen by illegal immigration. This great increase was bound to inflame the traditional anti-Semitism of the Rumanians. Indeed their feelings can up to a point be understood; in Germany only about 0·25 % of the population is Jewish, whereas in Greater Rumania the figure is 4·2 %. In many of the larger towns such as Czernowitz or Chişinau more than half the people are Jews. The Rumanians are not natural business men, and retail trade throughout the country has largely fallen into the hands of the Jews (it is said that Jews have never been able to establish themselves in Greece where the inhabitants can drive as shrewd a bargain as they). Peasants are often heavily in debt to Jewish moneylenders. Before the war there was no large Rumanian middle class; now that the family estates are no longer big enough to support them, the sons of landowners are being forced into business and the professions, and a generation of sons of priests and other peasants has been educated and is now ready for black-coated work. Both classes find their way barred by the Jews. In this soil it is not surprising that Iron Guard propaganda took ready root.

The obligation to allow Jews equal citizenship imposed on Rumania by the Congress of Berlin was evaded, but after the Minority Treaty of 1919 was signed they had to be allowed a place in the national life; the right of naturalisation was to be open to all Jews in Rumanian territory who did not possess any other nationality. During the six weeks' term of office of the Goga government at the beginning of 1938 plans were laid for drastic revision of Jewish claims to citizenship; it was estimated that more than 200,000 Jews might lose their rights, but the strong note sent by the British and French governments to the effect that this was an infringement of the 1919 Treaty helped to secure the dropping of the legislation. It was in any case too extreme to secure real support in the country; all were alarmed at the instant dislocation of financial life which followed the proposals.

All the same, the Jews are in a precarious position. Education is a difficult problem for them, especially in the minority districts. They may only send their children to a Hebrew or Rumanian school, not to a German or Hungarian one, even though their natural language be German or Magyar. The Hebrew school can give them no education that is of use for their future life, and in the Rumanian school they are unwelcome and sometimes ill-treated. This ill-treatment is more pronounced in the universities, where there have been many cases of brutality. Jews have difficulty now in getting permission to matriculate, and many are being excluded from the professions. King Carol's government is more moderate in its attitude to the Jews than the parties of the extreme Right, but it is doubtful if it will long be able to resist the strong popular feeling. It was said in the Press at the end of 1938, that the government proposed to send 150,000 Jews to Palestine in the course of the next three years. During the recent conversations with the Polish government, joint plans for the compulsory emigration of a large number of Jews were discussed. At present, however, it is estimated that only about 30,000 Jews will be considered unable to prove their citizenship, and will lose their rights.

THE TREATMENT OF THE MINORITIES

The minorities have certain grievances in common. They all complain of the unfair incidence of the land reform and of taxation and of the fact that very little money is spent on public works in their districts, while all goes to the capital. Even a stranger cannot help being struck by the violent contrast between the shabby, neglected appearance of the provincial towns and the magnificence of Bucharest. But this does not imply a discrimination against minorities. Jassy, the old capital of Moldavia, looks just as sad as Chişinau. The minorities also feel that they are not fairly represented in the national life and that their languages are unduly discouraged. It will be apparent from the preceding discussion that these complaints have different force in different districts, but that there is some substance in them everywhere. It was the Liberal Party that inclined to a narrow policy of centralisation; the National Peasants were much more truly liberal in their minority policy, but their tenure of office never lasted long enough for real reform to be effected. It was on the issue of minority legislation that Dr. Vaida Voevod broke off from the National Peasant Party. The other leaders would not admit his plan of a *numerus Valachicus* by which all firms would have to ensure that 75 % of their employees were 'ethnic Rumanians'.

The new Minorities Statute of 1938 does not make any startling concessions. The 1919 Treaty was quite fair, and the effect of the new Statute, as of the old Treaty, will depend on the spirit in which it is carried out. An important clause provides that the parents may now have the deciding voice in settling to which ethnic group a child belongs and what school it may therefore attend. Shop signs may now carry their inscription in the minority language as well as in Rumanian (if the minority name appears in larger letters there will be a tax!), but all sub-titles in the cinema must still be in Rumanian.

The new political groupings are beginning to break down racial feeling. Some of the most notable successes of the Iron Guard were obtained in minority districts. Codreanu was able to unite all other races in common hatred of the Jews. Recently the whole country has been divided up into ten new administrative districts cutting across the old provincial boundaries, in order to break down local racial feeling. Bessarabia, for example, has been shared out between four of these districts, and the Saxons of the Braşov region have been cut off from their fellows in Transylvania and joined administratively to Bucharest on the other side of the Carpathians.

The Rumanians are more lenient than their predecessors, though probably still at present less efficient. They themselves realise that their country is young, and has the tradition of centuries of bad government to shake off, and they are generous enough to admit that in spite of undoubted Hungarian oppression, the general level of the Rumanian population in the districts that had formerly been controlled by the Habsburg Empire was higher than that prevailing in the Regat. Some of Rumania's finest politicians, such as Dr. Maniu, come from Transylvania.

With give and take on both sides the minority problem should eventually solve itself, unless there is violent interference from without. As is shown in the following table the Rumanian population is increasing much more rapidly than the German or Hungarian, and some measure of assimilation will probably take place in time.

Excess of Births over Deaths:[1]

Rumanians	..	..	14·6 per 1,000
Magyars ..	..	..	5·5 per 1,000
Germans ..	..	..	4·7 per 1,000

IS AN EXCHANGE OF POPULATIONS POSSIBLE?

The Rumanian government would be willing in certain cases to consider an exchange of populations with other countries, but it is doubtful how far this would be practicable or acceptable to the aggrieved parties. An agreement has, however, been reached with Turkey to assist the migration of the 200,000 Turks in the Dobruja to their homeland; no exchange of people is involved in this case as there is no Rumanian minority in Turkey.

On the Hungarian frontier there are 400,000[2] Magyars inside Rumania as against only 20,000 or so Rumanians in Hungary. Again, in Ruthenia only about 30,000 Rumanians could be repatriated in exchange for the 225,000 Ukrainians over the border in Bukovina. On the Russian frontier the thing would be impossible. Even if the rumours about the removal of the Moldavian element from the Ukraine to Siberia are without foundation, both sides so cordially mistrust one another and are so reluctant to allow even one individual to cross the water in either direction that they would never admit large blocks of people infected with bolshevism or fascism.

Within the existing frontiers it would be difficult to do a deal with Bulgaria. The 500,000 or more Bulgars all live on the eastern side of Rumania, whereas the 70,000 Rumanians are in the west of Bulgaria. If southern Dobruja were restored to Bulgaria it might be possible to transfer the Bulgarians from Bessarabia and northern Dobruja against

[1] Quoted, *Nation und Staat*, February 1939, *Deutschtum in Rumänien*.
[2] Figures from C. A. Macartney, *National States and National Minorities*.

the Rumanians and Vlachs of southern Dobruja, but there again there would be too few Rumanians to make a balanced exchange and Rumania might not be willing to see the useful and industrious Bulgar market gardeners leave the still under-populated and under-cultivated regions round the Danube delta. The most hopeful field for exchange would be the Banat, where the 60,000 Serbs could easily cross over into the Yugoslav Banat and make room for the 70,000 Rumanians now in that part of Yugoslavia.

RELIGIOUS DIFFERENCES

Differences of religion sometimes accompany and some-times cut across those of language. The Orthodox Church is by far the largest religious body in Rumania, and nearly all those speaking Rumanian belong to it. There are roughly 10 million Orthodox in the country. Of the 2 million Catho-lics, only 230,000 are of the Latin rite, the others being Uniate or Greek Catholics, who were persuaded to abandon the allegiance though not the form of their faith by Austria-Hungary.

Of the Magyar minority 150,000 are Catholics, the rest being Calvinist and Unitarian. The Germans in Tran-sylvania are mostly Lutherans, while the Banat Swabians are Catholics. Though the State Church is Orthodox, Rumania has been very tolerant to other religions, with the possible exception of the Baptists, who have had some trouble recently. The 1927 Concordat with Rome is looked upon as a model.

Some Rumanians feel that it would have been more in keeping with their Latin culture and helped to link them with western progress had they acknowledged the Holy See, but the majority contend that Orthodoxy preserved their national character through the centuries of Austro-Hungarian domination. An outsider would feel that Catholicism would

have biased the nation unduly towards the west and
obscured her essentially dual nature.

3. THE NEW PROVINCES

IT has sometimes been claimed that Rumania got too
much out of the Great War, but it can never be suggested
that Greater Rumania was an artificial creation of the
Peace Treaties. It can be argued that in some cases the new
frontiers were too generous, but most of the new provinces
themselves voted for union with the Regat, or Old Kingdom,
and all contained a majority of Rumanians.

An examination has already been made of the size and
grievances of the various minorities. It is worth studying the
problems of the different provinces as a whole to see what
considerations were taken into account at the Peace
Treaties and what influences are operating today.

Transylvania, Crişana, Maramureş.—These three Hungarian
territories were assigned in a lump to Rumania, though the
Theiss frontier in the west, which had been promised in
1916, was not allowed. Such a frontier would have been
ethnically impossible, and it was fortunate for the Allies
that they were able to escape without loss of face from so
awkward a commitment. Rumania, by signing the separate
Peace of Bucharest in March 1918, was held to have broken
her side of the 1916 agreement, and thus to have absolved
the Allies from keeping theirs.

The historical controversy over Transylvania has already
been described. Though origins rest in obscurity it is certain
that the Rumanians formed the largest single element in the
population as early as the 18th century, and that in 1918
57 % of the total inhabitants were Rumanians. The Hungarian census of 1910 gave the Magyars (with whom were
incorporated the Jews) 34·3 % and the Germans 8 %.

Against this ethnic preponderance of Rumanians must be set the fact that the Magyars had ruled Transylvania for a thousand years. The Germans have been in the country nearly as long, for it was early in the 12th century that the Hungarian rulers sent a body of Saxon knights along with the Szeklers into the east of the province to guard the frontiers. These Szeklers form an awkward problem today. Whatever their origins, they have been so thoroughly Magyarised as to be equivalent to Hungarians, and there are 540,000 of them massed in the extreme south-east of Transylvania, exactly in the heart of Greater Rumania.

After the Turkish defeat of Hungary in 1526 Transylvania achieved *de facto* independence for 200 years, which proved to be her period of greatest prosperity. The three nations, Magyars, Saxons and Szeklers (the Rumanians, it may be noticed, were not counted), worked together in amity. When Hungary came under Habsburg rule at the end of the 17th century, Transylvania was included; but union with Hungary was not finally consummated until 1867. The Rumanian shepherds and peasants, though given little place in the national life, were not wholly inarticulate. They hoped for a federalisation of the Austrian Empire on national lines; Old Rumania had not been long enough a kingdom for them to turn to her.

Transylvania did not play an important part in Hungary's economy before the war, but now that she has lost Slovakia, Transylvanian timber and minerals would be useful to her. Most of the trade of the region was in any case directed to the south and east, as Vienna and Budapest were so far away. Industries were chiefly run by the local Germans, not the Magyars. Transylvanian minerals and natural gas are valuable to Rumania, for most of them are not found east of the Carpathians, and Transylvanian industries complement rather than rival those of the Old Kingdom.

Whatever may be the rights and wrongs of the case, it was not the Peace Conference which gave Transylvania to Rumania, but the vote of the people assembled at Alba Julia in December 1918, to which the German communities gave their assent a month later. Some would argue that the acquisition of so large a territory east of the Carpathians has weakened Rumania strategically. It looks neat on the map to let the Carpathians round off Hungary and leave Rumania with her back against them and her face to the Black Sea. But this ignores the undoubted fact that the Carpathians are the backbone, not the boundary of the race, which by its very character looks west as well as east. It is true that the Germans could overrun Transylvania in a war, but it would take time and prevent them from getting so quickly to the oilfields which lie very near the eastern slopes of the mountains. As far as symmetry is concerned the Rumanians maintain that their country is now a perfect circle which gives the maximum of territory with the minimum of frontier.

More sober Hungarian controversialists do not now claim the whole of Transylvania, though they would like to see it given some form of autonomy; what they do dispute is the western frontier of Crişana and Maramureş. Here Rumania's case is more difficult to maintain. Though the Theiss frontier was refused, she received a generous strip of plain on the west, including the predominantly Hungarian towns of Sătmar, Oradea Mare and Arad. A truer ethnic line would have run 20 kilometres to the east; the other was chosen so as to give Rumania the railway, but it might have been wiser to lend her money to build another. If the frontier were drawn in, it would satisfy 400,000 Magyars at the expense of 40,000 (some say 20,000) Rumanians.[1] This strip may some day prove a useful bargaining counter; it is the only impor-

[1] C. A. Macartney, *Hungary and her Successors*, p. 354.

tant concession which an independent Rumania could make to Hungary.

The Banat.—The Banat of Temeşvar which lies between the Theiss and the Danube, was also Hungarian. It had always formed an administrative unit and the whole of it was promised to Rumania in 1916, but this promise could not be fulfilled in fairness to Yugoslavia, for the Rumanian frontier would have been brought right down to the Danube opposite Belgrad. Rumanians again feel that this is their national home, for it is full of Roman remains and was the heart of Dacia. Though the tangle of races is almost inextricable, the Hungarian 1910 census gave the population as 37 % Rumanian in what is today the Rumanian Banat. The Germans were 24·5 %, the Serbs 13 % and the Magyars 14 %.

Though it was fair to give Belgrad a solid strip beyond the Danube, the frontier was not wisely drawn along the whole line. In one place the railway connecting Timişoara (Temeşvar) and Arad with the Danube was cut. In an age of disputes it is worth remarking that there has been no serious quarrel between Rumania and Yugoslavia over the Banat frontier, and their friendship has not been endangered.

The Banat is more industrialised than any other part of Greater Rumania. Only 72 % of the people are on the land, whereas in the rest of the country the figure is 80 %. The big Reşita iron and steel works are there. This area was much more closely linked with Hungary than was Transylvania. The industries filled an important place in Hungarian economy and the trade was directed to Budapest.

The Bukovina.—The Bukovina is regarded with more affection by Rumanians than any of the other new provinces, though it is no great economic asset, and is the smallest of them all.

The historic case is clear. It had always been an integral

116

part of Moldavia until 1775, when it was handed over to the Habsburgs by Turkey as a reward for Austrian support against Russia. The family of Gregory Ghyka, who was executed for protesting, have tears incorporated in their coat-of-arms in grief for his death and the loss of the province. The country is singularly beautiful, and hidden in the wooded hills are a group of remarkable monasteries, covered inside and out with frescoes which are some of the finest examples of Rumanian art. Bukovina was the scene of many of the exploits of Stefan cel Mare, the favourite national hero.

The problem of the country is the large Jewish and Ukrainian minority. More than half the population of Czernowitz is Jewish, and there are about 225,000 Ruthenes adjoining their fellow-countrymen in Ruthenia and Polish Galicia. The Austrian administration was comparatively efficient and benevolent and has not left unpleasant memories; most of the people speak German, and there are a large number of Germans still in the province. Some of the more violent recent activities of the Iron Guard were centred on Czernowitz. Hitler might find a field for the exercise of his self-determination policy there. On the other hand, if Rumanians felt inclined to adopt a more liberal Jewish policy, the two problems might cancel out.

Bessarabia.—Bessarabia is another province about whose Moldavian origin there is no dispute. Russia only held it for 100 years after she had succeeded in extracting it from the Turks in 1812. Part she ruled for an even shorter period; she had to return the southern districts down to the Danube after the Crimean War. It was Russia's insistence on re-taking Southern Bessarabia at the Congress of Berlin, when Rumania had so recently fought as her ally against the Turks at Plevna, that greatly embittered subsequent Russo-Rumanian relations. On the outbreak of the Russian revolution in 1917, Bessarabia, after a brief period of union with the Ukraine, proclaimed itself an independent Moldavian Republic, with a Constituent Assembly, the Sfatul Ţarii. Independence for such a small agricultural state was obviously impossible, and the Assembly shortly afterwards enthusiastically proclaimed union with Rumania. The Peace Conference did not endow Rumania with Bessarabia. Indeed, some time elapsed before the acquisition was recognised.

The population of the province is mixed, especially in the south, but here again the Rumanians are in a majority. Though ethnic and historical considerations join here in favour of Rumania, the economic factor comes into play on the other side. Bessarabia was California to Russia; to Rumania she is almost Siberia. There are hardly any industries in the country, the main products being fruit, wine and cereals, which have to compete for scarce markets with the rest of the Kingdom. Twenty-six per cent of the arable land of the whole country is in Bessarabia, but money needs to be spent before it can be turned to great profit.

Russia was said to have exploited the country, and she did cut the timber ruthlessly and unscientifically, but she absorbed all Bessarabian production. The main railway lines are all directed eastward; only one line connects the main centres with the Rumanian Danube ports. Rail transport is thus inadequate and is inordinately costly, roads are non-existent in bad weather, and the closing of the Dniester has removed the main artery of trade. All sections of the population have been hit by the collapse of trade. There are about the same number of Ukrainians as in Bukovina; one block is in the north adjoining the Ruthenes of Bukovina, and the other in the south, where German colonies are interspersed. It is interesting to note that during the war Germany threw out a suggestion that she needed a port of her own at the mouth of the Danube, and that the presence of her colonists in Southern Bessarabia gave her a claim.

The Dobruja.—Rumania was given Northern Dobruja, a strip of country bounded by the Danube on the north and the Black Sea on the east, in 1878, when Russia succeeded in persuading the Congress of Berlin to restore to her Southern Bessarabia. The Bulgars, though still under Turkish suzerainty, regarded this area as an integral part of their territory; Rumania had no wish for it, as there were very few of her nationals in the province. She wanted to keep Southern Bessarabia, peopled by her own Moldavians, but as this was impossible she accepted with a bad grace the compensation offered. Once having set foot south of the Danube, however, she was not averse from further extension, and readily seized Southern Dobruja at the end of the Balkan War of 1913. When Germany was in the ascendant in the Great War, it was restored to Bulgaria, but Paris gave it back to Rumania.

Northern Dobruja has a very mixed population, mostly Turks, and it seems reasonable that Rumania should control both sides of the Danube, but very little justification can be found for her holding Southern Dobruja; indeed, it would hardly seem to compensate her for the hostility of Bulgaria, which its possession involves. Many statesmanlike Rumanians are willing to admit this, but they argue that in these days of German intrigue it is impossible to be sure that Bulgarian friendship would be finally bought at the price, and if Bulgaria had the Dobruja, the new frontier would run within thirty miles of the Rumanian naval base at Constanza. More serious still, any territorial concession might be seized on as a precedent by the vigilant Hungarians, and the whole fabric of Greater Rumania, the fruit of so many centuries of hope and effort, would be broken up. It is difficult to see how this argument can be countered.

4. ECONOMIC STRUCTURE

AGRICULTURE

Rumania has had a troubled agrarian history. In early days the peasants had a traditional right to the use of the land, the Cnez or headman being entitled only to a tithe. As time went on, labour dues of increasing severity were imposed, but the right to the land was still guaranteed. In the days of Turkish overlordship the rulers appointed by the Porte were foreigners whose tenure of office was short; they had no need to attach the local boyars to themselves by granting feudal privileges. It was not until Russia assumed a virtual protectorate over the Principalities in 1772 that the rights of the peasantry suffered their first serious diminution. Russia insisted on the appointment of native princes, and they had more interest than the passing Phanariots in securing privileges for the members of their own class. The Organic Statutes of 1832 not only increased the labour dues but altered the whole system of land tenure. The boyar was recognised as proprietor of the land, and for the first time the modern conception of property as an absolute right was introduced into Rumanian law.

From then on the position of the peasants became increasingly miserable. Cuza's reform in 1864 effected some redistribution of land, but it was purely a political move and hardly touched the economic problem. Serfdom and labour dues were abolished, but not enough land was distributed to encourage peasant proprietorship on a solid basis; on the other hand, had no land been distributed at all, a class of wage labourers would have been created (which was what the landlords wished) and this might have led to greater economic prosperity all round than the system adopted.

Rural distress continued, and there were several peasant

risings, the most violent being in 1907 when 10,000 peasants are said to have been killed, but still no serious steps were taken by the government. Some idea of the position may be gained from the fact that as late as 1913 0·5 % of the population owned in large estates 42·5 % of the arable land of the country. The peasants who crossed the Danube in the Balkan War of 1913 were stirred by seeing better conditions prevailing among the Bulgars than they themselves enjoyed, and reform was already in the air; after the Great War it could no longer be delayed. Rumanians from the Old Kingdom mixed in the field for the first time with their fellow countrymen from Transylvania and Bukovina and were roused to common action, and from Bessarabia the ideas of the Russian revolution spread over the whole country. Events in Russia have always influenced the Rumanian peasantry. Cuza's 1864 reform followed on the emancipation of the serfs in 1861. The 1907 rising happened closely after the 1905 rising in Russia and it was the 1917 Russian revolution which was the forerunner of the great agrarian reform in Rumania.

Already in 1917 King Ferdinand promised land to the peasant soldiers, and a scheme of expropriation and distribution was worked out. There was a setback when the conservatives under Marghiloman came back in 1918 after the collapse of the eastern front and the signing of the Peace of Bucharest, but by 1919 the reform could be deferred no longer. The new provinces had already taken matters into their own hands, and the Old Kingdom could not lag behind. M. Mihalache, Minister of Agriculture in M. Vaida Voevod's Coalition government, proposed a reform similar to that already carried out in Bessarabia; each individual landowner was not to be allowed to keep more than 100 hectares[1] and forests were to be included in the expropria-

---

[1] 1 hectare = 2·4 English acres.

tion; 4-6 hectares were to be distributed to each peasant family.

This proposal caused the fall of M. Vaida Voevod's government and it was left to a conservative Minister of Agriculture, M. Garoflid, to carry out the reform in its final shape. The expropriation ultimately decided on applied in the Old Kingdom to properties and not to proprietors; a landowner could keep up to 500 hectares of arable land on each of his estates, and vineyards and forests were altogether exempt. A second expropriation had to follow in 1921 as the first fell short by 450,000 hectares of the amount required, and this reduced the discrepancy between landowners in the Old Kingdom and the new provinces. The decree for Bukovina was similar to that for Bessarabia, though in Bukovina the landowners could keep 250 hectares instead of 100. In Transylvania also the reform was of the same character, but was modified by a wide series of exceptions. Hungarian landowners, however, calculated that in practice they were seldom left with more than 115 hectares. The peasants received from 6-8 hectares in Bessarabia and from 3-5 in the Old Kingdom and other provinces. The compensation was paid to the owners in state bonds; the peasants paid less than the price received by the owners and the difference was made up by the state. But as the peasants are the bulk of the taxpayers they in fact paid the major part of the expropriation price which was remitted in form. Owing to the depreciation of the leu, however, and the fall in values on the Stock Exchange, the bonds came to be worth practically nothing, and it has been calculated that most of the owners have not in fact received more than 3·2 % of the value of their property.

The reform thus broke the power of the boyars; in return it has raised the status of the peasants, but it is doubtful if it has materially improved their standards. Production as a whole has fallen in quantity and in quality. The yield of wheat per hectare in Rumania is lower than that in almost any other country in Europe. Large-scale wheat farming needs machinery for which the hedgeless Rumanian fields are as well suited as the Russian plains, but it is not worth the while of the landowners to use machinery on their reduced estates, and the peasants cannot afford it, nor would it be of much advantage on their small and often scattered holdings. Not only the fall in production, but the drop in world agricultural prices from 1929 onwards has prevented the Rumanian peasant from winning the expected benefits from the reform. League of Nations figures show that the 1930 harvest fetched less than half the price per bushel which was obtained in 1929, and though the peasants do not grow for export on the same scale as the big landowners did in former times, so catastrophic a price fall made it difficult for them to pay their taxes, and removed all hope of their being able to raise their standard of living by increasing purchases.

Today, in spite of an industrial drive, 80 % of the population are still engaged in agriculture, and pressure on the land is increasing. Five hectares was small enough for a family to live on in 1918 (in practice the average amount distributed to each smallholder was only 2·6 hectares) and in twenty years a new generation has grown up which also needs land. There are now 100 inhabitants per square kilometre of arable land in Rumania, whereas in Denmark, where cultivation is much more intense, there are only 35·6. No more land can be squeezed from the owners, and it looks as though a new agrarian crisis might arise. The solution of the problem would seem to lie in the development of co-operative farming and marketing, improvement of cultivation methods, a substitution of fruit and dairy and market garden produce for some of the wheat, an active development of road transport and the negotiation of a larger foreign market. This was the National Peasant policy, but the party was not in office long enough to try it. Industrialisation as pursued by the Liberals has not raised purchasing power. The Iron Guard has been able to step in and make capital out of rural discontent and the failure of the older parties to relieve it. Codreanu, who was a very handsome young man, captured the imagination of country people by arriving in the villages in national dress, mounted on a large white horse. His slogan, 'omu si pogonu', an acre a head, though it meant little, caught on like wildfire.

The real poverty of the peasants which still persists and the heavy losses sustained by the landowners owing to the reform, the lack of markets and the collapse of world agricultural prices explain why Rumania could not avoid signing a trade agreement with Germany. It suited both countries for Germany to assist in the growing of diversified crops, and to provide a guaranteed market for them when harvested; and this certain economic benefit outweighed, in Rumanian eyes, the probable political disadvantages of such an agreement.

INDUSTRY

The Liberal policy of industrialisation received added impetus after the economic crisis. With Italy and Germany encouraging food production at home, the agricultural countries of the Danube were naturally inclined to accelerate their industrial production, and the general rearmament drive of the last few years has accentuated this tendency.

The policy has not, however, had the desired effect of raising rural standards of living, at any rate in Rumania. This may have been partly the result of the way in which industrialisation was carried out. The Liberal Party was opposed to borrowing on the foreign market; national savings had not been built up on a scale to allow sufficient capital expansion on the home market, and an orthodox monetary policy precluded heavy state borrowing; industrialisation was therefore only achieved at the expense of agriculture. If rural standards were to be raised, money would first have to be spent on improving agricultural technique, on combating soil erosion (which is proceeding apace in Moldavia and Bessarabia), on irrigation projects and on transport development. Not enough was forthcoming, for industry had been given first claim on the limited supply of available capital. Further, the new industries needed foreign machines and raw materials. Some of these are obtained from Germany and Italy by regulated exchanges, but the equivalent in foreign exchange of about 3½ million lei has to be found to pay for the rest. This naturally reduces the amount of devisen available for the import of consumption goods. Home production of consumption goods has increased by 40 % since 1927, but 60 % less are now imported.

No country today can remain purely agrarian, but the National Peasant policy of building up agriculture first and developing industry later might have had better results for the people as a whole. For some time to come Rumanian industrial products will still be sold mainly on the home market, so it would have been more natural to provide first for the increase of home purchasing power. Rearmament has of course somewhat obscured the need of finding a market for industrial goods. The National Peasant Party also wished to foster industries based on agriculture and using local materials rather than those dependent on imports.

Total industrial output is about 1½ times as high today as in 1927. The main industries are in the textile, chemical, metallurgical and food groups.

Under a new five-year economic plan there is to be a big development of road, rail and water transport. Three hundred miles of new railway are to be built, and double tracks laid (at present there are only 200 miles of double track in the whole of Rumania). Import duties on cars are to be reduced, and motor transport encouraged, navigation on the Pruth is to be developed, and an ambitious scheme of canal building is planned.

TRADE

Rumania is rich in natural resources, but not rich enough to attempt autarky. Home production can now supply all coal needed for the railways, there are big salt mines, bauxite is being extracted in increasing quantities and in Transylvania are found natural gas (methane), gold and silver and other metals.[1] There is not enough iron, however, for the needs of industry. Iron and steel, machinery, chemical products, rubber and textiles have to be imported in large quantities, and Rumania has therefore to live by her exports of oil, cereals and timber.

In the first half of 1938 Rumania's six best customers were Germany, Czechoslovakia, Greece, Italy, France, and Great Britain in that order, and her six main sources of supply, Germany, Czechoslovakia, Great Britain, France, Belgium and the U.S.A. Nazi ideas of a *Wirtschaftsraum* in south-east Europe are not new. Even before the war, German influence

[1] According to Rumanian figures, 4,684 tons of bauxite were produced in 1937, with a 50·7 % aluminium content. The deposits near Bihor are estimated at from 3 to 10 million tons, and it is calculated that Rumania could supply the world's requirements of aluminium for 10 to 15 years. German figures for Rumanian production of the various metals are ·

	1934 (Tons)	1935 (Tons)	1936 (Tons)	1937 (Tons)
Manganese ore ..	12,057	19,795	30,576	50,749
Iron ore	83,590	93,818	108,429	128,592
Pyrites	4,001	9,855	10,000	10,717
Copper	887	1,241	1,580	1,125
Bauxite	1,458	1,468	2,039	6,016

was penetrating Rumanian commercial life more and more, until in 1913 she was supplying 40 % in value of the imports of Old Rumania, though she only took 7 % of Rumania's exports. After the war, however, trade was given a new direction, and Rumania tried to deal mainly with her allies. This succeeded up to a point, but there were inherent difficulties, which time did not remove. France did not need to import a large quantity of cereals and Britain's hands were tied after Ottawa. With the exception of Czechoslovakia, Rumania's fellow members of the Little Entente and the Balkan Entente were also mainly agriculturalists and their exports competed with hers. Several efforts were made to fill the economic gap left by the disappearance of the Austro-Hungarian Empire from the Danube basin, but none was wholly successful. The Little Entente endeavoured to promote mutual trade after the setting up of the Economic Council in 1933, but no great advance was made until the adoption of Sanctions temporarily removed Italy from the lists. Czechoslovakia's trade with her allies increased materially after 1936. As the war danger drew nearer, she bought more wheat and oil from Rumania and sold her more armaments; trade both ways in the first half of 1938 was nearly double what it had been in the corresponding period of 1935. Most of this trade was with the Sudeten districts, so after Munich the increase merely served to swell the German volume, and now that Czechoslovakia has gone and Rumania's first and second trading partners are amalgamated the preponderance of Germany in Rumanian trade is overwhelming.

Rumania in 1936 presented an ideal field for the adoption of the trading technique of Messrs. Funk and Schacht which has since become so familiar. Markets were difficult to find, for Rumanian internal prices were often higher than world prices owing to the heavy taxes on industry, the high tariff on imports and the prohibitive cost of transport. The position was aggravated in relation to the free exchange countries by the over-valuation of the leu, which was kept nominally at its old gold parity after 1931 by means of exchange restrictions. All foreign exchange obtained by exporters from their sales had to be sold to the National Bank, which in turn supplied all exchange with which to pay for imports. The Reichsmark also remained officially at the same level as before the crisis; the pound was thus undervalued in relation to the Reichsmark and sales to Britain did not produce a sufficient return in lei; this should have been compensated by the greater cheapness of British goods for the Rumanian importer, but the clearing system set up by Germany, whereby Rumania was compelled to take German goods in payment of her sales to Germany, prevented events from taking their natural course. Trade between Rumania and Great Britain noticeably declined, while trade both ways between Germany and Rumania doubled between 1933 and 1936, and continued to increase in volume until in 1938 Germany took about 35 % of Rumania's exports and supplied 41 % of her total imports.

Rumania is glad to trade with Germany, whose needs and geographical position make her a natural customer and source of supply, but she does not wish to see complete German domination of her economic system, and has taken what steps she can to promote trade with free exchange countries. In 1935 a law was passed allowing a premium of 38 % to exporters trading with strong exchange countries, but even this rate did not provide an adequate return, and recently a compensation system has been set up for certain classes of goods; exporters can now sell the foreign exchange obtained by their sales direct to importers less a varying percentage which has still to be sold to the National Bank at the official rate plus 38 %. A new agreement has recently been signed with Great Britain whereby exporters have to sell 40 % of their takings to the National Bank (at the official rate plus 38 %), but can transfer 60 % to importers at a free market rate. This rate was in practice between 900 and 1,100 lei to the pound at the end of 1938, the old rate before the introduction of the new arrangements having been 490. This raises the value of sterling in relation to the leu and secures a better price for the Rumanian exporter, but it makes British goods more expensive for the Rumanian importer. Germany by her currency manipulation and state control of trade can sell her machinery cheaply to Rumania and buy Rumanian products at the same unduly high price that they would fetch on the home market.

Many people argue that Germany is Rumania's natural trading partner; Britain has her own trading spheres and why should she adopt German methods and interfere in German spheres? The answer would seem to be that provided reasonable outlets are secured for Germany here or elsewhere, it is obviously to Britain's interest not to let the Balkan countries fall entirely under German domination, and as their strongly expressed wishes coincide with British interests there would seem to be a clear case for action. It is not only sentiment on the part of the Balkan countries: Rumania, for example, cannot sell all her exports to Germany, otherwise she would never be able to pay the interest on her foreign debts to other countries.

It may be difficult for Britain to buy more Rumanian produce, but the grant of a credit for the development of agriculture and transport and the financing of Rumanian trade with other countries such as Poland and the Scandinavian states would ease the position. (Thirty millions is the figure suggested in Bucharest.) In Poland fruit is scarce and you cannot get a cheap table wine. France has a trading preference there, but her products are expensive and many people do without.[1] Over the border in Bessarabia are thousands of gallons of delicious wine that cannot be sold and fruit that lies rotting for lack of transport and a market.

As for the import of British goods, British machines are still preferred in Rumania, but it is found that the German machines will work, and as they are so much cheaper they are not unnaturally installed. If action is to be taken, Britain would have to adopt German methods to the extent of allowing some state organisation and subsidisation of export. It would be possible to set up British factories in Rumania employing local labour. At present, for example, there are comparatively few bicycles in the country, and those there are imported from Germany. An assembly plant for bicycles, the parts being sent out from England, might be a great success, especially if at the same time credits were given for the development of roads, which are still in an embryo state.

A consortium of British firms might set up a joint shop in Bucharest (it would have to be handsome and impressive) for the sale of plated goods and porcelain.

Against this background, the signing of the new trade agreement with Germany at the beginning of 1939 can be understood. Rumania has not changed her policy. She did not wish any single country to dominate her economic system, but after the incorporation of Czechoslovakia in the Reich, Germany was already in a dominating position and it was only reasonable that Rumania should get what advantage she could from the situation.

Capital was badly needed and no other country was

[1] Poland has the lowest wine consumption of any country in Europe —·04 litres per head per annum, against 145·9 in France, 107·5 in Italy, and 31·4 in Rumania. Rumania is the largest Balkan wine producer, and ranks fourth or fifth among world producers. The output is 9,500,000 hectolitres in an average year, compared with 58,000,000 hectolitres in France, 45,000,000 in Italy, and 3,000,000 in Hungary.

willing to take the risk of a large enough loan; markets were also needed and no other country would buy. Under the agreement Rumanian agricultural production is to be adapted to Germany's needs,[1] a mixed German-Rumanian company is to exploit new oil fields and work mineral ores,[2] and the Rumanian road and railway transport system is to be extended with German help. Germany is to supply Rumania with war material. She has agreed to buy 400,000 tons of Rumanian wheat annually. (Already in the first 10 months of 1938 Germany was taking 39·3 % of Rumania's cereal exports.)

There is a feeling in Bucharest that the subsequent Anglo-Rumanian Trade Agreement is nebulous and limited in scope compared with the German. The original £5,000,000 credit was felt to be on far too niggardly a scale, and even the additional £5,000,000 of June 1939 left the total still inadequate. The interest rate at 5 % was also regarded as onerous in present market conditions. The striking contrast between the lengthy negotiations needed to secure even this sum and the eagerness of the Allies to lend the money to Rumania in 1916 did not fail to be observed. Further, the credit only referred to trade, and there was no question of capital investment in Rumanian industries or development.

The only purchase the British Government guaranteed to make was to buy 200,000 tons of the new crop of Rumanian

---

[1] Soya bean cultivation, introduced by Germany into Rumania in 1934, is to be extended. It is a popular crop, as the market is guaranteed, and the peasants get 5,000–6,000 lei a ton for soya beans, which is about double the world price. Germany does not buy soya beans cheaply from Manchukuo because of shortage of foreign exchange, and the excessive price she has to pay in Rumania is only apparent because of the over-valuation of the Reichsmark (41·5 lei = 1 RM.).

Germany is now trying to introduce the planting of flax and even cotton in Rumania.

[2] Germans are to exploit the copper pyrite gravel of Dobruja, the chrome ore of the Banat, and manganese from Broșteri.

wheat if it was available at the world price.[1] From what has been said above, it will be clear that the Anglo-Rumanian Agreement has failed to help Rumania in the provision of the two essentials—capital for development, and a market for her produce.

But Rumania is not confining her hopes of trade expansion to the British and German markets. Apart from the negotiations with France and Italy at the end of 1938, there were trade talks with Russia in the spring of 1939. It was suggested that Rumania should provide Russia with cattle for breeding, leather and shoes, and receive machinery in return.

There have been interesting developments also in the prospects of trade between Rumania and the Near East, and talks have taken place between representatives from Rumania on the one side, and from Palestine, Syria, Turkey, and Egypt on the other. It is thought that the Near East might provide a good market for the newly developing Rumanian industries.

NOTE ON OIL

At present the production of oil is falling off. In the peak year 1936, 8,704,000 tons of crude oil were extracted, but in 1937 this declined to 7,150,000, and in 1938 to 6,600,000. The estimated production for 1939 is 5,900,000. In 1936 the output averaged 26,000 tons daily; today the figure is only 17,500, and refineries are working at half capacity. Rumania has fallen from third to fifth place in the list of world producers; her output is about one-fifth of that of the USSR. This decline is largely due to the exhaustion of existing fields. Crude visible reserves are estimated at 60,000,000 tons, which would only give the industry a further ten years of life. Crude invisible reserves are put at 120,000,000 tons. Exploration of new areas is needed, but domestic capital is scarce, and there are irritating restrictions

[1] The question may not arise this year, as the harvest is comparatively poor. It is estimated that the exportable surplus will only be 500,000 tons instead of the hoped-for 2,000,000.

which discourage foreign prospectors. Under the new agreement with Germany a mixed German-Rumanian company is to exploit new fields.

Rumania's own consumption of oil was 1½ million tons in 1937, and this may be expected to expand rapidly in the future with the inevitable development of road transport and the use of agricultural machinery.

At present Rumania comes third on the list of Germany's oil suppliers, and provides about 16 % of the total German consumption of fuel and lubricating oils. Germany took in 1938 about one-eighth of the Rumanian output (about one-sixth of her exports) and the agreement of December 1938 gave her the right to acquire one-quarter of the total production. Though nearly half the capital invested in the industry is British, oil supplies from Rumania only come sixth on Britain's list.

German figures give the following percentages of capital invested:

Anglo-Dutch capital	..	42 %
Franco-Belgian capital	..	23 %
American capital ..	..	6 %
Rumanian capital ..	..	29 %

DESTINATION OF EXPORTS (PETROLEUM PRESS BUREAU)

	Metric Tons		
	1936	1937	1938
Germany	1,072,402	435,281 ⎫	703,732
Austria	341,804	91,710 ⎭	
Italy	653,222	575,800	556,535
United Kingdom ..	846,276	580,182	549,227
France	866,322	603,868	289,338

It is interesting to note the provisions for Rumanian oil that Germany made at the treaty of Bucharest in 1918. All the oil fields owned by the state were to be leased to an Austro-German company for thirty years (the lease was renewable for two further periods of 30 years); no other foreign capital was to be admitted, and this company was to have the exclusive right to export petrol and control Rumania's internal consumption. Luckily for Rumania the oil fields lie east of the Carpathians. If she can remain friends with Russia and Bulgaria, she might be able to keep Germany out of them in the event of war. It has been suggested that as the wells could so easily be put out of action, Rumanian oil would not be of great value to Germany in war time, but unless the destruction were more thorough than in the last war, considerable quantities would still be available. The British military mission helped to fire and block the wells and to destroy storage tanks and refineries in November 1916, but by July 1917 the Germans were securing 1,470 metric tons per day, and by the armistice two-thirds of the pre-war quantity were being produced, though it was not until 1924 that the full 1913 level was reached.

TOTAL PRODUCTION OF CRUDE PETROLEUM

Metric Tons

1913 ..	.. 1,885,225
1916 ..	.. 1,244,093
1917 ..	.. 517,491
1918 ..	.. 1,214,219
1921 ..	.. 1,163,623
1924 ..	.. 1,851,000

After 1924 there was a rapid increase, until the peak production of 8,704,000 tons was reached in 1936.

5. SOCIAL CONDITIONS

THE land reform, though it removed the greater discrepancies of wealth, has not altered the structure of Rumanian life. The boyars are still distinct from the other sections of the community. Their political power as a class went with their lands, though individuals among them have of course had political careers since the war as members of other parties, but their social influence remains. Since the establishment of the royal dictatorship, however, they have still less place in politics. The old struggle between the King and the barons is going on, and very few of the Crown councillors or heads of departments are boyars. It would have been better for the Magyar and Russian minorities if the boyars had had more influence after the war. There is class free-masonry above as well as below, and the Rumanian aristo-crats would have understood the troubles of expropriated Hungarians and Russians and been more ready to mitigate them than the liberal oligarchy which was actually in power.

The middle class is composed partly of the former liberal business men and partly of the sons of priests and peasants who are gradually being educated. Salaries are low, even in proportion to the cost of living, and now that a year of national service is compulsory as well as the two years' military service, a man will have to wait a long time to marry.

The mass of the people (80 %) are still peasants: they are beautifully dressed in hand-embroidered clothes, their houses are clean, attractively painted and decorated inside with hand-woven rugs, but for food they often have little but mamaliga, a traditional dish of boiled maize. The children rarely get milk, and the peasant does not eat enough meat to keep himself in shoe leather.

Since the reform they have gained in self-respect but not much in pocket. They do sometimes get bread now, however, as a change from the eternal mamaliga. The birth rate is high, but the infant mortality rate the highest in Europe. The new scheme for sending teams of students into the villages was King Carol's idea. These teams of four or five students in their last year, accompanied by a similar number of fully qualified people, spend three months of each year in the villages living in the cottages. The medical students, with their accompanying doctor, set up a dispensary and give free advice which is most acceptable, as at present there is only one doctor to about 8,000 people. The agricul-tural students give instruction in manuring and suggest the planting of diversified crops. By growing maize on mountain slopes instead of apples, the peasant makes a loss of 150 %. The girls deal with infant welfare. The teams go back three years in succession to the same village. Apparently the peasants do not resent being given good advice, but more than advice is necessary if standards are really to be raised.

At present only 7·6 % of the population is engaged in industry, 37 % of this number being employed in small artisan workshops and 61 % in enterprises employing over six workers. Wages are not high and housing is on the whole poor. Most of the industrial workers come from Transylvania and the Banat, and were well organised in trade unions and practised in social struggles through their experience in the Austro-Hungarian Empire. In 1937 there were about 60,000 trade union members in Rumania. It is significant that of the 78 strikes that took place in 1935,58 were in Transylvania.

There is little unemployment among artisans, but in the professions it grew serious after the economic crisis of 1931. There were over 6,000 black-coated workers unemployed in March 1937. This surplus has largely been absorbed under improving economic conditions, but many people with professional training still have posts and salaries below their capacity and qualifications. It is interesting to note that the citizens of the Old Kingdom, who may find that their only outlet is state employment, which is very poorly paid, are worse off than members of the minorities, who can often get comparatively good posts in business. This lack of adequate openings for clever young men was also one of the causes of Iron Guard success.

Women are employed in industry, mostly in the textile works, and there are openings for them in the professions, though the general lack of professional opportunity has hit them too. Some women have made good careers at the Bar, and it is possible that a woman would have held Cabinet rank if the National Peasant Party had again come into power. There is one woman senator in the new Parliament.

EDUCATION

Roughly half the population was illiterate when the new Rumanian state was formed after the war, but great strides have since been made in the field of education, largely on the initiative of the peasants themselves, who have voluntarily contributed land, money and labour for the building of schools. Agricultural education has not been neglected, though it has not been pursued so systematically as in Bulgaria. By 1924 there were 101 agricultural schools in Rumania, and in 1936 there were 3,795 pupils taking agricultural courses. Rumania has not escaped the usual difficulty of the unwillingness of the educated, or even the semi-educated, to live on the land. It was found in 1924 that less than 10 % of the pupils from the agricultural schools settled down to farming. Nearly all took state employment. The National Peasant Party passed a law in 1929 designed to make the education provided by agricultural schools more practical, and King Carol's teams already described are doing their best to educate peasants without enticing them away from the land.

There are about 590 trade and professional schools in Rumania and four universities, in Bucharest, Jassy, Cluj, and Czernowitz, the last two being in minority districts. In 1934 there were altogether 30,424 men students, 21,883 women; 5,165 of the students were Jews, but their numbers at the universities are diminishing each year.

6. DOMESTIC POLITICS

THE present royal dictatorship can only be understood in the light of political history. The Principalities were endowed on union with a democrátic constitution on the western model, and before the war liberal and conservative governments succeeded one another with quiet regularity. There were no startling differences in home or foreign policy. France had taken such a prominent part in the founding of the new kingdom and her cultural influence was so strong that neither party could be anti-French, though the Liberal Party, which represented the newly emerging bourgeoisie, gave France more unqualified allegiance. One section of the Conservative Party, which was formed from the boyar class, had sympathy with Germany, and another was inclined to be pro-Russian, but it is a significant indication of the state of public feeling that King Carol I did not feel able to reveal to either party his secret treaty of 1883 with Austria and Germany.

The war changed the whole balance of political life in Rumania. Pro-German policy was discredited, and the loss of their estates in the Reform destroyed the influence of the boyars: the Conservative Party in its old form was dead. The new provinces brought new political alignments into the country. The National Party of Transylvania, composed of men whose political apprenticeship had been served in resisting Hungarian rule, fused in 1926 with the Peasant Party of M. Mihalache and provided the main opposition to the liberals. The two parties had already formed a coalition under Dr. Vaida Voevod after the fall of M. Bratianu and the liberals in 1919. This new National Peasant Party, though not socialist, was the Rumanian equivalent of post-war parties of the Left. Socialism proper or communism could not take root in a country where the vast majority of the population were peasants turned into smallholders by the land reform. The Liberal Party had a long spell of power after the war. The Bratianu brothers who led it carried on the traditional policy that their family had evolved. The liberals favoured private enterprise against state ownership, but were strictly nationalist and opposed to the use of foreign capital. Their industrial policy has already been discussed. It is true that it was under the liberals that Rumania had achieved much of her success, but their failure after the war to adapt their policy to the times did much to cause the breakdown of parliamentary government. They left untouched the system whereby all local government officials were changed at each election, and did nothing to check the prevailing corruption and graft, while their centralising policy alienated the minorities.

The National Peasants had their first experience of office almost exactly at the same time as the second Labour government in England, and the economic crisis similarly caused their downfall. There was no time to carry out their programme of decentralisation, the development of agriculture and more liberal treatment of minorities. The influence of the party was further diminished by the estrangement of its leader, M. Maniu, from King Carol. M. Maniu was largely responsible for the King's return from exile in 1930, which had been strongly opposed by the liberals, but he must have sensed even then King Carol's intention to be more than a constitutional monarch, for relations between them became strained almost at once. M. Maniu's openly expressed dislike of Madame Lupescu and the Court *camarilla* brought matters to a head, and he resigned the premiership towards the end of 1930, never to resume it, though he still led the party. His rigidity has been criticised by many of his followers, who feel that it has compromised the party's prospects, but men of all parties join in respect and admiration for one of the finest political figures that Rumania has produced.

The Liberal Party could not solve the country's economic problems, and the National Peasant Party had no chance to try. This gave their opportunity to politicians of the extreme Right, and fascist groups began to come into prominence after the great depression and the severe Rumanian banking crisis of 1932. It was easy to fasten responsibility for the economic troubles on to the ever-unpopular Jew, and these new groups quickly found a following, especially among young men from the universities who saw little chance of finding a career. The most important of these groups, M. Codreanu's Iron Guard, was inspired by Professor Cuza's pre-war Christian Defence League. The less violent National Christian Party was led by a venerable Transylvanian poet, M. Goga. Rumania is proud that political assassination is not among the national traditions, but this clean record was broken by the Iron Guard, who after an unsuccessful attempt to murder M. Anghelescu in 1927, killed the Liberal Premier, M. Duca, as a reprisal for the suppression of the party in 1933 (it was promptly resurrected under the title 'All for the Fatherland'). Later some of M. Codreanu's associates were sent to shoot in cold blood a former comrade who was lying ill in hospital. Such was the position of the main parties at the end of 1937, when an election was due.

Parliaments are elected for four years, but it is rare that a ministry can last in office as long. By the end of 1937, however, M. Tatarescu's liberal government had had its whole four years, and the country was thoroughly tired of it. When a ministry falls as the result of a vote of censure in the Chamber, the normal procedure is for the King to call on the leader of the next largest party to form a cabinet and 'make' the elections. By the electoral law of 1926 only 40 % of the votes is necessary to secure a majority in the Chamber; those who get 40 % or more of the poll are given half the seats in the Chamber, plus a share in the remainder in proportion to the number of votes obtained. The elections

are literally 'made' (the party in control has been known
to forbid voting in a village of doubtful allegiance by closing
the polling stations on the ground of a visitation of plague),
and until 1937 no party in charge had ever failed to secure
the necessary 40 %. But M. Tatarescu's government was so
thoroughly unpopular that the unheard of happened.
Though his party headed the poll, they failed to get the
40 %. The National Peasant Party came second, and had
M. Maniu been put in charge of the elections, as according
to ordinary procedure he ought to have been, there is no
reasonable doubt that he would have won, especially as he
had made an electoral pact with the Iron Guard. This pact
at first sight seems surprising and almost shocking to the
outsider, but both parties, in spite of their fundamental
divergence, could join in opposition to corruption and the
Court *camarilla*; M. Maniu thought he could deal satisfac-
torily with the Guard once he was in office, and the
Guard thought that a National Peasant government would
be more ready to allow the right of free association than
the liberal. The Iron Guard came next on the poll, and
last of all M. Goga's National Christians with 10 % of the
votes.

The King was determined not to have the National
Peasants in office, partly because of his personal dislike of
M. Maniu and partly because it would not have suited his
plans to have a strong democratic party in power. The Iron
Guard he mistrusted (there could not be two dictators in a
country, and Codreanu was undoubtedly determined to be
one) and therefore he called on M. Goga to form a government, realising no doubt that it would prove a *reductio ad
absurdum*. This expectation was fulfilled. The Goga government in its 45 days provoked the hostility of everyone at
home and abroad with its violent anti-Semitic measures;
all economic and financial activity was thrown into chaos,

and the stage was well set for King Carol's coup and the establishment of the new constitution in February 1938.

For a year parliament was suspended; all political parties were dissolved, and martial law and a strict censorship established. The King governs, assisted by a Crown Council consisting mostly of former ministers, but not including the most outstanding figures. In December 1938 the formation of a new single party, the Front of National Regeneration, was announced. The party is formed on a semi-corporative basis, and is controlled by an Executive Committee of 150 and a Directorate of 24. The minority parties have joined this front. The Magyars and Germans each have one seat on the Directorate and six on the Executive Committee.

Once the new party was formed and consolidated, it was possible to consider the re-opening of Parliament, and King Carol announced an election for June 1939. The new Parliament was to consist of Chamber and Senate as before, but was to be elected from the members of the one party on a corporative basis, the electoral body consisting of three colleges, one each to represent agriculture and manual labour, commerce and industry, and the liberal professions.

Between them these colleges elected 74 deputies to the Chamber; 30 for agriculture and manual labour, 11 for the merchants (commerce), 11 for industry, and 22 for the intellectual occupations, which are subdivided into various sections. Only those over 30 are now entitled to vote, and the illiterate and unemployed are disfranchised. There were thus only about 2 million electors in 1939, whereas in 1937 there had been over $4\frac{1}{2}$ million. A fine of 1,000 lei for not voting was imposed in the true Solonic manner, and 85 % of those entitled to vote in fact went to the polls.

Voting was by districts in 11 constituencies, the 10 new provinces and Bucharest. As explained above, the new provinces cut across the old provincial boundaries, and this weighted the scales against candidates belonging to minority races. For the 258 seats in the Chamber there were 524 candidates, among whom were 18 Hungarians, 11 Germans and 5 Bulgars. In spite of the rearrangement of the constituencies, 8 Germans, 7 Hungarians, 1 Bulgar and 1 Turk were elected. It is interesting to note that the Hungarians, who are nearly three times as numerous as the Germans, have secured fewer seats.

For the Senate only those over 40 and on the boards of professional organisations may vote, so that for the 88 elected seats there were only 1,108 voters. Of the 88 elected senators, 14 were to represent manual labour, 11 industry, 11 commerce, and 22 the professions. For the 88 seats there were 171 candidates.

Under the new constitution, as under the old, those who had been elected 10 times to the Chamber became senators automatically, and this brought in many of the great Parliamentary figures of earlier days, such as Maniu, Mihalache, and Diner Bratianu. Their membership proved short-lived, however, for they were turned from the door of the Senate House for refusing to take the oath to the new constitution and wear the new uniform of the National Regeneration Front. They were not finally expelled, but suspended for the 8 or 9 years' intended duration of the present Parliament.

Five Hungarians, 5 Germans and 1 Bulgar were candidates for senatorial seats, and of these the 5 Hungarians and the Bulgar were elected, but none of the Germans. The King, however, is able to redress any inequality in the balance of the Senate that he may consider undesirable, as he nominates 71 members. Further, the heads of religious denominations are entitled to senatorial seats if their Church has at least 200,000 adherents. This has secured the only

Parliamentary seat for a Jew, the Chief Rabbi being a senator by right.

In the final result, the Germans have 3 seats in the Senate, the Hungarians 7, the Bulgars 2 and the Jews 1.[1] It is to be noted that there are no Russians or Ukrainians in either house.

Women are entitled to vote, and may be candidates for the first time in Rumanian history, but only for the Senate. Only about 30 % of those elected were members of former Parliaments. There are now 30 peasants in the Chamber, and it is claimed that so many genuine peasants never had seats even in the heyday of the National Peasant Party. The cost of the election also is said to be 20 times less than in former days.

It may be asked why so much importance was attached to the election when Parliament has no initiative in legislation, and can merely draft and examine bills presented by the Crown Council. There is no doubt, however, that the election aroused great interest in the country and that the minorities set much store on obtaining seats. It is possible that the new Parliament may be a beginning of return to democracy, but meanwhile all power remains as surely as before in the hands of the King.

One is tempted to look on King Carol as a Shavian Magnus. His astuteness in breaking up the older parties by playing off one politician against another is unrivalled, and much though an Englishman may regret the collapse of parliamentarism, it is possible that democracy is not suited to Rumania at her present stage. The King has taken many points from the programme of his rivals. His interest in the

[1] Previous elections—Hungarian members of Parliament:

		Chamber.	Senate.
1926	.. ..	14	12
1937	.. ..	19	3

improvement of village life is as keen as that of the National Peasants, and his stand against corruption as strong. The youth movement (Strajeri) that he has started strongly resembles that of the Iron Guard. Though a Hohenzollern by race, and having much sympathy with Germany, he is yet determined to maintain his country's independence. In a moment like this when Germany is trying to break up each state by making use of factions within, it must make for the safety of Rumania to have undivided control.

The weakness of King Carol's system is that, like all dictatorships, it can make no allowance for opposition, which has to be ruthlessly suppressed. The execution of Codreanu and his companions last autumn and the manner in which it was done, made a deep impression in the country; not only supporters of the Guard were indignant. The National Peasants still feel that democracy is the only ultimate way of educating the people. Some would admit that King Carol's government is better than any possible alternative at the moment, but they argue first that the throne should be a steadying force above politics, and secondly that King Carol by making all the main decisions himself is not training a future generation of politicians. When he goes there will be no one with knowledge or the experience of responsibility to step into his shoes.

7. FOREIGN POLICY

1918–1938

Since the war Rumania has no longer had to fear that she would be crushed between the rivalries of three empires. The change of heart in Russia and Turkey and their resulting friendship, and the collapse of Austria-Hungary has removed the old danger, but a new one has arisen. German designs on Rumanian wheat and oil are well known. If it came to war between Germany and Russia, Rumania as well as Poland would be the battle ground, and she also lies across Germany's transversal Eurasian axis from Hamburg to Basra. Nearer home are other potential enemies. The doubling of Rumania's territory and population after the war, however just, was not achieved without rousing resentment among her neighbours, and the three aggrieved neighbours, Hungary, Russia and Bulgaria, had a far greater length of frontier with Rumania than her fellow successor states, Poland, Czechoslovakia and Yugoslavia.

Since the war, then, Rumanian foreign policy has necessarily been based on an endeavour to maintain the *status quo* and protect herself against aggression. She fell naturally into place beside the other satisfied Powers, and was from the first a conscientious member of the League of Nations. Its decisions were loyally accepted, even when they conflicted with Rumanian interests, as in the case of the claims of the Hungarian optants in 1930 or the adoption of Sanctions against Italy in 1935. But it was felt that the League of Nations alone did not offer adequate safeguards, and a careful system of regional pacts was built up to supplement collective security.

It was her eastern frontier which at first gave Rumania the most anxiety. Even now Russia has not officially recognised the acquisition of Bessarabia, and in the early years after the war there were frontier incidents in that province. The first engagement, therefore, into which Rumania entered outside the League of Nations was the defensive alliance with Poland, which was signed by Prince Sapieha and Take Ionescu in March 1921 to guarantee the eastern frontiers of both countries. This alliance has since been renewed at intervals of five years, and was strengthened after 1936.

Under the influence of M. Titulescu, who became Foreign

Minister in 1927, relations with Russia continued to improve. With the signing by both countries in 1933 of the Conventions of London defining the aggressor, Russia's entry into the League in 1934, and the exchange of letters between Titulescu and Litvinov later that year, most people regarded the question of Bessarabia as settled. Unfortunately traditional Rumanian distrust and dislike of Russia under whatever government prevented Titulescu from securing the agreement with the Soviets which would have crowned his policy. After he had left the Foreign Office an article appeared in *Pravda* in July 1937 attacking the Rumanian-Polish alliance and asserting that the Bessarabian question could once more be regarded as open. The Province still appears as Russian on Soviet maps, with the inscription 'In Rumanian military occupation'.

Having secured her eastern frontier, Rumania turned to the west. Hungary's whole remaining territory was no larger than Transylvania and the Banat which she had lost to Rumania, and she made no secret of her active dissatisfaction with the Treaty of Trianon. Rumanian armies, which had occupied Budapest after the war, might well feel able to meet Hungary in the field, but her discontent might obviously be used as a cat's-paw by other Powers. It was natural that Yugoslavia and Czechoslovakia, who also had much to fear from Hungarian revisionism, should join with Rumania in forming the Little Entente, which grew out of the original bilateral pacts signed in 1921 between the three countries concerned.

Take Ionescu, the Rumanian statesman, had originally envisaged a more ambitious Baltic-Aegean *bloc*, comprising Poland, Czechoslovakia, Rumania, Yugoslavia and Greece, which would have acted as a buffer between Germany and Russia, but this idea was rejected by Benes, who preferred to confine the Entente to Hungary's immediate neighbours.

Perhaps the coolness always existing between Poland and Czechoslovakia influenced his decision. With the rise of Nazism in Germany, the bonds between the members of the Little Entente were strengthened. The alliance entered a new constructive phase. A Pact of Organisation was signed in 1933 and a Permanent Economic Council set up.

The southern frontier remained. Bulgaria could not forgive the loss of Southern Dobruja. She also claimed parts of Macedonia incorporated by the Peace Treaties in Yugoslavia and Greece, and once again the states who had something to lose joined together for protection. The Balkan pact between Rumania, Yugoslavia, Turkey and Greece was signed early in 1934. M. Barthou's plan for a general Eastern pact aroused enthusiasm in Rumania, but was wrecked by Hungary and Poland. The more modest Balkan Pact aroused less opposition. In view of unconcealed Bulgarian revisionism one might have expected the Pact to be concluded earlier after the war, but Balkan memories are long and it was only the increasing pressure of external events after 1933 which made it possible for the states concerned to sink their differences. The Pact was left open to Bulgaria and Albania, which showed that the Balkan Entente was something more than a mere anti-revisionist front. It aroused general pride and satisfaction among the people of the Balkans, who felt that their peacefulness was becoming a model of behaviour to western Europe.

Going outside the circle of her immediate neighbours, Rumania concluded pacts of friendship and collaboration with her two 'Latin sisters', France and Italy. Both were signed in 1926 'in the spirit of Locarno'. The Italian Pact lapsed in January 1934. Italy was becoming increasingly pro-Hungarian (the Rome Protocols were signed only two months later); in any case it could not have survived the adoption of Sanctions by Rumania. The Pact had the result of securing Italian recognition of Bessarabia, which had been withheld until 1927.

With France, Rumania has had the closest cultural ties since 1848, and it was to French support that she largely owed the achievement of independence and unity. The Liberal and National Peasant parties who controlled Rumanian politics until 1937 were strongly pro-French; sympathy with France went, therefore, far beyond the letter of the 1926 Pact.

Rumania was thus well fenced round by pacts and alliances. The weakness of the system was that both the Little Entente and the Balkan Entente too rigidly supported the *status quo* and neither were satisfactory economic units. It is possible that the Little Entente by lining up against Austria and Hungary, helped to make the Anschluss inevitable. Even on the political side there were cracks in the structure. Yugoslavia proved an uncertain partner in both alliances. It was she who blocked the Turkish proposals of 1936 for an Euxine Pact which was to include the riverains of the Black Sea and Greece. Her alliances with Italy and with Bulgaria in 1937, even though ultimately condoned by her fellow members of the two Ententes, went outside the spirit, if not the letter of the agreements, and she came more directly under German economic and political influence than any of the other countries concerned.

Between Rumania and Turkey there was a possible conflict of interests over the question of the Black Sea and the remilitarisation of the Straits. The Straits are of vital importance to Rumanian trade, and any suggestion of treaty revision aroused nervousness and distrust lest it should be used as a precedent. However, an amicable settlement was fortunately reached, and Rumania accepted the Montreux decision in 1936. Finally, the Franco-Soviet and Czech-

Soviet Pacts were viewed with suspicion by Rumania, who was becoming increasingly alienated from the USSR.

1938 AND AFTER

The Anschluss brought down this whole structure like the proverbial pack of cards. The immediate effect was to make all Danubian peoples review their position and try to agree with their enemies quickly while they were in the way with them. In July an important agreement was signed between the states of the Balkan Entente and Bulgaria, whereby the clauses of the Treaty of Neuilly forbidding Bulgarian rearmament were repealed. Then in August the new Rumanian Minorities Statute, announcing further concessions to the minorities in her territory, was published and immediately after, at the August session of the Little Entente at Bled, an agreement with Hungary was concluded on the lines of the earlier Salonica agreement with Bulgaria; the states concerned mutually renounced the use of force and allowed Hungary to rearm.

After Munich the inadequacy of these expedients became obvious; Rumania has had to work out a more radical revision of her system. The keynote of her policy still remains anti-revisionism. 'Rumania has nothing to give, and if anything something to take', said Titeanu, the Under-Secretary for Propaganda, in a speech addressed to the representatives of the minority Press last autumn. There are about a million Rumanians outside the country, but Rumania had at that time anyhow no thought of profiting by the general scramble. For, with collective security and the Little Entente gone, her concern is to keep what she has, and while she gratefully accepted British and French guarantees in April 1939, she is still undecided where her safest allegiance lies.

Political parties are at present suppressed in the country, but the tendencies they represent are still there. The would-be fascists say that their pro-German policy is triumphantly vindicated by Munich. The western democracies have proved themselves useless, decadent, and rotten with Jews. Russia is not only a menace to the social structure but the hereditary enemy. The obvious solution is for Rumania to come of her own accord into the German orbit. There she will find a strong partner who will buy her products, help her to get rid of the Jews and train her rising generation to be Nordic heroes.

The would-be democrats have a more difficult case to make, but they would answer that though France and Great Britain are not altruists they must be alive to their own interests, and realise that it would be unwise to let Germany push through via Rumania to Iran. This would not suit Russia either. Further, if a Four-Power Conference were called, it would be in Rumanian interests to have the friendship of Great Britain and France, for Germany and Italy, though not prepared to go to war for the sake of Hungary, could hardly fail to support her claims through diplomatic channels.

King Carol's government would seem to incline to neither of these views, but to be watching to see what use can be made by Rumania of the Entente-Axis rivalry for influence in eastern Europe, and to build a new system on what remains of the old.

The Balkan Entente still stands. It was thought that the Bucharest Conference in February 1939 would see the inclusion of Bulgaria, but the hopes raised after the rapprochement of August 1938 were disappointed. The present members of the Entente are still unwilling to make territorial concessions and Bulgaria is not prepared to forgo her demands; indeed, since that date Bulgarian politicians have made several revisionist pronouncements, and there have been rumours of troop movements on the Dobruja frontier. The recent ugly incident at Belitsa, when 22 Bulgarian komitadjis were shot down by Rumanian gendarmes in doubtful circumstances, has further inflamed feelings, though the Rumanian government has done its best to make amends. It is significant that for the first time at a Balkan conference no mention was made of fidelity to the League of Nations, and the usual reference to the prolongation of the Balkan Pact was omitted. Turkey is evidently unwilling to commit herself for another 5 years. This does not mean, however, that she undervalues her Balkan connections. A Turkish paper recently pointed out that the Balkan Entente united 60 to 70 million people, and could put into the field for defence between 3 and 4 million soldiers. (Bulgarians estimate a possible Balkan Entente army at 7 millions.)

It appears that Litvinov's new plan for a Black Sea Pact between Russia, Turkey, Rumania and some of the Balkan states was discussed at the Conference, though no decision was reached. Yugoslavia again opposed the suggestion, and fears have been expressed that Yugoslavia and Bulgaria might allow the Rome-Berlin Axis to push through across their territory to the Black Sea, thus isolating Rumania and Greece.

The Italian seizure of Albania has tended to draw the remaining Balkan countries together, but Great Britain's policy of guarantees and a Peace Front has increased the strains within the Balkan Entente. Yugoslavia looks askance on the Anglo-Turkish Pact, and Turkey is reviving the idea of a Black Sea Entente containing Russia, Rumania, Bulgaria and Turkey in case Yugoslavia should break away.

Turkish attempts to overcome the Bulgarian difficulty by getting Rumania to lease the Dobruja to Bulgaria for 100 years hardly appear likely to be acceptable to either party.

Of the former system the Polish alliance also remains.

There was a definite cooling in Polish-Rumanian relations in October 1938, when Poland attempted to gain Rumanian support for the establishment of her common frontier with Hungary. Colonel Beck is said to have offered Rumania a slice of Ruthenia containing a number of Rumanians, variously estimated at between 20,000 and 40,000, as the price of assent to the partition of the rest of the province between Hungary and Poland. Rumania's indignant rejection of the offer was largely the result of loyalty to her ally Czechoslovakia, but she also felt that any concession to Hungary based on historical and not ethnic considerations might have dangerous repercussions in Transylvania, and she did not want another 93 miles of frontier with Hungary. Also it was difficult to believe so soon that the old system had entirely gone, and Ruthenia was the only link between Rumania and Czechoslovakia. But in 1939 the position altered. With German pressure on Czechoslovakia increasing daily, it may well have seemed to Rumania that a common frontier between Poland and Hungary would be less dangerous than a German-controlled Ruthenia, which could be used as a centre for spreading Ukrainian propaganda in Bukovina and Bessarabia. The *bloc* of Ukrainian population is continuous from the Uz to the Don. This would seem to explain the withdrawal of Rumanian opposition to the Polish proposal, which M. Gafencu, the new Rumanian Foreign Minister, was able to give Colonel Beck on his visit to Warsaw in March 1939.

The visit greatly strengthened the ties between Poland and Rumania. The two nations were plainly once more trying to form a *bloc* between Germany and Russia, and were engaged in the feverish political arithmetic which occupies all the states of eastern Europe. What combination would provide a number of men to balance Germany's 80 millions? Pilsudski's Polish-Hungarian-Rumanian *bloc* would have raised 60 million people. The idea had been revived, but it is doubtful if it would have found favour in Rumania. Of great importance were the proposals discussed by M. Gafencu and Colonel Beck for a Baltic to Black Sea canal system terminating at Galatz where the Pruth joins the Danube. It was possible that Rumania would grant Poland a free zone in Galatz to compensate for Danzig and Gdynia.

Though the Italian pact has lapsed, there is growing sympathy with Italy in Rumania, which still persists in spite of the coolness engendered by the occupation of Albania, and an attempt to detach her from the Axis would probably find considerable support in Bucharest. The present trend of Rumanian political thought is undoubtedly towards the corporative ideal; alienation from the western democracies is not merely the result of Munich. German friendship would be too dangerous, but Italy would be the ideal partner. The fascist government is not slow to take advantage of this tendency, which has been accentuated since the Spanish Civil War. Most Rumanians hail General Franco as the protector of religion and the family against communists and Jews. The Italians are setting up handsomely built institutes in all Rumanian towns, and Rumanians are flocking to learn Italian. The propagandists point out how delightful it is for Rumania, when one Latin sister had fallen into the hands of Jews, to find another and a purer one closer at hand. All the same, a 'semaine du livre français' had a phenomenal success last winter in Bucharest, nearly all the books being sold in two days, and in March 1939 a Pact of Intellectual Co-operation was signed between France and Rumania, providing for the general development of cultural relations between the two countries, exchange of university students and professors, promotion of travel, etc. Old attachments do not die so easily.

The weakness of Rumanian foreign policy has been that her ideological sympathies and desire for rigid maintenance at all costs of all existing frontiers have conflicted with her real interest in preserving herself as an independent nation. It is obviously important for the USSR to prevent German political or economic domination of Rumania, but apart from this she has no real interests to advance in that area. The Rumanian oilfields lie on her side of the Carpathians and she wants no more oil, having plenty of her own. Bulgaria was the weak spot in the last war. The Carpathians, though not an impassable barrier, offer a serious obstacle to an army, and it was only through her Bulgarian alliance and consequent ability to cross the Danube that Germany was able to smash Rumanian resistance. It would seem worth while to conciliate Bulgaria and forgive Russia for swallowing the Rumanian treasure sent to Moscow in 1916. On the other hand, a guarantee of existing frontiers by Germany could be too dearly bought. If Germany does not back Hungarian claims, it cannot mean genuine friendliness towards Rumania, but an intention to control both Hungary and Transylvania separately herself.

Since the disappearance of Czechoslovakia some may wonder how Rumania has been able to stand up to Germany at all, while others are surprised that she has not thrown herself wholeheartedly into a peace front with the USSR, the Balkan states and the western democracies. Three things have to be remembered. First, that Rumania does not wish to make concessions to Bulgaria if she can avoid doing so; second, that she hesitates to place all her confidence in Great Britain and France after Munich; and third, that experience in the war led the Rumanian people to fear their Russian allies more than their German enemies.

The occupation of Prague and subsequent German threats to Rumania have once more tilted the balance.

After a rapid series of visits to Berlin, London, Paris, Rome, and the Balkan capitals in the spring of 1939 M. Gafencu advised his government that national independence was more likely to be secured by the British guarantee than by listening to German promises. There has been a still greater swing of popular feeling in Bucharest; things German are looked on with increasing disfavour, and Rumanians are even prepared reluctantly to agree to accepting Soviet assistance if it can be received.

Rumania has one of the greatest futures in Europe before her, if she can but keep her independence secure during the next few critical years of consolidation and growth.

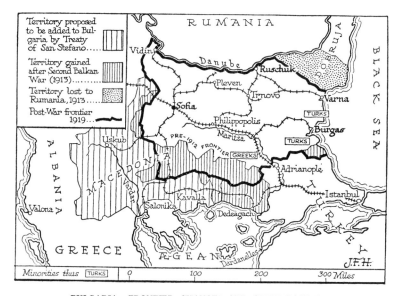

BULGARIA—FRONTIER CHANGES AND CHIEF RAILWAYS

BULGARIA

CLARE HOLLINGWORTH

1. POLITICS

BULGARIA UP TO THE ACCESSION OF FERDINAND OF COBURG

Bulgaria is a country situated in the eastern part of the Balkan Peninsula, having a coastline on the Black Sea, the greater part of its northern frontier being formed by the River Danube. The Balkan Mountains form its spine; the Rhodopes its southern boundary. The narrow plain of western Thrace, between the Rhodopes and the Aegean, belongs to Greece. The area of Bulgaria is 40,000 square miles, and its population some 6 million. Eighty-three per cent of the inhabitants are members of the Orthodox Church and 14 % are Moslems. The majority of the latter are Turkish speaking, but there are a considerable number of Pomaks or Bulgar-speaking Moslems.

Bulgaria is essentially a peasant country, 80 % of its people being engaged in some form of agriculture. There are two great classes: the poor peasant smallholders, and the bourgeoisie of the towns. Over this people there reigns a King of the House of Coburg, whose style derives from the medieval Bulgarian Czars—Boris III.

The nation has been formed from a blend of two main elements: a conquering Turki tribe, the Bulgars, and the previous inhabitants, mainly belonging to the Slavs, who had overrun the Peninsula in the 6th century, and the earlier Thracians whom they had absorbed. The Slav element predominates in the Bulgarians; the language is definitely Slav in vocabulary and form, except for the presence of a few words of Turkish origin (even these are attributable to

159

the later Turkish conquerors); and the use of the Turki article suffixed to nouns. The language is written in the Cyrillic script.

The condition of backwardness prevailing in the Balkan Peninsula today is due to the fact that the collection of medieval Christian states occupying the Peninsula in the 14th century was overwhelmed by the Turks. The recession of the Turkish wave, only completed in our own days, has uncovered a Balkan world singularly like the one which existed before the Turks arrived in Europe; Bulgaria, Serbia and Greece resumed their game of 'power politics' where they had been forced to put it down.

The Balkans are now devoting themselves to the acquisition of civilisation; but that which they possessed a few years ago, and that of the mass of the people even today, is really nothing but a top-dressing of imported modern inventions; essentially, the Turks embalmed for the future the civilisation which existed before they came. They did not set out to destroy Balkan culture, though they burned many books and pictures in the monasteries; having nothing to put in its place, they contented themselves with arresting the development of Balkan civilisation, save in so far as the subject population continued to sing the stories of bygone heroes such as the Bulgar Czar Simeon or Marko Kraljević. A proportion of the lads who ought to have supplied the flower of the nation for literary or political rebellion were taken away for the Corps of Janissaries, and brought up as Mussulmans.

LIBERATION

Bulgaria was only the fourth of the Balkan states to be liberated from the Turkish yoke. This was largely due to the attraction exercised by Constantinople and foreign countries upon those qualified by their abilities for leadership. The monk Paijsij led a literary revival; but the peasants were not aroused until the foundation of the first Bulgarian school in 1835, and over 50 more schools in the next 10 years. In 1844 a Bulgarian newspaper was printed outside the country; but as late as 1877 there was only one printing press in Bulgaria. The cultural and religious movement resulted in the liberation of the national Church from the control of the Greek Oecumenical Patriarchate; after which nationalism passed to the men of action, *comitadjis* and conspirators, who with bomb and rifle maintained the Bulgar cause until Russian armies liberated their country.

The Russians endeavoured to secure, in 1877, the creation of a large Bulgarian state in dependence upon the Czar. They were thwarted by Great Britain, which dreaded the extension of Russian influence. Disraeli need not have been so anxious; in seven years Russia and Bulgaria had quarrelled. As Bismarck wrote:

> Liberated nations are not grateful but exacting. All these races have gladly accepted Russian help for liberation from the Turks; but since they have been free they have shown no tendency to accept the Czar as successor of the Sultan.

He added that the calculation as to the permanent dependence of Bulgaria upon Russia:

> Even if the peace of San Stefano had been carried out intact . . . would probably have proved false.

The Congress of Berlin erected a Principality in the northern part of Bulgaria, and gave autonomy, under a Turkish Governor, to the southern half, known as Eastern Rumelia. Alexander of Battenberg became Prince, and in 1885 Eastern Rumelia threw off its Governor and united with Bulgaria. Alexander accepted the *fait accompli*, and thereby incurred the hostility of Russia, which procured his downfall. Ferdinand of Coburg was chosen as the new Prince.

THE MACEDONIANS

It is necessary to break off the chronological story of Bulgaria in order to introduce a particular factor which has decisively influenced Bulgarian politics from the period of her liberation until the present day. Between the Pirin mountain massif in the east and the Lake of Ohrid in the west, between Skoplije in the north and Salonika in the south, there lies the country of Macedonia. It is the contention of all Bulgarians and a large part of the Macedonians that this country ought to form part of the Bulgarian Kingdom. At the present time, only a small portion, around the Pirin, is included in Bulgaria; the southern part is in Greek hands, and has been almost completely Hellenised; while the bulk of Macedonia forms the southern Banovina of Yugoslavia. From 1878 until 1918, Balkan politics centred mainly upon the eventual attribution of sovereignty over Macedonia; from 1919 until 1934 the foreign relations of Bulgaria, particularly those with Yugoslavia, were kept in a perpetual turmoil by the activities of Macedonian terrorists; Bulgarian domestic politics during the same period were equally disturbed by the same agency; and since the suppression of the terrorists in 1934 there has always been the fear that their influence was not dead. Moreover, in 1939, when the states of eastern Europe are deciding their attitude towards Germany and Italy and the western Powers, in view of possible territorial changes and an all-too-probable war, the lure of Macedonia is a factor in the minds of the statesmen at Sofia.

The population of Macedonia is a *mélange* of all the Balkan races, the predominant speech being claimed by the Bulgars as Bulgarian and by the Serbs as a dialect of Serbian. (In this connection, the use of the Bulgarian article-suffix is significant.)

It is difficult to give an impartial yet accurate account of the position occupied by the inhabitants of Macedonia, between the claims of the Bulgars and the Serbs. Macedonia, like Bulgaria itself, was overrun by the Slavs in the course of their original invasions. The arrival of the Turki Bulgars resulted in the formation of a Bulgarian people mainly Slav in blood and speech, but differentiated from the Serbs in character and appearance, and to some extent in language. Macedonia was the main battle-ground between the three rival Balkan peoples in the Middle Ages, and was accordingly from time to time part of the dominions of each ascendancy, the Greek, the Bulgar and the Serb. It has evolved a Macedonian people differing in some of its characteristics from each of its neighbours; yet able to be regarded as an outlandish brand either of Serb or of Bulgar when either of those nations has been ruling it for a sufficiently prolonged period. From the time of the liberation of Bulgaria until the end of the Great War, it would appear that Bulgarian affinities prevailed; but in the contest for possession of Macedonia, Serbia, not Bulgaria, was successful.

In the sixties and seventies of the last century, when Serbia and Greece had already established their independence, though in restricted frontiers, Bulgaria and Macedonia looked forward to the day when the hated rule of the Turks would be overthrown. It still seemed possible in those days that Macedonia would form a separate Principality; but if that should not happen, it was a matter for speculation which of the three little kingdoms would acquire the bulk of the province. Greece had a strong position, through her control of the Church, and, consequently, of all Christian education, until the Sultan recognised the Bulgarian Patriarchate, and the non-Greek Macedonians, whether of Serbian or Bulgarian sentiment, rallied to the Slavonic as against the definitely foreign culture.

The Treaty of San Stefano proposed to give nearly the whole of Macedonia to Bulgaria. Had that peace been carried out, when the Macedonians had not yet proceeded far in their internecine rivalry, probably Macedonia would have settled down quite naturally as a part of Bulgaria. The interests of the Great Powers, however, caused Macedonia to be restored to Turkish rule for another 34 years, and during this period each of the three Balkan states did its utmost to prove its title to the whole province. Each one, sometimes supported by a protector among the Great Powers, spent money upon propaganda and upon arms, to enable the Greek, Serb and Bulgar factions to exterminate each other.

By the end of the 19th century, the misrule of the hapless Macedonian Christians by the Turks had become such a public scandal that, in order to prevent the intervention of the three European Empires in the interests of their Balkan protégées, Great Britain endeavoured to compel Turkey to carry out administrative reforms. A Christian gendarmerie was enrolled, with European officers supplied by the Great Powers. This scheme was not taken very seriously, except by the British, and Austria eventually sabotaged it. The Balkan states much preferred to deal with the matter themselves by tearing the province from Turkey in the First Balkan War of 1912–13.

Greece, as was expected, obtained the southern portion of Macedonia, and, to the disgust of the Bulgars, captured Salonika, the one important town and port of the province. Subsequent events, including an exchange of minority populations, have confirmed the Greek ethnographic character of this region.

The rest of Macedonia was mainly Slavonic (using the term to include Serb and Bulgar) and was (according to the terms of the Balkan Alliance) to be partitioned between

164

Bulgaria and Serbia. The wedge between the Rhodopes, the Greek frontier, and the line Ohrid-Kriva Palanka was to go to Bulgaria; from there northward to the Šar Planina was to be allotted according to adjudication by the Russian Czar. Unfortunately, Serbia was deprived of her anticipated gains on the west (where she had hoped for an outlet to the Adriatic through northern Albania) and claimed to be compensated in Macedonia. The zone agreed to be arbitrated she proposed to hold for herself, and desired further a share of the Bulgarian zone, so as to obtain a common frontier with Greece. Since the operations of the war had led to the occupation of Macedonia by Serbian troops, there was nothing for the Bulgars to do but to try to push out the Serbs. With a combination of diplomatic incompetence and military miscalculation, the King of Bulgaria (Ferdinand of Coburg) let himself in for general condemnation as a blustering aggressor, and for a crushing military defeat. The consequence was that Bulgaria obtained a mere fraction of the anticipated share of Macedonia. Intervention in the Great War was expected to restore the lost territory, but, by choosing the losing side, Bulgaria only forfeited some of what she had previously won.

In the days of the Bulgarian Patriarchate and the liberation of Bulgaria, various secret societies were formed, having for their object the liberation of Macedonia from the Turks. Among these movements the most popular was that which was fostered by Bulgarian influences, namely the Internal Macedonian Revolutionary Organisation. This body obtained arms and money from Bulgaria and elsewhere, and prepared rebellion against the Turks. It spread chiefly among the Bulgarian schoolmasters, and it looked forward to a liberated Macedonia which should be either independent or attached to Bulgaria. Its members held up an American lady to ransom, and spent the proceeds on dynamite with which they blew up the Ottoman Bank in Salonika. In 1903 they staged a rising which for several weeks overthrew the authority of the Turks; but the subsequent vengeance of the victorious Moslems was extremely horrible.

Many of the members of the terrorist movements formed themselves into bands of *comitadjis*, or irregulars, and fought alongside the armies of their respective allies during the liberation of their homeland by the Balkan Allies in 1912. Unfortunately, however, the I.M.R.O. had envisaged a Bulgarian liberation, and when the liberated province was annexed to Serbia, they felt that here was no true liberation at all. Having long considered themselves as Bulgar, they were little disposed to accept the rule of the rival faction, the Serbs. They therefore devoted themselves, after the war, to the further 'liberation' of Bulgarian Macedonia from Yugoslav rule. The Serbs not unnaturally met the challenge by proving extremely drastically that the inhabitants of Macedonia were not outlandish Bulgars but outlandish Serbs; this they did by 'Serbifying' the names, the language, and (if repression could manage it) the sentiments of their new subjects. The Macedonian grievance was thus given food for its perpetual nourishment.

One small portion of Macedonia remained in the hands of Bulgaria. This was the district of the mountain mass of the Pirin, to which flocked all those Bulgar-Macedonians who had made Yugoslav Macedonia or Greek Macedonia too hot to hold them. This mass of refugees and brigands, used to the pursuit of freedom, gun or bomb in hand, formed a powerful and utterly ruthless organisation inside the Bulgarian state. The all-powerful Revolutionary Organisation ruled the Pirin as a *de facto* autonomous state within the Bulgarian Kingdom, and when King Boris's tax-gatherer received the money owing to the King, he also received a further sum as taxes due to the Organisation, and for this he gave a separate receipt in the name of the Central Committee.

The Organisation did not stop at playing at brigands in the recesses of the Pirin. It established an advanced base in Sofia, from which it waged a second war, on the home front, against any of the men in Bulgarian political life who sought to make friends with Yugoslavia, or who threatened to put down the terrorists, or even to punish any of them for their crimes. What finally ruined the Organisation was that the central control fell into the hands of an ambitious villain named Mihailov, who eliminated his rival Protoguerov and waged a civil war of extermination within the Organisation itself. The great days of I.M.R.O. were over when it attached more importance to the shooting of a rival Macedonian than to the bombing of a Yugoslav express train, or the assassination of a Serbian judge or general.

The Internal Macedonian Revolutionary Organisation set itself to keep awake the consciousness of Bulgarians and Macedonians that Macedonia was being oppressed, and needed to be liberated. It did this by numerous raids over the border into Yugoslav territory, until the Serbs fortified their whole frontier with a dense wire entanglement; even so, there would be twenty people killed in a normal week up near the Dragoman Pass. When a number of students were tried in Skoplije, and sent to prison for subversive activities— largely because they insisted upon calling themselves Bulgars —a patriotic Macedonian woman took upon herself the task of avenging their fate, and went to Skoplije, where she assassinated the judge who had condemned the youths; immediately she had accomplished her object, she committed suicide. The wife of Mihailov assassinated an alleged renegade from the Organisation by shooting him in a box in the Vienna Opera. Trains were frequently bombed or mined. No Serbian general felt safe.

All this murderous activity was kept alive by the raising of contributions in Bulgaria itself, the collecting of money from charitable persons abroad who thought the cause of Macedonian liberty was something philanthropic, and by engaging in the illicit drug traffic. Subsidies were also obtained from Italy.

So long as the terrorists carried on their activities unhindered by the government at Sofia, Bulgaria's reputation abroad was deplorable. In particular, harmonious relations with Yugoslavia were impossible. That, from the Macedonian point of view, was all to the good. The fate they most feared was that Bulgaria would shelve the Macedonian question for the sake of friendly relations with her neighbour—as eventually happened. To this end, any Bulgarian statesman who made a gesture of friendliness to the Yugoslavs, or tried to enforce the law against a terrorist, was dispatched by the Organisation's gunmen. That was the fate of the agrarian prime minister, Stambuliski, who was overthrown by the army, then seized and murdered by the I.M.R.O.

Tzankov, Stambuliski's successor, owed his position to the Organisation. The next Premier, Liapćev, was himself a Macedonian. Liapćev's successor Mušanov was compelled (after the rival factions of Macedonians had fought a pitched battle outside the Royal Palace) to 'clean up' the Macedonian quarter of Sofia; but he took the precaution of allowing the leaders to escape first. It was eventually the military government of Colonel Gheorghiev that smoked the brigands out of their nest in the Pirin, and 'restored the authority of the state in the whole of its territory'. Many terrorists were imprisoned or transplanted to other parts of the country; huge stores of arms were captured; Mihailov and his friends escaped into exile. There are still secret societies, and there are still Macedonians, but the decisive power of a state within a state, which ruled everything, is a nightmare which has passed away.

Before leaving the subject of Macedonia, it is difficult to forbear a survey of the possibilities of a final solution, taking a longer view than is possible to those who, with bomb or baton, are immediately engaged upon subverting or maintaining order.

It should be recollected that in our own country, too, there are deep-seated differences of type, of speech, of mentality. This is particularly noticeable as between English, Scots and Welsh; but it is also true of the inhabitants of different parts of England. These differences give rise to a certain regional patriotism, as who should proudly say: 'I am a southerner'; but none desires to hate or to kill his fellow-citizen, or to separate his own region governmentally from the rest of England. Even the most ardent Scottish Nationalist desires a measure of autonomy, but not secession from the United Kingdom.

These considerations give us a certain clue to the eventual solution of the problem of the Slavonic Balkans. The difference in blood, in the shape of the head, in the speech and (purely artificial, this) in calligraphy, is not a sufficient cause for Serb and Bulgar to be set up as antithetical conceptions; rather, they are kindred peoples with everything to gain by unity.

One of the great disasters of modern history was the assassination of Prince Michael of Serbia, who was planning the First Balkan War just half a century before it actually took place. In those days Bulgaria had not been liberated from Turkish rule; the bitter and partly artificial national consciousness of the contending factions in Macedonia had not been stimulated; there was no valid reason against a Bulgarian people, liberated by the Prince of Serbia, forming a part, and a grateful part, of a Great Yugoslavia. But Prince Michael died, his scheme unrealised.

The establishment of the Bulgarian Exarchate and the liberation of Bulgaria ought to have been accompanied by a solution of the Macedonian question, but were not. The Berlin settlement of 1878 established the new Bulgarian state, which was attacked by Serbia in 1885, and the separate existence of Serbia and Bulgaria were therefore fixed for at least a long period of years. At the same time, Macedonia was erected into a formidable cause of dispute between the sister nations. Thus, the machinations of the Great Powers have created division where union was desirable in the interests of the peoples themselves, and ultimately of their neighbours and the rest of Europe. The tide began to turn towards union during the rule of Stambuliski in Bulgaria, but ebbed again at his death. During the last five years the tendency has been to closer and closer rapprochement between Bulgaria and Yugoslavia, and, until the birth of Prince Simeon, it did not seem altogether visionary to hope for a personal union of the two crowns by the marriage of King Boris's daughter with the young King Peter. The new contest among the Great Powers for influence in the Balkans may again create hostility; but, on the other hand, it may initiate a move towards some sort of federation between peoples essentially similar. A federal state comprising the present components of Yugoslavia (which find themselves too closely knit politically) and Bulgaria, which is too much separated from them, is one of those consummations that one recognises as eminently desirable, but hardly dares to hope for. The spirit expressed by the slogan: 'the Balkans for the Balkan peoples', however, has increased in recent years, and under the stress of strong external pressures there is no telling how the peoples themselves might react.

FROM FERDINAND TO THE MILITARY COUP OF 1934

The reign of Ferdinand.—Ferdinand was a Catholic, and had large estates in Hungary. He transferred his Principality from the Russian to the Austro-Hungarian orbit. About the same time Serbia, the neighbour and rival of Bulgaria, which had attacked her but had been beaten off in 1885, moved in the opposite direction, when in 1903 the Austrophil dynasty of Obrenović was replaced by the Karadjordjević. In 1908, with the connivance of Aerenthal, Ferdinand threw off his allegiance to the Porte and proclaimed himself Czar of all the Bulgars.

The chief events of Ferdinand's reign were the three wars of 1912, 1913 and 1915. In alliance with Serbia, Montenegro and Greece, Ferdinand defeated the Turks in 1912, and Turkish rule in Europe was confined to eastern Thrace. Bulgaria extended her territory to the Aegean Sea—an outlet which she has ever since been anxious to recover. However, the main prize of the First Balkan War was intended to be Macedonia, and this had been occupied by Serbian forces. Afraid of being defrauded of his share, Ferdinand tried to push out the Serbian and Greek forces, and thus involved himself in the Second Balkan War. In this Bulgaria found herself isolated before a coalition of her three former allies plus Turkey and Rumania. The Peace of Bucharest deprived her of parts of her recent acquisitions, and of a strip of the Southern Dobruja, ceded to Rumania.

Ferdinand resolved to recoup his losses by bringing Bulgaria into the Great War on what he imagined would be the winning side. His people were at that time unwilling to fight against brother Slavs, but Ferdinand was a master of trickery, and succeeded in committing his country. Efforts by the Allies to buy over Bulgaria beforehand broke down upon the refusal of the Serbs to give up Macedonia. Bulgaria thus joined the Central Powers and shared in their defeat. Ferdinand, entirely discredited, abdicated. He is still living in exile.

Stambuliski.—In October 1919 there took office in Sofia a Cabinet led by Alexander Stambuliski, the leader of the Agrarian Party. He remained Premier until his overthrow and death in June 1923. During these four years Bulgaria was ruled in the interests of the peasants, who form four-fifths of the population.

Stambuliski was a peasant who obtained a High School education and studied abroad. He was an arrogant, boastful man, but possessed immense energy and driving-force and was a powerful speaker. He made his name in the Agrarian League, which became a political party a little while before the Balkan Wars.

There are two classes in Bulgaria: the peasants and the townspeople. The peasants scratch a hard living from the soil, and live in primitive conditions. Those who manage to emerge from this life form a town-dwelling class which attempts to achieve elegance and ease through the professions, the civil service and politics. The object of the Agrarian League was to bring education and the amenities of life to that vast section of the people which must always remain attached to the soil. Its driving-force was in the school-teachers, one of whom, Madame Stambuliski, maintained her husband from her earnings in order that he might be free to work for the Agrarian League by speeches and organising. By 1915 Stambuliski was leading the Agrarians in the Sobranje and was one of those who warned Ferdinand against the fratricidal crime of attacking their brother Slavs, the Serbs and Russians. Stambuliski spent much of the war years in prison, and was released and taken into the government when disaster came upon the Central Powers. Just before the end, Stambuliski attempted a Republican coup, but upon its failure he resumed his place in the Cabinet and gave his blessing to the new King, Boris, upon the departure of Ferdinand. In the election of August 1919 the Agrarians emerged the strongest Party, and a mainly Agrarian government was formed.

At first Stambuliski had a very small majority, and his party openly adopted the time-honoured practice of Bulgarian governments, beating and imprisoning opponents, and faking elections. However, there was much that an Agrarian government could do for the peasants, and Stambuliski thought that peasant rule had come to stay. He anticipated forty years of power; and in the elections of 1923 he obtained an overwhelming majority.

Stambuliski is painted by reactionaries as extremely Red, partly because he had a working alliance with the Bulgarian communists. In fact, however, he was not even a determined republican, for he made no attempt to overthrow the monarchy at a time when Ferdinand was discredited and Boris had not had an opportunity to gain the affections of his people. There was, it is true, an 'Agrarian Reform', or breaking up of the larger estates; but this was a small affair in comparison with the similar operations in other countries, for there was no class of wealthy landed proprietors. Three causes combined to procure the downfall of the 'Peasant Dictator'. He had to bear the burden of the oppressive peace terms imposed by the Allies; he earned the hatred of the class of bourgeois politicians who had hitherto enjoyed a monopoly of power; and he stood for friendship with the Serbs and the aim of a union of all the South Slav peoples. This tendency appeared as treason to the narrow Bulgarian faction, especially strong in the little piece of Macedonia that Bulgaria had obtained, and among the exiles from Yugoslav Macedonia, which hated the Serbs with a bitterness ever augmented by bloody deeds on either side. Stambuliski was eventually destroyed by an unholy alliance of the bourgeois reactionaries, the military, and the Macedonian terrorists.

The Agrarians had come to power through the discrediting of the war policy, to which they had been opposed, and the sheer voting power of the peasants. The elections of 1920 had given them 110 seats in a parliament of 228; but their majority was assured by the practical support of 49 communist Deputies. Personal grievances played their part in the eventual downfall of the Party, for the bourgeois politicians had been ousted from their preserves. By 1923 Agrarian rule was bearing somewhat heavily upon the bourgeoisie; the burden of Reparations was felt, and the loss of the outlet to the Aegean. The chauvinists were alarmed at the policy of friendship with Yugoslavia. Moreover, in their later period, the Agrarians ran their politics by the same repressive measures that had been practised by the bourgeois politicians. In the end, they were defeated by the magnitude of their own victory, for the elections of April 1923 gave them no less than 212 seats, and it was plain that they could never be overthrown by constitutional means. Despairing of ever getting rid of the Agrarian Dictator by ordinary political measures, his enemies organised a *coup d'état*, the brain behind which was that of Colonel Damian Velćev. Stambuliski, on holiday at his country villa, was seized by troops of the regular army. From their charge he was carried off by the Macedonians, who first made him dig his own grave, then shot him and put him into it.

The reactionaries.—Stambuliski was succeeded as Premier by Professor Tzankov, who remained in office from June 1923 until January 1926. Substantially the same team held power under Liapćev until April 1931. Both governments were reactionary, that of Tzankov being especially brutal in its suppression of agrarianism and communism. Technically, only communism was forbidden; but the term could be applied loosely to the agrarians, and also to the socialists. Some thousands of persons were imprisoned or shot, and of the former many were never seen again. Army, Macedonians, intellectuals, bourgeois, all supported the government which had replaced the hated peasant leader. The bourgeois reaction began ferociously, and when, in 1925, some desperate men plotted first the assassination of the King, and then the blowing up of the Cathedral at Sofia, during a funeral service which was to be attended by the whole government, the authorities had another opportunity to intensify the terror, for they alleged that the peasants were responsible for the crime. The leader of the anti-Left persecution was the War Minister, General Volkov.

Genuine communism, sometimes masquerading as agrarianism, did in fact exist, and was fostered by Russia during the 'World Revolution' period of Soviet history. Four Russian fishing boats were once found deserted at Varna, their crews having landed without passports to make propaganda among the peasants.

Tzankov in due course gave place to the milder Liapćev, an upright man, much liked and respected, who allowed the agrarians to re-form their party, and enabled some of the artisans to form trade unions. But he kept many of the Left Wing leaders in prison, as he said, to ensure their safety against fascist gangs! By introducing Proportional Representation, Liapćev added to the confusion of political parties that was one of the chief misfortunes of parliamentary government in Bulgaria.

The fall of Democracy.—In May 1930 there was a constitutional crisis, arising from a quarrel between Tzankov and Volkov. The latter was thought to be plotting a military coup. The Cabinet was reconstructed without Tzankov, and Volkov was sent as Minister to Rome.

In the following spring Liapćev held elections. He was

confident of success, saying: 'We are not giving the power
to fools!' However, the elections went against him. Malinov,
a pre-war Premier, who has since died, formed a Cabinet
which included the agrarians. On taking office, Malinov
announced: 'I do not find a single leva in the Treasury!'
Malinov soon afterwards became ill, and the leadership of
his government was taken over by Mušanov. With various
reconstructions, this government lasted until May 1934,
when parliamentary government was abolished by a military
coup.

The democratic régime of Mušanov, known as the 'National
Bloc', allowed the worst vices of the Bulgarian parliamentary
system to flourish. Parties spent their energies in lobbying for
position, and crises were precipitated not on matters of policy
but upon considerations of bargaining for portfolios among
the groups composing the government *bloc*. There was little
legislation. Mušanov himself, an ordinary politician without
special ability, had much ado to keep his 'National Bloc'
together, for his largest party, the agrarians, was perpetually
at issue with the smaller bourgeois groups in the government,
most of whom had split off from the parties in the Opposition group of Liapćev. In the spring of 1934, the clamour of
the agrarians for a fourth portfolio brought down the government, and while negotiations were afoot for a new Cabinet,
the military effected a coup. Mušanov perceived one morning
a large number of troops in the square outside his house.
Ringing up the War Office to enquire the reason, he was
told that private citizens were not allowed to telephone, as
the city was under martial law.

'But I am the Prime Minister', replied Mušanov.

'Oh no you are not!' replied the War Office, and
rang off.

The fall of Mušanov marks the end of the system of government by parliamentary coalitions and ordinary democratic parliamentary procedure. It is interesting, therefore, to analyse the parties and the political factions as they existed at the moment of their dissolution; for the military government which emerged from the coup of 19 May was not slow to declare the total abolition of all the political parties; nor has their revival since been permitted.

It was said of Bulgaria, as of other countries where parliamentary systems have been abolished, that there were too many political parties. But it is only fair to remember that the parliament of the United Kingdom contains eight separate parliamentary parties, without counting independents, dissident conservatives, or those parties which exist outside the Palace of Westminster. This fact should be borne in mind when criticism is levelled at the multiplicity of parties existing in certain Continental political systems. In Bulgaria, at the time of the *coup d'état* of May 1934, there were some half-dozen parties, three of which had broken up into sections, under various would-be leaders.

The Agrarians.—There are three tendencies in Bulgarian political life: *chauvinist, liberal-bourgeois, and peasant.* Eighty per cent of the population is composed of peasants, whose primitive conditions of life form a sharp contrast with the position of the town-dwellers; thus, the most obvious line of cleavage is between the men of the soil and those who, in this generation or in the past few generations, have managed to leave behind the discomforts of peasant life and to acquire some of the attributes of 'civilisation'. The *Agrarian Party*, when not subjected to suppression, and when given a fair field in the elections, usually obtained the largest representation in Bulgarian parliaments. Like other Labour Parties, the agrarians inevitably included men who desired to use the movement as a spring-board for their personal advantage. They hoped by its means to leap out of the peasant class and find themselves a position in the political bourgeoisie. There were others, however, who, in the spirit of the party's aims, sought to extend to the peasants the advantages of education and civilised amenities, a softening of the rigours of country life, and security for their economic position.

Socialists.—There were other Left Wing parties besides the agrarians. The small industrial proletariat was represented by the Social Democratic Party, and in 1927 there appeared five representatives of an Artisans Party. But the main allies of the agrarians were the communists. After the fall of the agrarian government in June 1923, the communists were suppressed, but reappeared in the guise of a Labour Party. On several later occasions this group was again suppressed in order to enhance the relative size of the government *bloc* at the moment.

Agrarian factions.—The agrarians themselves, after their eclipse in 1923, were rehabilitated by Liapćev, and took part in the Coalition of Mušanov; but meanwhile they had suffered the process of fission, so common in the political parties, and were represented inside the movement by three sections. Of these, the faction that participated in the government was led by those who had filled the places of leaders driven into exile. Mušanov amnestied the exiles, who returned to Bulgaria to find themselves excluded by their successors from the leadership of the party. They therefore formed a section known as the Pladne Agrarians.

The bourgeois parties.—The Left Wing of the bourgeois parties was formed by the radicals. The two main groups were the liberals and the democrats. The former were on the whole the more conservative party; but there is not very much in the distinction. Both liberals and democrats were split up into several factions, and the Right Wing of the democrats, under Professor Tzankov, moved off so far to the Right that it became the most conservative group of them all, and eventually developed into a separate chauvinist and fascist party, modelled upon the Nazi Party in Germany. Professor Tzankov from time to time goes to the Reich to learn the technique of Nazism. His party is now called the 'National and Social Movement'.

The sequence of groups.—An attempt to arrange the political parties of Bulgaria, as they were at the time of their legal dissolution, after the coup of May 1934, in a progression from Right Wing to Left Wing, would work out something like this:

1. The Macedonians. These were distinguished by their chauvinism and bitter anti-Yugoslav policy, and their willingness to use the extremes of violence and secret terror for the prosecution of their aims. After the smoking out of the Terrorist centre in Macedonia in 1934, they emerged as a charitable society; but ever since 1927 they had held seats in parliament as a political party.
2. Tzankov's National and Social Movement, formerly part of the Democrat Party.
3. The Smilov group of Liberals.
4. The main body of the Liberal Party, under Kachakov and Bojadev.
5. A similar group of Liberals, forming the personal following of Petrov.
6. Liapćev's section of the Democrats.
7. Burov and Mollov's section of the Democrats. These two sections (6 and 7) represented big business. It must not be forgotten that Liapćev himself was a Macedonian.

It is at this point that the cleavage may be said to come between conservatives and liberals, according to English standards.

8. The Malinov–Mušanov section of the Democrats, who were the nucleus of the governments of 1931–34. Malinov died in 1938; he was a pre-war Prime Minister.
9. The Radicals.
10. The Agrarian Party, representing the interests of the peasants.
11. The Pladne Agrarians, whose return to Bulgaria put the government Agrarians on their mettle, in the period immediately before the military coup.
12. The Social Democrats and the Artisans.
13. The Communists or Labour Party.

POLITICS SINCE THE MILITARY COUP

The coup of 19 May 1934 was engineered by two over-lapping movements, the Officers' League and the Zveno Club. Two other bodies, the League of Reserve Officers and the organisation of Professor Tzankov, were forestalled by the actual coup from undertaking revolutions of their own.

The Zveno Club, with which Colonel Velćev was in close touch, was a 'clean politics' movement of intellectuals. The Officers' League, of which he was Secretary, was composed of serving and retired army officers. Both bodies were disgusted at the jobbery and ineffectiveness of parliamentary government as practised at that time, and both desired to substitute something more authoritarian. They had supported Tzankov, and later Liapćev, and for a time had hoped for reforms through the governments of Malinov and Mušanov; but by 1934 they had given up all the political parties and leaders as hopeless. Apart from the cleaning up of politics, the two bodies were in sympathy with fairly Left Wing measures, such as were included in the programme of the democrats and the Right agrarians.

Professor Tzankov was leading a political movement that was too openly fascist for the Zveno and the Officers' League, and a meeting of his was projected for 20 May. Another military body, the League of Reserve Officers, while also anxious to clean up political life, was of conservative tendencies. On 18 May this League placed its demands before the King, who promised to consider them. Thus, the Officers' League was forced to act quickly. Velćev, who had organised the overthrow of Stambuliski, was ready with a new conspiracy. On 19 May, in the small hours of the morning, the conspirators (having occupied the city with dependable troops) waited upon the King, and Colonel Gheorghiev was appointed Premier.

The government of the Officers' League and the Zveno Club undertook the promised overhaul of the political system in a series of decrees reducing the salaries and privileges of Ministers and abolishing the 'spoils' system. The existing parliament was dissolved, and the political parties were suppressed. The administrative system was overhauled, and the number of provinces was reduced from sixteen to seven. Various economic measures were projected.

The two most important aims of the new government were the improvement of relations with Yugoslavia, and the 're-establishment of the authority of the state throughout Bulgarian territory'. Both of these objects required the liquidation of the Macedonian Terrorist organisation, which maintained a state within a state in the Macedonian province, and which added to the confusion of internal politics by continual assassination of politicians. The feud within the Organisation, between the Mihailovists and the Protoguerovists, had resulted in a campaign of mutual extermination and the weakening of the Macedonians; Mušanov had under-taken a round-up of the Macedonian establishments in Sofia itself. Gheorghiev's government marched troops into Bulgarian Macedonia, and smoked out the hornets from their nest. The back of the terrorist movement was thus broken. The Zveno Club wished to demonstrate its good faith, and dissolved itself shortly after the coup. Tzankov's organisation was forcibly dissolved some months later. The Officers' League, however, continued in being. Meanwhile, Velćev was planning a great reduction of the authority of the King, and the constitutional issue came to a head at the beginning of 1935. Velćev broke his teeth upon the royalism of the army officers, who began to distrust his personal ambition. The royalist members of the Officers' League staged a counter-blow, and the Gheorghiev government gave place to a Cabinet under General Zlatev.

Zlatev's government of royalist generals lasted from January until April, when Tzankov's faction again became dangerous. Tzankov and some of his supporters were arrested, whereupon two of his representatives who were in the Cabinet resigned. To avoid further strife, Zlatev resigned, and was succeeded by the Cabinet of Tošev, a Professor of Botany, who had been Bulgarian Minister to Serbia, Turkey and Austria at various stages of the war. The Tošev government set to work upon the draft of a new constitution, which was to restore parliamentarism without the political parties.

Colonel Velćev left Bulgaria soon after the appointment of Tošev, but in November he returned, apparently in the hope of leading a new coup. He was caught, tried for treason, and condemned to death. The sentence was eventually commuted to life imprisonment, largely owing to a movement in western Europe in favour of clemency. Opinion, however, was becoming enraged with the subversive activities of the soldiers, and Tošev gave place to the non-military Cabinet of Kiosseivanov, who has succeeded in maintaining himself in office, at the head of successive Cabinets, down to the present time.

King Boris III.—It is difficult to write of reigning sovereigns in a dogmatic manner, since about most of them, in countries where considerable power rests still in the hands of the monarch, there is acute controversy as to whether they cherish autocratic aims, possibly concealed under a cloak of democratic professions, or whether they are genuinely seeking to maintain as much liberty in their states as is consistent with tolerable efficiency, in circumstances where order and efficiency are sometimes hard to obtain.

The former King Ferdinand pursued a foreign policy of a dynastic nature, imposed his will upon his people by trickery, and gambled unsuccessfully with his country's fortunes. Upon the collapse of Bulgaria as a belligerent it is remarkable that there remained a throne for his son to mount. King Boris, however, by avoiding the courses of his father, and by showing a simple yet courageous disposition, has made himself more popular than King Ferdinand ever was. Sofia boasts no showy Court, no synthetic 'High Society', no extravagant Court functions. The King converses with the peasants about their crops, and gives the impression of a serious-minded and well-disposed man. Nevertheless, in the period succeeding the military coup, the path which he pursued was by no means that of a Victor Emmanuel, allowing a dictator to usurp his functions. When Colonel Gheorghiev allowed the newspapers to appear on New Year's Day with his photograph and that of Velćev, but without that of the King, it was not long before his government came to an end. Controversy rages, and will continue to rage, as to the relative merits of the King's and of Velćev's constitutional ideas, and as to the degree of personal motive actuating either of them; if the proof of the pudding be in the eating, Bulgaria has taken considerable steps back towards genuine democracy, as the replacement of generals by civilians in the Cabinets of Tošev and Kiosseivanov shows, and as has been markedly illustrated by Kiosseivanov's restoration—though in a modified form—of a parliament in which there is a distinguishable opposition.

Restoration of Parliament.—Kiosseivanov took up the task of providing for the representation of the people without restoring the evils of the former system of political parties. He maintained the prohibition of parties, but prepared a law for the election of municipalities, and afterwards a law for the election of a new Sobranje. For the former parties, with their long lists of candidates submitted to the electors, Kiosseivanov substituted single-member constituencies, and drew up careful lists of qualifications for voters and candidates, including a declaration by every candidate that he did not belong to a political party. Votes were given to women over the age of 21 who had borne children in lawful wedlock.

In March 1937 there were held elections for the local government bodies, which had been reorganised so as to contain a majority of elected members. Since there were no political parties, it was difficult to claim any specially favourable result; but the government was able to point to the failure of the parties to organise a boycott of the elections.

In the autumn the government proceeded to the elaboration of a law for the election of a Sobranje, based, like the law for municipal elections, upon the idea of securing upright and independent men as representatives of the nation. There were to be 160 Deputies, each representing a constituency of not less than 20,000 or more than 40,000 inhabitants. Election meetings, posters and manifestos were permitted, but no agents of party organisations. The voters' registers were prepared, and the elections took place in March 1938.

The Sobranje was opened by the King on 22 May, four years and three days after the termination of the life of its predecessor.

The new parliament was intended to act rather than to talk. In a two-day debate, all the decree-laws of the past four years were submitted to the Sobranje for ratification, and, to the number of 1,761, were duly ratified.

The government claimed 104 pledged supporters in the Sobranje of 160; and after the Committee of Credentials had procured the invalidation of three mandates, on the ground that these members had stood for a party—the Communist—the Opposition walked out, and stayed away for several days. The government supporters thereupon proceeded to debate a reply to the speech from the Throne, and enjoyed themselves with jibes at the abstentionist tactics of their opponents. The Sobranje was duly prorogued for the summer recess, and on its return it defeated the Cabinet and brought about its reconstruction, still under Dr. Kiosseivanov.

2. ECONOMIC STRUCTURE AND POLICY

BULGARIA'S ECONOMIC STRUCTURE

Bulgaria is an agricultural country; no less than four-fifths of the population is composed of peasants. The agricultural products are of four kinds: tobacco, cereals, fruit and vegetables, poultry and eggs. Bulgaria has always been a country of smallholders, and when, at the end of the war, an agrarian reform was carried out, there was little land held in the form of great estates which could be cut up and distributed among landless peasants; the agrarian reform was therefore predominantly a distribution of former Crown lands among the new nationals who arrived either as refugees or in the course of the exchange of populations between Bulgaria and Greece.

The following sections will describe the co-operative

system, which plays an important part in the economic life of the people; the foreign loans that have been raised before and after the war; and the distribution of Bulgaria's foreign trade, in which Germany takes an extraordinarily large share.

In the year 1930 Bulgaria's exports amounted to 234·8 millions of Swiss francs, of which tobacco accounted for 41·5 %, grain for 11·9 %, eggs 11·6 %; other important exports were hides and skins, essence of roses, livestock and poultry, and silk cocoons. The crisis caused a great contraction in the export of attar of roses, and of late years cereals have become increasingly important. (Except for 20,000 tons sold to Germany in 1936, cereals have been reserved for export to countries of free currency.)

In the same year, 1930, imports amounted to 249 millions of Swiss francs, of which machinery and motor vehicles accounted for 17·3 %, cotton yarns and manufactures for 15·8 %, iron and steel manufactured goods for 14·8 %; and the total of manufactured goods for 69·2 %.

Before the war tobacco played a less important, cereals a more important rôle; but the loss of the wheat-growing Dobruja and the acquisition of tobacco-growing country in Macedonia and Thrace altered the balance.

Few industries have been established. The most successful is the localised production of attar of roses. The fishing industry had, after the war, to make a fresh beginning in Bulgarian hands, as the Greek fishermen of the Black Sea coast were repatriated to Greece. Roads are few and railways fewer.

The great social cleavage in Bulgaria, since there is no aristocracy, is between the middle class of the towns and the peasants. The latter scratch a difficult and precarious living from the soil, contending with a perennial shortage of water. The villages are desolate and muddy. The aim of the pre-war agrarian movement, which became the Agrarian Party, and enjoyed a spell of power under Stambuliski, was to counteract the preoccupation of the ruling bourgeoisie with the concerns of the towns and to bring the amenities of civilisation to the peasants in their villages. The movement concentrated upon education, and there are now 24,000 trained teachers, over 90 % of the children of school age actually attending school. A recent measure has been the requirement that young, newly-qualified doctors should spend a period in the country on a salary basis, ministering to the needs of the peasants, before setting up in private practice in the towns.

THE CO-OPERATIVE SYSTEM

In agricultural countries there is always need of supplies of credit to farmers, because their income is seasonal, and the variations in the amount of crop from year to year and of the prices of agricultural produce lead to frequent resort to borrowing. If lending is left to private banking systems, the security is not attractive; while if the lending is performed by Jewish publican-moneylenders, the interest charged is apt to be exorbitant. Two methods have been adopted in eastern Europe and elsewhere for supplying the necessary credit to farmers, namely, mortgage credit banks set up by the state, and the development of farmers' co-operative banks. In Bulgaria mortgage credit banks are on a small scale, and exist only to serve the somewhat different needs of the towns; but the co-operative system, established in 1882, is well developed. Unfortunately as yet it supplies only short-term credit.

In 1907 the state began to encourage the co-operatives, and during the Stambuliski régime of 1919–23 the agrarian government greatly expanded the system. At the end of 1930 the co-operatives, which did not share the disfavour accorded by subsequent governments to Stambuliski's other projects, had about 350,000 individual members and 1,350 corporative members. Out of 1,870 co-operative associations, 1,599 were in rural districts.

The economic crisis, during which large amounts of agricultural produce either could not be marketed at all or were marketed at catastrophically low prices, led to a great increase in the demand of the farming population for credit, together with an inability to pay the service of the debts already contracted. The state was obliged to intervene to relieve the debtors of part of their obligation, and this measure naturally prejudiced the position of the co-operative associations and of the Central Co-operative Bank from which they obtained their finance. In October 1934 Colonel Gheorghiev's government effected an amalgamation of the Central Co-operative Bank with the State Agricultural Bank, the combined body being known as the Agricultural and Co-operative Bank.

By this time the co-operative movement had more than doubled its strength of four years previously, and it continues to increase. At the end of 1936 there were 5,300 co-operative associations with 914,230 individual members. Enormous assistance had been rendered to the farmers, who were enabled to purchase seed and implements, and to arrange among themselves for the sharing of those agricultural machines which can be used by several farms, and are of too great a capital value to be purchased by a single small proprietor.

The Agricultural and Co-operative Bank is indeed the lynch-pin of the government's direction of agriculture—the livelihood of four-fifths of the population. Its importance, and the need for it to co-operate closely with the government, was recognised by the Minister of Agriculture, Mr. Bagrianov, in a speech which he made to the staff of the

188

Bank in December 1938. The legislation of Gheorghiev's government (enacted by decree, but ratified by the Sobranje when at length it met in the early summer of 1938) endowed the Bank with large powers of control over the co-operative movement, including the power to give or to withhold permission for the formation of new co-operative associations. It is much to be hoped that this control will not result in such a regimentation of the co-operatives that they cease to be attractive to the farmers.

The importance of the co-operatives in Bulgarian life is illustrated by the fact that Dr. Kiosseivanov's government, when preparing in the winter of 1936–37 for the election of the local authorities, invited the co-operatives to instigate candidatures, and in consequence many co-operators obtained seats upon the municipalities and district councils.

NUMBERS AND CLASSIFICATION OF CO-OPERATIVES, 1936

Scope of the various co-operatives	Societies	Members
Production	572	145,723
Commerce	268	98,559
Public works, hygiene and art.. ..	30	16,365
Total of these three categories ..	870	260,647
(Of the above, consumers' co-operatives)	154	84,640
For the purpose of CREDIT	2,125	419,416
(Of these, agricultural co-operatives)..	1,744	166,888
For the purpose of INSURANCE ..	2,253	224,734
(Of these, for insurance of cattle) ..	2,243	95,554
Unions and Centrals	52	9,433
Total	5,300	914,230

It will be observed that, by number of societies, two-fifths of the total exist to supply credit, one-third of the total being for agricultural credit. By number of persons, nearly one-half of all the co-operators are concerned with credit, not quite two-fifths of these (a little under a fifth of the total) with agricultural credit. Rather more than a tenth of the co-operators co-operate to insure their cattle in a very large number (over two-fifths) of the co-operative societies; but eight big co-operatives for general insurance have substantially more members than have the 2,243 small cattle-insurance societies.

FOREIGN DEBT

At the end of November 1938 Bulgaria bore a burden of floating debt of 2,781·6 million levas and consolidated debt 19,235·8 million levas. The consolidated debt was made up of a little over 13 milliard levas of foreign indebtedness, a little over 6 milliard levas of internal loans; besides about 3½ milliard levas owed to the National Bank.

The outstanding foreign indebtedness consisted of a series of pre-war loans and two big post-war loans of 1926 and 1928. The pre-war loans carried interest at rates from 4½ % to 6 % and the amount outstanding was 9·2 milliard levas. The loans of 1926 and 1928 were issued under the auspices of the League of Nations, the former for the settlement of refugees, the latter for stabilisation of currency, etc. The 1926 loan at 7 % and the 1928 loan at 7½ % had respectively 1,158·8 million levas and 2,489·9 million levas outstanding, and there were miscellaneous foreign debts for a further 287·8 million.

Like most of the debtor nations, Bulgaria had been obliged to make agreements with her creditors for the transfer of sums less than the agreed service of these various loans. By an agreement which expired at the end of 1938, she had been paying 32·5 % of the sums due. In November 1938 a financial mission proceeded to London and negotiated a new agreement by which $38\frac{1}{4}$ % of the sums due in 1939 would be transferred—$36 \cdot 5$ % of the first half-year coupon and 40 % of the second. The bondholders represented in London included the United Kingdom, United States, France, Holland, Switzerland and Belgium. Other creditors included Yugoslavia, Rumania, Hungary and Greece.

FOREIGN TRADE AND PREDOMINANT POSITION OF GERMANY

For a year or two after the war Italy and the United States supplied the bulk of Bulgaria's imports, while her exports went mainly to Italy, the United States and Czechoslovakia. Germany then entered the field, and constantly supplied about 22 % of Bulgaria's imports in the years from 1922 to 1929, after which the proportion rose considerably. Germany's share of Bulgaria's exports reached approximately 30 % in 1929, and has risen further in the last few years. The British share of imports was $4 \cdot 6$ % and of exports $4 \cdot 3$ % in 1935.

From 1933 to 1935 Germany increased her share of Bulgarian trade in both directions, reaching $53 \cdot 5$ % of imports and 48 % of exports in the latter year. Then came the great drive of Dr. Schacht for trade with the Balkans, and in 1936 Germany supplied no less than 61 % of Bulgaria's imports.

Dr. Schacht's now famous tours in the Balkans in 1936 found these countries embarrassed by the increased difficulty of marketing cereals, and cut off from trade with Italy by half a year of Sanctions. The advent of a large-scale buyer of foodstuffs and other primary products was a godsend to agricultural countries at their wits' end for markets, and immense quantities were sold to Germany on credit. A crisis occurred, however, when the time came for these deliveries to be paid for. German currency could not be exported, and it was a difficult matter to find goods which the Balkan states could purchase in order to realise the sums standing to their credit at the Reichsbank. In June 1936 the trade debts of Germany to Bulgaria amounted to some 10 million Reichsmarks.

Germany's aim was to secure free currency to enable her to purchase materials for rearmament. In order to obtain goods from the Balkans on credit, she paid prices about 30 % higher than the prevailing world price; she then obtained the required free currency by re-selling her Balkan purchases at or below the world price. The deal was an expensive one, but Germany was able to buy what she required. To her Balkan creditors, however, she declared that she had no foreign exchange with which to pay for her purchases, and asked them to accept German manufactured goods, especially armaments. Trusting in Germany's credit, the governments had themselves facilitated the German purchases by advancing the purchase price to the growers, and the commercial debts of Germany to the Balkans were thus debts to the Balkan governments. In order to get paid, the creditor nations were obliged to take from Germany manufactured goods which in previous years they had obtained elsewhere. Thus, Germany secured a hold on the Balkan markets which gave her a very strong position in their economy. Part of the cunning of the manœuvre lies in the fact that countries which eventually bought the Balkan primary products at second hand from Germany did not thereby gain the share of Balkan markets to which their purchase of Balkan exports would normally entitle them.

In several of the Balkan states the German raid upon their trade provoked resentment; but Bulgaria found it good business. In the spring of 1936 Germany was absorbing 63 % of Bulgaria's exports, including more than half of the tobacco crop. Germany encouraged Bulgaria to increase their mutual trade by growing special crops for the German market, such

as oil seeds and soya beans. Nevertheless, a Bulgarian economist pointed out that the tying up of Bulgarian trade
with a single foreign state is without precedent anywhere
in the world, except for the trade of Mexico with the United
States. Denmark and Finland send very large proportions
of their exports to England, but are not similarly confined
to a single source for their imports. Bulgaria sees her trade
in both directions dominated by Germany.

The autumn of 1938 saw a further attempt by Germany,
this time under the management of Dr. Funk, to establish
a monopoly of Bulgarian trade. Germany now offered to
buy, at prices agreed at the outset, the whole of Bulgaria's
surplus of a number of commodities for a period of twelve
years. The goods to be sent to Bulgaria in payment were
also specified, with the prices, and provision was made in
the proposal for the services of a number of German experts
to direct Bulgarians in the use of the weapons and machinery
and in the construction that was envisaged. The offer was
turned down. Had she accepted it, she would have become
so tied to German economy as to be unable, by selling goods
to countries with free currencies, to purchase any goods not
forthcoming from Germany. Moreover, by the severing of
all her trade connections, she would have placed herself
entirely at the mercy of Germany whenever the latter
desired to obtain further advantages, whether economic or
political.

The close of the year saw the visit to Sofia of a French
commercial mission, headed by M. Alphand.

The effect of Germany's predominance in Bulgaria's trade
is temporarily to create relatively boom conditions in the
structure of local prices, and to ease her financial position.
The less fortunate consequences have not yet developed,
but are not difficult to foretell.

Recent tendencies are illustrated in a comparison between

the monthly trade returns for the period January to October in the years 1937 and 1938. Germany's share of imports decreased from 59·3 % to 50 %, while her share of Bulgarian exports increased from 47·6 % to 55·1 %. Compare this with Britain's share. Though her proportion of imports rose from 4·7 % to 7·6 % in this period, the corresponding figure for exports fell from 13·8 % to 6·4 %.

GERMANY'S SHARE IN BULGARIAN TRADE
(Percentages of whole)

Years	Imports	Exports
1922	21·8	16·5
From 1926	Fluctuates between	Fluctuates between
to 1931	21·0 and 27·9	19·5 and 29·5
1932	25·9	26·0
1933	38·2	36·0
1934	40·1	42·7
1935	53·5	48·0
1936	61·0	47·6
1937	58	47
1938	52	59

Note the sharp rise which begins with the figures for 1933.

These figures give the percentage of German trade to the whole of Bulgaria's export and import trades respectively, calculated by value in levas.

3. FOREIGN POLICY

BULGARIA AS AN IRREDENTIST STATE

When the Balkan peoples recovered their freedom from Turkish rule, each nation hoped to obtain as great an estate as it had enjoyed during those periods of medieval history in which it was the most important kingdom in the Balkan Peninsula. Certain parts of the Peninsula were obviously Bulgarian, or Serbian, or Greek; other regions had belonged, centuries ago, now to the one empire and now to the other, and those districts became the prizes for which the Balkan states strove among themselves, and fought and worked and plotted. From the time of the Treaty of San Stefano onwards, Bulgar, Serb, Greek and Rumanian cast their eyes upon territories which they thought they ought to acquire, but which were also coveted by one or other of their neighbours. The frontiers between the various states were from time to time changed as the result of wars, and it is not impossible that further changes will still be made; the countries which might hope to gain territory in any such alteration of frontiers are Albania and Bulgaria.

Of the territories which might have formed part of the Bulgarian kindgom but do not, the first to be lost was the Northern Dobruja, given to Rumania as compensation for the cession of Bessarabia to Russia in 1878. At the same time, the Congress of Berlin deprived the Bulgarian Principality, then being created, of practically the whole of Macedonia, which Russia had intended to give to her protégée.

The expansion of Bulgaria to her present frontiers, and something beyond, dates from the First Balkan War of 1912-13. The principal prize of this war was to have been Macedonia, but we have already described in earlier sections the manner in which the greater part of the province eluded the grasp of King Ferdinand. The small portion of Macedonia allowed to Bulgaria after the Second Balkan War was further reduced at the end of the Great War, and other strips of territory, small in extent, near the Dragoman Pass and in the Timok district, were transferred to Yugoslavia.

The first 'irredenta' is Macedonia; the second is the South Dobruja. In the First Balkan War, Rumania was neutral, for she had nothing to recover from Turkey; but in the second she intervened against Bulgaria, and took as her spoil the 'Quadrilateral' of the South Dobruja. During the Great War, Bulgarian troops won back the Quadrilateral, which was given to Bulgaria by the Treaty of Bucharest, forced upon the defeated Rumania by the Central Powers. When Bulgaria was defeated, the Allies did not at first intend immediately to restore the Quadrilateral to Rumania; but Rumanian troops occupied it, and by the Treaty of Neuilly, Bulgaria was compelled to restore it to Rumania. The Southern Dobruja is one of the regions which Bulgaria would like to recover, partly because it has a large Bulgarian population, partly because its corn-lands form the commercial hinterland of the port of Varna. This port was ruined by the loss of the Quadrilateral, and had to make shift to turn itself into a holiday resort.

In the south, Bulgaria obtained by the Balkan wars a territorial corridor to the Aegean. Western Thrace, from Xanthi to the River Maritza, gave her a coastline containing two potential ports, Kara Agatch (or Porto Lagos) and Dede Agatch. Of this gain, too, she was despoiled by the Treaty of Neuilly, by which she was obliged to cede it to the Allies, who undertook to make a settlement which would assure Bulgaria her maritime outlet. The words of the Treaty do not specify that the outlet is to take the form of a territorial corridor, but that was the interpretation placed upon them by the Bulgarians. By the eventual settlement, western Thrace was given to Greece, which now has a common frontier with Turkey along the Maritza. The prospects of a territorial rectification were diminished by the subsequent transfer of population; the Bulgarians of Greek territory being sent back to Bulgaria, partly by forcible expulsion, partly by an agreed exchange of minorities. The place of the Bulgars was filled by Greeks migrating from Smyrna and other regions now secured to Turkey.

The Allied Powers made a move at the Conference of

Lausanne to fulfil their pledge of an outlet to the Aegean
for Bulgaria, but their proposals took the form of transit
rights and a free zone in an Aegean port, and this did not
satisfy Bulgaria. The refusal to accept the Allied offer
resulted in no settlement being arrived at, and Bulgaria was
left without her outlet. On several subsequent occasions
negotiations have taken place between Greece and Bulgaria,
but always without result. The Greek proposals have
generally taken the form of a request to Bulgaria to choose
an Aegean port in which she would have a free zone; to
link up her railway system with the port; and to join with
Greece in placing the proper working of the zone and the
railway under the supervision of a League of Nations Commission. From time to time there are rumours of an accommodation being reached; but up to the present nothing has
come of them. It is exasperating for the Bulgarians to be
obliged to send their goods round from Burgas by the Black
Sea and the Straits to a sea which washes the coast only
about twenty miles from their frontier; or else by way of
Constantinople, or up through Central Europe.

The anniversary of the Treaty of Neuilly is usually made
the occasion for revisionist demonstrations, particularly by
chauvinists such as the supporters of Tzankov.

BULGARIA AND HER BALKAN NEIGHBOURS

Yugoslavia.—Bulgaria and Serbia were rivals in the Middle
Ages. What is now Yugoslav Macedonia formed in turn part
of the dominions of Bulgaria under Czar Simeon and under
John Asen, and of the Serbs before the arrival of the Bulgars,
and again under Stephen Dušan and Marko Kraljević. In
1885, when Prince Alexander of Bulgaria accepted the
allegiance of Eastern Rumelia, Austria-Hungary egged on
Prince Milan of Serbia to attack his neighbour. Russia
refused to support her former protégée and withdrew her

officers from the Bulgarian army. The Bulgarians, left with no officer above the rank of captain, nevertheless gave the Serbs a sound beating at Slivnitza. In 1912 the two kingdoms were allies; in 1913 and again in the Great War they fought upon opposite sides. Macedonia was the bone of contention.

There have always been men in Bulgaria who wished for close relations between Serbia and Bulgaria; among them was Stambuliski, who owed to this cause the enmity of the Macedonian terrorists. These violent men set their faces sternly against any attempt to acquiesce in the *status quo* in regard to Macedonia, and when Stambuliski was overthrown they secured possession of the fallen Premier and murdered him. For some years thereafter they successfully kept the Yugoslav-Bulgarian frontier in a turmoil, and not until their power diminished was it possible for the two kingdoms to achieve any sort of reconciliation.

In the summer of 1933 Mušanov's government made an attempt to clean up the nest of terrorists in Sofia. The sequel was the visit, in December, of the King and Queen of Bulgaria to King Alexander in Belgrade. During the next summer the military government of Colonel Gheorghiev smoked the terrorists out of their lair in the Pirin, and in September King Alexander paid a visit to Sofia. The two kings got on well together, and the rapprochement between Yugoslavia and Bulgaria was well under way, a Pact of Friendship being in course of preparation. Immediately after this visit, however, King Alexander was assassinated at Marseilles.

Meanwhile, the series of Balkan conferences had resulted in the conclusion of the Balkan Pact between Yugoslavia, Rumania, Greece and Turkey. To this Pact Bulgaria could not adhere without appearing openly to abandon her claims for eventual territorial revision. But in 1936 relations between the two countries had so far improved that at the

end of that year Bulgaria proposed to Yugoslavia the conclusion of a Pact of Friendship. This was signed in January
1937.

The Pact was made in advance of public opinion, and its
signature occasioned rioting in Belgrade. But the more
enlightened men in both countries welcomed the agreement
as the beginning of a new era. The barbed-wire entanglements were in due course removed from the frontier, cultural
relations improved, and the Macedonian question was placed
in cold storage. The good work was carried a stage further
by the conclusion of the Pact of Salonika between Bulgaria
and the Balkan Entente in July 1938.

Albania.—Bulgaria and Albania were the two countries
which stayed outside the Balkan Pact. In both cases the
obvious reason was their territorial claims (in the case of
Albania, against Yugoslavia; with Bulgaria, claims against
Yugoslavia, Rumania and Greece). Albania was further
deterred from signing by the pressure of Italy.

While territorial claims were at the bottom of the difficulty,
the respectable form in which such rivalries could be publicly
discussed was the question of the treatment of minorities.
Sometimes a Balkan country would rather have its minority
ill-treated by a neighbouring state, so as to keep warm a
grievance that might be used as a basis for later territorial
claims; but in public every Balkan politician professes only
to want his co-nationals in neighbouring states to have fair
minority treatment. The Balkan conferences became more
complicated and acrimonious when minority questions were
being discussed; and at one time Bulgaria threatened not to
attend the conference unless minorities were discussed, while
Yugoslavia did not propose to attend if they were on the
agenda. In the event a compromise was arrived at, and
minorities were allowed to be discussed in a minor key. But
by way of setting an example of public-spirited solicitude

for the welfare of the unhappy people living under alien rule, Bulgaria and Albania solemnly signed a Minority Treaty with each other, guaranteeing certain privileges to the Albanian minority in Bulgaria and the Bulgarian minority in Albania. The point of the gesture lay in the fact that for both these countries the foreign minorities in their territories are much smaller than the minorities of their own people ruled by foreigners; thus they are, as it were, on balance creditor nations in this respect. Furthermore, the Bulgarian minority in Albania and the Albanian minority in Bulgaria are practically non-existent!

Since April 1939, however, relations with Albania have become merely an aspect of relations with Italy. The presence of Italian troops on the other flank of Macedonia might well tempt Bulgarians to a renewal of irredentism.

Rumania.—From time to time Bulgarian politicians feel it necessary to protest against Rumania's treatment of the Bulgarian minority in the Dobruja. Rumania has not always been happy in her treatment of minorities, and has generally felt it necessary to plant Rumanian colonists in the districts near her borders. Bulgarians have complained at various times of discrimination against them; unfairly operated agrarian measures, lack of the promised minority schools, forced purchase of their land by the government for the benefit of colonists, and other oppressive treatment. When the Balkan conference was held in Bucharest, Titulescu was induced to promise some redress; but Maniu was the most benevolent ruler from the point of view of the minorities, and even he did not entirely reverse the policy of his predecessors.

The frontier between Bulgaria and Rumania, except where it runs to the sea along the southern edge of the Quadrilateral, is formed by the Danube. Along the whole length of the river frontier there is no bridge. At various times there have been proposals to bridge the river between Ruschuk and Giurgiu, and to link up the railways which approach the river on either side at this point. At long last a train ferry has been instituted.

The swift changes in Europe in the spring of 1939 gave rise to speculation whether, after all, Rumania might not buy the adherence of Bulgaria to the Balkan *bloc*, and dissuade her from adventures with the Axis by concessions with regard to the Dobruja. But Rumania refuses to cede territory, for fear of setting a precedent for Transylvania; and even were she to give in, it appears that Bulgaria will not promise in exchange her adherence to the Balkan Entente.

Greece.—The principal cause of difference between Bulgaria and Greece is the question of the lost 'Aegean Outlet', to which reference has already been made. The two countries were allies in 1912, enemies in 1913 and 1917. Greece was fortunate enough to end up, more by good luck than good management, on the winning side, and this unfortunate 'irredenta' was then created in her interests by the Allied Powers.

Finance has also played a big part in Greco-Bulgarian relations. The movements of population after the war gave rise to arrangements for compensation to the migrants for their property, and under this head Greece became the debtor of Bulgaria. On the other hand, Bulgaria, as a defeated state, was mulcted in Reparations, partly payable to Greece. The debts in either direction were eventually consolidated in the Mollov-Kaphandaris agreement, by which Bulgaria made certain annual payments in respect of the excess of her reparation debt to Greece over Greece's compensation debt to her. During the economic crisis Bulgaria was granted by the Allies a moratorium in respect of her Reparations obligations; and the Greeks naturally interpreted this as a suspension of the Mollov-Kaphandaris payments. The Bulgars claimed, however, that only Reparations payments were suspended, not compensation payments, and that Greece should continue paying her side of the account. This gave rise to a short controversy, ended by a compromise. Greek holdings in Bulgarian loans were among those which were the subject of negotiation in the 1939 London Bondholders' Conference.

Venizelos, during his last long spell of power, wanted to make a settlement with Bulgaria; but he fell before he could carry out his intention. He did, however, make pacts with Yugoslavia and Turkey, and these were afterwards consolidated into the Balkan Entente. One of the fruits of these arrangements was the partial mobilisation of Turkey during the Greek rebellion of March 1935, by way of dissuading Bulgaria from succumbing to the temptation of intervention. The Greeks were again nervous when the Bulgars signed a Pact of Eternal Friendship with Yugoslavia in January 1937, lest the putting into cold storage of Bulgarian claims upon Macedonia might portend a greater concentration upon the pursuit of an Aegean outlet.

It was General Metaxas who, in July 1938, signed on behalf of the Balkan Entente the Pact of Salonika, by which Bulgaria's neighbours released her from the restrictions placed upon her armaments by the Treaty of Neuilly.

Turkey.—During the Second Balkan War, Turkey, which had been decisively defeated in the First Balkan War, made shift to recover some of the territory in eastern Thrace taken from her by Bulgaria. The fortresses of Lule Burgas and Adrianople (Edirne) were recaptured and now form part of the Turkish Republic. During the Great War, when Turkey had already intervened on the side of Germany, but Bulgaria had not yet committed herself, the Germans induced Turkey to grant Bulgaria some frontier rectification as an inducement to her to join the Central Powers.

After the war, the renunciation by the Turkish nationalists of all idea of a great Ottoman Empire removed the occasion for further hostility between Turkey and Bulgaria, and had a tranquillising effect. The sequel was the signature of a Pact of Friendship in 1925. This was the first, and remained for a dozen years the only, pact between Bulgaria and the neighbouring Powers. In the post-war years much of Bulgaria's foreign trade passed through Istanbul.

The Balkan conferences and the Balkan Entente.—The general drawing together of the Balkan states was given a great impetus by the series of Balkan conferences held from 1930 onwards. These conferences were unofficial, and were held at the instance of a body known as the International Peace Bureau. They were taken up, however, by the authorities in the various countries, which took pains to secure the presence of persons whom they considered suitable. Economists, politicians, trade unionists, peasants, private persons, undertook to discuss their differences round a table. The first of the conferences was opened in Athens in October 1930, and an Englishman, long resident in the Balkans, observed that the mere meeting of the conference was nothing short of a miracle.

It would be out of place to discuss here the details of the conference. It was a great beginning that citizens of the rival states should come together in friendliness and take stock of each other. Bulgaria nearly did not participate because it was proposed not to discuss minorities; a compromise was effected by which this subject should be discussed 'in principle only'. A pious resolution was passed, urging all governments 'to fulfil their engagements in accordance with the Minority Treaties'.

Among the subjects discussed, and on which resolutions were passed, were public health, tariffs, agriculture, banking, transit and intellectual co-operation. The discussions, and the conclusions arrived at, were not without their practical consequences. The conferences became an annual event. Three resolutions were passed on the subject of political co-operation. One of these resolutions expressed the hope that the six Foreign Ministers would meet each year to exchange views and discuss means of 'assuring solidarity between their respective countries'. A second proposal contained an outline for a Balkan Pact, based upon the outlawry of war, peaceful settlement of disputes, and mutual assistance against aggression by one of the members against another. Thirdly, a committee was set up to examine further the project for a pact.

The third conference, held at Bucharest, was decisive from the point of view of Bulgarian participation in the proposed pact. A draft had been prepared; but Bulgaria would not consider it until a satisfactory solution was found for the minorities question. Unfortunately no such settlement could be reached, and Bulgaria withdrew from the negotiations. Greece, Yugoslavia, Rumania and Turkey signed the Balkan Pact in May 1934 without Bulgarian participation.

The abstention of Bulgaria altered the nature of the Pact, which took on the appearance of an alliance to oppose the irredentist claims of Bulgaria, analogous to the Little Entente against Hungary. The Pact itself, however, provided for the eventual adhesion of Bulgaria and Albania.

The four partners to the Pact bound themselves in a mutual guarantee for the security of their frontiers; but it was afterwards made clear that this obligation did not extend to participation in a war against one of the Great Powers. Thus, the guarantee was in practice a provision against attack by one of the signatories, or Austria, Hungary, Albania or Bulgaria.

The signatories to the Pact bound themselves to concert measures among themselves in the case of 'eventualities affecting their interests'. From this provision has grown the custom of periodical meetings of the Ministers of the Entente, on the lines of the former Little Entente conferences. The states further undertook to give each other notice of any political action towards a non-signatory Balkan state, and not to assume obligations towards such non-signatory Balkan states without the consent of their partners. Thus, when Yugoslavia entered into a Pact of Friendship with Bulgaria, in January 1937, it was necessary first to secure the approval of the other three kingdoms.

Bulgaria felt aggrieved by the signature of the Pact. Mušanov, who was then Prime Minister, regarded it as a diplomatic defeat, and said that its signature was super-fluous, as all that was valuable in its provisions was already contained in the Covenant of the League of Nations. It must be pointed out that this was in 1934, before the League system had suffered defeat over Ethiopia. Mušanov complained that his government had not been kept informed of the course of the negotiations; an allegation which was stoutly denied by Greece.

Since the signature of the Balkan Pact, Bulgaria has drawn nearer to the grouping there formed. First came her rapprochement with Yugoslavia in January 1937; then, in July 1938, the Pact of Salonika, in which the Balkan Entente acted as one unit, Bulgaria as the other, and a Pact of Friendship was signed, including the release of Bulgaria (consented to by the other signatories of the Treaty of Neuilly) from the restrictions placed upon her armaments.

There have been frequent rumours that Bulgaria would join the Balkan Entente. Sometimes these rumours are accompanied by the suggestion that the pathway might be made smoother for her by concessions on the part of her neighbours.

BULGARIA AND THE GREAT POWERS

USSR.—In spite of the antagonism among the Bulgarian governing circles to communism, there exists in the Bulgarian people a traditional sympathy with the Great Slav brother; though what is revered is not the present USSR, and not the government of the Czars, which deserted Bulgaria, but the Slavdom of which Russia is necessarily the head. There is a sort of sentimental affinity, strengthened by similarity of language, for a speaker in Russian at a Bulgarian Rotary Club was quite well understood by his audience.

Political relations are another matter. In the active stage of Comintern activities, much was done by Moscow in Bulgaria. The episode of the four Russian boats at Varna has already been mentioned. Tzankov and Volkov suppressed communism with great determination, and the anxiety of the Bulgarian authorities on this score has been exemplified quite recently, when certain persons elected to the 1938 Sobranje were declared to have forfeited their seats on the ground that Moscow supported their candidatures.

Great Britain.—The relationship between this country and Bulgaria is largely concerned with finance and commerce. Great Britain took up substantial 'tranches' of the two post-war loans, and it was in London, in December 1938, that the Bulgarian Finance Minister, Božilov (more commonly transcribed as Bojilov), who has the reputation of being pro-German, met the foreign creditors of Bulgaria to negotiate a settlement of the payments for the present year upon the service of these loans. The British share of Bulgaria's imports has of late increased; but Britain does not take a proportionate share of her exports. One difficulty is that Virginian tobacco has supplanted Balkan tobacco in the British popular taste; another that the Ottawa system involves making the main purchases of cereals from outside Europe.

Mr. Robert Hudson declared late in 1938 that if the peculiar trading methods of Germany resulted in a serious diminution of British trade in the Balkans, Great Britain might have to take countervailing measures. Among such measures might well be the use of diplomatic agents in support of British business men. The German Legation and Consular staffs mix freely with the local people and thus facilitate the commercial negotiations of their salesmen. Many of the British officials in the Balkans, and especially in Bulgaria, are reluctant to mix with the 'natives'. They do not, like the Germans and Italians, sit about in the cafés, and many educated and English-speaking Bulgarians have told me that they find it quite impossible to get on to friendly terms with the staff of the British Legation. There are, of course, exceptions, who have learnt the language and become friendly with the people; but for the most part they miss the opportunity to spread British ideas and make this country popular; they regard Sofia as a godforsaken spot, which they will be glad to leave, and meanwhile they discharge their duties, and thereafter play bridge together and read *The Times* and the *Tatler*. On Sundays they explore by motor-car the more accessible parts of the country.

France.—Bulgaria, as a revisionist state, did not belong to the constellation of anti-revisionist Powers revolving in the French orbit. Now, however, that the French system of alliances has to all intents and purposes collapsed, the friendship of France is to be enjoyed by any country that is afraid of Germany; though that friendship does not always take the form of strict alliances.

Commercially, the exchanges between France and Bulgaria cannot, in the nature of the case, be on a grand scale, for the economics of the two countries are parallel rather than complementary. Nevertheless, a group of bankers in Paris, assisted by a credit-guarantee, gave Bulgaria a loan of relatively short duration in the summer of 1938. The total sum, amounting to 375 million francs, is to be repaid in two annuities, beginning in 1940.

Towards the end of the year, M. Alphand led a commercial mission which surveyed in Bulgaria the field for economic relations between the two countries. On 6 December the Bulgarian Prime Minister and the French Minister signed at Sofia a new agreement, dealing with the method of payments, and with an extension of the most-favoured nation privilege to a new range of Bulgarian exports, and to importation into the French colonies.

The total volume of trade effected will probably prove to be relatively small; but such relations have a psychological effect exceeding their economic importance. Both France and Great Britain may be said to be drawing closer their relations with Bulgaria.

Italy.—In so far as Bulgaria may be said to have attached herself to the orbit of any Great Power, that Power is Italy. From that country King Boris obtained a wife; and though the Italians are supposed to have subsidised and armed the Macedonian terrorists in order to preoccupy Yugoslavia with her eastward border, relations between Bulgaria and Italy have been uniformly good. There is a constant flow of junior Bulgarian officials to visit Rome with a view to establishing 'closer cultural relations'.

The policy of Bulgaria may well be compared with that of the other small revisionist state, Hungary. Both were left out in the cold by their neighbours, and by France; both were courted by Italy. Hungary went so far as to form part of the 'Rome Bloc'; Bulgaria maintained a greater degree of independence.

Professor Toynbee, writing in the Chatham House Survey of International Affairs for 1936, said:

> Europe was being spared the infliction of a third danger zone by the action of Bulgaria, who eschewed the policy of clientage and ensued the alternative policy of detachment in spite of all temptations to follow the examples of Hungary and Austria by enrolling herself in the suite of Italy.

Since 1936 the Rome-Berlin Axis has become a larger factor on the European scene, and the increasing power and drive to the south-east of Germany has involved these relatively small Powers, willy-nilly, in the game of power politics. Hungary, as an immediate neighbour of Germany, professes attachment to the Axis, but particularly desires to belong to the southern rather than the northern department of that Axis; in this she is less successful than could be wished. Bulgaria has thus far maintained a greater degree of independence in her policy, and has also kept a tighter hold upon the southern, as opposed to the northern, end of the Axis. Commercially, Italy is now the second most important Bulgarian market, and ranks third among the suppliers of Bulgaria's imports.

The seizure of Albania by Italy in April 1939 was followed by fierce contention between the Axis Powers and the Peace Front Powers for the sympathies of such states as Yugoslavia and Bulgaria. It is difficult to estimate what change may take place in the relations of Bulgaria and Italy in the near future.

German propaganda.—Germany's economic preponderance in Bulgaria has been described earlier in this chapter. Her political influence, based partly upon commerce and partly upon propaganda, remains to be discussed.

According to the Nazi political philosophy, the flag follows trade. The famous tour of Dr. Schacht in the Balkans, and the acquisition by Germany of an enormous share of Bulgaria's trade, were not ends in themselves, but destined to form the basis of a general cultural propaganda and the extension of German political influence. During the Great War, when Bulgaria was ostensibly an independent state in alliance with Germany, the Germans treated her practically as a colony, installing their own customs officers at her frontiers and commandeering for removal to Germany the produce upon which the Bulgarians had hoped to live. Among the older generation of Bulgarians, therefore, Germany is not popular. But the realities of present-day trade have brought to the Ministry of Finance, Božilov, who has a Pro-German reputation; and the former Prime Minister, Tzankov, is an admirer of Nazi political methods. In December 1938 a number of Bulgarian army officers were awarded German decorations.

Germany does not neglect her propaganda. Much German money is devoted to this purpose, though the effects are not as obvious as in Hungary or Yugoslavia. In Sofia there are no big shops with illuminated diorama, illustrating the beauties of the Tyrol or the Black Forest; but the bookshops, which four years ago stocked numerous French books and a few English, today are filled with German literature of all kinds, well printed in Latin script, easy to read and extremely cheap.

The younger generation of Bulgarians, lacking the memory of the war, is impressed with the achievements, actual and reported, of the Nazis. The German Legation supplies plenty of opportunity for the young people to visualise Germany as a land flowing with milk and honey. Young people who learn German are entertained at the German Legation, their fares paid for holiday visits to the Reich. Students wishing to go to German universities are given favourable terms, and on their return the German Legation does not lose touch with them. The returned students are aided to play the host in cafés to willing admirers, who learn that in Germany there is no unemployment, the workers have paid holidays, with ski-ing and cheap accommodation thrown in, and that Germany is a strong and loyal friend but a dangerous enemy.

Much German propaganda is carried on by supposed commercial travellers. Sometimes it is possible to see four or five such men at one time in a village with no shops and only a muddy market.

German propaganda in Bulgaria (and in other Balkan countries too) is part of the general German policy of south-eastward penetration. If it were only commercial, it could be regarded as the legitimate development of trade, and might be thought to conduce to the economic prosperity of Bulgaria, of Germany, and of the world at large. In its political aspect it is inevitably bound up with the general European situation, and cannot but be regarded as dangerous to democratic ideology and to the interests of the democratic Powers.

PRESENT OUTLOOK

Without attempting to survey the international situation as a whole, or even to consider Germany's progress in south-eastern Europe, or the likelihood that this will be the direction of the next German advance, it is relevant to observe the reaction of Bulgaria to the circumstances of 1939. At the end of January, Dr. Kiosseivanov, Prime Minister and Minister for Foreign Affairs, gave an exposition in the Sobranje of Bulgaria's present foreign policy. Some extracts will indicate the lines along which the most responsible person was then thinking.

> In the times in which we live, in which international events create anxieties and dangers which oblige the peoples, great and small, but above all the small, to reinforce their friend-

ships and to seek new ones, in order to be in a position to defend their rights, their national interests, perhaps also their existence, I consider it extremely imprudent to encourage hopes and ambitions which correspond neither to the strength nor to the possibilities of our country, and which could only cause bitter disillusionment in the afflicted Bulgar soul, and strike a blow at the faith of the Bulgarian people.

That is why the Government, at the risk of incurring unpopularity, is going to continue the foreign policy of peace and understanding which it has adopted during the last years, fully conscious of the responsibilities which it assumes towards the Bulgarian people, and with the firm conviction that in this way it is defending the interests of the latter in the best way.

These introductory sentences give the key to the speech. One must presumably read into them a refusal to cherish hopes of any drastic revision of the Treaty of Neuilly. The reconquest of western Thrace, Macedonia and Southern Dobruja are evidently included among the aims which 'correspond neither to the strength nor to the possibilities of our country.' No doubt, in pursuance of this policy, any slight ameliorations which might be accorded to Bulgaria would be welcomed by a minister exposed to chauvinist criticism. It should be remarked that in September 1938, on the anniversary of the Treaty of Neuilly, revisionist demonstrations were unusually big and took a pronounced pro-German character.

Dr. Kiosseivanov claimed that this policy had been well understood by Bulgaria's neighbours, and had given rise to a desire to settle peacefully all the questions in suspense, and to collaborate in defence of the general interests of the Balkans. Here one may perceive the hope of modest settlements of Bulgaria's grievances, opening the way to the solidarity of the Balkans against an outside menace.

'This realistic policy has drawn our country out of the

dangerous situation of isolation in which she found herself five years ago, upon the conclusion of the Balkan Pact.' To this policy the Minister attributed the improvement of relations with Yugoslavia and the conclusion of the Bulgaro-Yugoslav Pact. With Turkey, it had made relations even more cordial than before; with Greece it had created the conditions for the resumption of economic bonds broken some years ago, and a commercial agreement would probably follow. The same policy would allow of the re-establishment of friendly relations with Rumania.

Dr. Kiosseivanov then spoke of the great diplomatic achievement of the year—the Pact of Salonika.

> The relations of friendship and confidence which have been so happily established, and the pursuit of this pacific foreign policy have created the necessary conditions for the signature, on 31 July last year, of the agreement of Salonika, in virtue of which Bulgaria has been freed from the restrictive —I should rather say humiliating—military clauses imposed by the Treaty of Neuilly. Thus, twenty years after the end of the war, Bulgaria has resumed her rights as an absolutely independent state, and the Bulgarian army has re-conquered at the same time its pride and its freedom to prepare itself for its sacred destiny—that of defending the frontiers of the country and the interests of the Fatherland. The agreement of Salonika . . . is the first pacific revision accomplished in virtue of the provisions of Article 19 of the Covenant of the League of Nations, and in agreement with the Great Powers. It is incontestably a great success for Bulgarian foreign policy.

With regard to security in general, Dr. Kiosseivanov regretted the decline in the authority of the League of Nations, to which Bulgaria was particularly grateful. Bulgaria therefore pursued an independent policy, and avoided entanglements with any Great Power, lest it should incur the enmity of others. In advocating this policy, free from 'adventures and entanglements', Dr. Kiosseivanov made an oblique reference to the errors of King Ferdinand's efforts at aggrandisement:

> In the history of the Bulgars there are numerous sublime pages, of which a people may justly be proud; but there are also dark pages, which we ought often to read, so as to avoid the fatal steps of the past, because the same causes can produce the same disillusionment, and the same sufferings for our martyr country.

Finally, with no attempt to gloss over the anxieties of the time, Dr. Kiosseivanov appealed for unity in the face of danger:

> In these alarming days, which may bring new trials for the Bulgarian people, the Fatherland has need of all its children, who must form a single force, a single spirit, a single will, in order to help Bulgaria to march resolutely on her historic road, and to occupy a place worthy of her in the family of nations.

To these utterances may be added three pieces of recent evidence as to Bulgaria's political attitude:

1. Gafencu could not get Dr. Kiosseivanov to promise Bulgarian alliance or entry into the Balkan entente even should Rumania concede territorial revision.

2. On the occasion of an incident, when twenty-two of the Bulgarian Minority in the Dobruja were shot—the Rumanians say for brigandage—irredentist societies demonstrated noisily in Sofia; but the government tried to keep news of the incident from the public.

3. The King in conversation asserts his determination to preserve neutrality—provided it does not prove impossible to restrain the chauvinists.

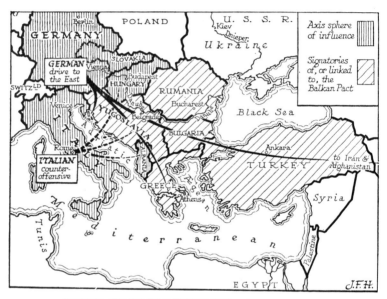

GERMAN AND ITALIAN PENETRATION OF THE BALKANS

GREECE

VANDELEUR ROBINSON

1. INTRODUCTION

Greece is the most southerly of the Balkan states. Its northern regions are indeed Balkan, but the heart of the kingdom is European rather than Balkan; Athens compares in its appearance and character rather with Rome than with Belgrade or Sofia. Thus, Greeks are called 'South-East European' rather than Balkan to their faces.

This old friend of Great Britain, spiritually much akin to ourselves, and now taken under the protecting 'guarantee' of Mr. Chamberlain and the British Fleet, is a monarchy under King George II, and is governed by General John Metaxas according to openly professed authoritarian principles. The area of the kingdom is 50,270 square miles and the population nearly 7 million.

The first part of this chapter will describe the vicissitudes of the Greek people before, about three years ago, they fell under the dictatorship of General Metaxas; the second will attempt to survey the nature and condition of Greek affairs under the existing régime.

No estimate of the duration of the dictatorship is attempted; for one must beware, on the one hand, of the superficial estimate of the British journalist who visited Athens during the Pangalos régime, and whose article, beginning, 'The dictatorship of General Pangalos has come to stay', appeared on the day of the dictator's fall; and, on the other hand, of the facile wishful thinking which always buoys itself with hopes of the inherent instability of any uncongenial system.

2. DOMESTIC POLITICS

THREE CIVILISATIONS IN THE AEGEAN BASIN

The Greeks enjoy the distinction of having produced no less than three times in history a national civilisation. The present-day Greeks are the lineal heirs in blood and language of the Hellenes of the Classical period, whose thoughts and achievements have had so notable an influence upon the general culture of Europe. Like the Jews, their nation seems to have been wonderfully preserved.

The men of the Greek city-states, from whom much of our European culture is derived, brought the art of living to a high perfection. Politically, Macedonia conquered Hellas; but only to widen the geographical range of its culture. The Roman conquest had a similar effect, and the Greek language and ideas were preserved and spread over the Mediterranean Basin and the Middle East.

When the Roman Empire in the west broke up, the eastern part remained. Much of Greece was overrun by the Slav invaders; but the East Roman or Byzantine Empire survived for a thousand years. When Constantinople recovered some of the ground lost to the Slavs, there emerged a second Greek civilisation, the Byzantine, based upon the Orthodox Church, the Greek language, and the law and order and bureaucracy of the Roman Empire. The Byzantines developed their own distinctive forms in pictorial art and in architecture, and in their turn exercised a powerful influence upon the Slavonic world, and to some extent also upon the west.

During the Middle Ages the Balkan Peninsula formed politically a miniature Europe, in which Greek, Serb and Bulgar strove for supremacy, each in turn enjoying a period of paramountcy under some specially powerful ruler. The Greeks had the further duty, towards the end of the period, of defending eastern Christendom from the attacks of the new Mahommedan Powers upon its eastern flank. In this duty it was hampered not only by the rivalry of the Serbs and Bulgars, but also by the occupation, for half a century, of Greece itself by a horde of western adventurers masquerading as a Crusade. Eventually the Turks overran the Balkans and captured Constantinople itself, and the second Greek civilisation came to an end. With the Battle of Kossovo eastern Europe entered upon its Dark Ages, which only came to an end with the liberation of the Balkan Kingdoms in the 19th and 20th centuries.

Under the Turks, Greeks enjoyed a privileged position among the subject populations; they were the traders and the bureaucracy; their Patriarch was the head of the Orthodox religion or *millet*. But only with the War of Independence which began in 1821 did Greece arise as 'a nation once again'.

The War of Independence was a long drawn-out affair. The rebels were brave and resourceful, but seized every opportunity to quarrel among themselves, in accordance with the intense individualism which characterises Greek political action. However, despite their feuds the Greeks were successful. Unable by means of his own resources to put down the revolt, the Turkish Sultan called upon the help of his vassal Mahomet Ali, an Albanian who had become Pasha of Egypt. Mahomet Ali sent his son Ibrahim with Egyptian troops to suppress the Greeks in a fierce war of extermination. The Greeks were saved by the intervention of the western Powers, which imposed an armistice, and enforced it by sinking the Turkish and Egyptian fleets at Navarino. The Sultan, with a Russian war upon his hands and his Egyptian ally's sea communications cut, relinquished the control of a large part of Greece, which was set up as an independent state under international guarantees.

The new Greek state began as a Republic, but was at once torn by internecine feuds. President Capo d'Istria was murdered, and the Powers then supplied a foreign sovereign in the person of Prince Otto of Bavaria. Otto and his German advisers tried to establish a police dictatorship *à la* Metternich, until the Greeks rose and extorted from him a constitution. In 1862 they expelled him altogether, and a new King was found from the royal house of Denmark.

King George I of Greece reigned for fifty years, all but a few months. In 1913 he was assassinated, at the moment when the work of years had just been crowned by an immense extension of territory, northern Greece having been liberated from the Turks by means of the Balkan War.

The word 'Greece' means to us, geographically, the southern part of the Balkan Peninsula, together with some islands in the Aegean. Historically, the extent of the Greek world has been subject to various changes, for at times it embraced Asia Minor and the coast of the Levant. Essentially, the Greek civilisations belong to the Aegean Sea, its coasts and its islands, with occasional expansion to other coasts. Before the coming of the Turks Asia Minor had become Greek-speaking. The Turkish invasions, however, changed the language and religion of that country and made it the homeland of the Ottoman Empire. In the 19th century, and until 1922, the predominantly Greek-inhabited lands included Smyrna and an extensive hinterland, but this was lost by the victory of the Turks in their war of nationalist liberation after the Great War, and the Greek population was partly massacred and partly expelled. Greece, therefore, now means the mainland as far north as Albania and Yugoslavia; the Macedonian and West Thracian coastal plain along the north shore of the Aegean as far as the River Maritza; and most of the Aegean Islands.

The state that was set up after the War of Liberation

included only the southern part of mainland Greece; the majority of the Greek lands remained under the Turkish flag. The politics of the new state were, therefore, directed far less to the organisation of the Kingdom than to the eventual redemption of the Greek irredenta. This redemption occurred progressively. At the accession of King George I, Great Britain ceded the Ionian Islands. Later, an unsuccessful war was fought against the Turks; but before the end of the century Turkey was obliged to give up Thessaly, while the large island of Crete became autonomous. In the Balkan War of 1912 Greece obtained all the Aegean Islands (Imbros and Tenedos, near the mouth of the Dardanelles, were eventually restored to Turkey), except for Rhodes and the Dodecanese, then in Italian occupation and since annexed to Italy. On the mainland, southern Epirus and southern Macedonia were added to Greece, and western Thrace, which in 1913 was given to Bulgaria as a corridor to the Aegean, reverted to Greece at the end of the Great War. Thus the unification of the Greek-inhabited lands (as they now are) under the Greek flag is substantially complete. Cyprus, Rhodes and the Dodecanese are the only lands with a Greek majority now outside Greek frontiers.

After the Smyrna disaster the age-old quarrel with Turkey was made up. The respective territorial spheres of the two countries having been defined, and neither being left in possession of lands properly (that is, ethnographically) belonging to the other, the residual minorities, with small exceptions, were compulsorily exchanged, so that each state should have as nearly as possible a homogeneous population. Drastic as was this measure from the point of view of the unhappy people who were uprooted, it certainly achieved the object of reconciling two old enemies by removing the one remaining bone of contention between them.[1]

[1] (See p. 276).

VENIZELISTS VERSUS ROYALISTS, 1914–35

The dominant factor in Greek politics from 1914 till 1935 was the profound schism between the Venizelists and the Royalists.

Eleutheros Venizelos began his career as a leader of anti-Turkish insurrections in Crete. From Crete he came to Athens, where, as Minister to King George I, he helped to prepare Greece for the approaching Balkan Wars. His policy brought the Greek Army in triumph to Salonika; but there King George was assassinated.

The Great War produced a profound divergence of opinion between Venizelos and the new King Constantine. The former desired to attach his country to the Entente Powers, which were offering glittering prizes for Greek co-operation. The King, however, was a brother-in-law of Kaiser Wilhelm, and was convinced that Germany would win; he therefore conceived it his duty to save his country from the disaster of intervention on the losing side, and to this course he obstinately adhered, notwithstanding a treaty of alliance with Serbia, the advice of nearly all the Greek politicians, and the result of a general election. The King was supported by his Chief of Staff, General Metaxas, who had been treated with extraordinary lack of tact by the British military authorities.

Venizelos went so far as to invite the Allies to land an army at Salonika, which they did on the day after the Greek Premier's fall from office. The commanders of this force found it necessary to disallow the authority of King Constantine's government in the area of their occupation, and Venizelos set up a rival government in Salonika, justifying this course by the claim that the King had transgressed the constitution. The upshot was that the Allies landed troops at Athens, and King Constantine was compelled to abdicate.

His second son, Alexander, became King, and brought Greece into the war on the side of the Allies, under the Premiership of Venizelos.

When the war ended, Venizelos departed to Paris to obtain Greece's reward from the statesmen at the conference. While there, he offered to become the mandatory of the Allies in forcing compliance with the Treaty of Sèvres upon the recalcitrant Turkish Nationalists; hence the war in Asia Minor. But, unfortunately for Greece, two disasters now befell; King Alexander was bitten by a monkey and died, leaving the way clear for the return of Constantine; and Venizelos held free elections at an injudicious moment, under the system of majority voting, with the result that a defeat by a relatively narrow margin of votes gave his opponents a large parliamentary majority. The Greek Army in Asia Minor was by these events turned into an agent of the pro-German King and his anti-Venizelist Ministers; the Allies washed their hands of it, and, under royalist corruption and mismanagement, it encountered not merely defeat but utter disaster.

The fall of Smyrna in September 1922 finished the career of King Constantine. A group of officers, including Colonel Gonatas and Generals Kondylis and Plastiras, demanded the deposition of the monarch whom they held responsible for their misfortunes. King Constantine abdicated and withdrew to Italy, and his eldest son, King George, ascended the throne. The officers formed a military government, whose principal exploit was the trial and execution of five former Ministers and the Commander-in-Chief for treason in connection with the management of the Turkish War. The shooting of 'The Six' left a scar upon Greek society which refused to heal, and accounted for an immense amount of bitterness in political life. Years afterwards, commenting upon an unsuccessful attempt upon the life of Mr. Venizelos, a Greek lady remarked at a party: *dommage que ça a ratté*! For Venizelos was held (quite unjustly) responsible for the slaying of 'The Six'.

The short first reign of King George II was marked by a royalist rising, designed to free the King from the control of the military, and led by General Metaxas. The rising failed, and the military government immediately held elections. The discrediting of King George, and of the royalists who had staged the unsuccessful rising, led to a Venizelist victory. Venizelos again became Premier, but he resigned, owing to ill health; his lieutenant, Kaphandaris, succeeded him as Premier and in the leadership of the Liberal Party. Kaphandaris' short administration was followed by that of an out-and-out republican, Papanastasiou, who sent the King on a holiday while the Assembly voted the abolition of the monarchy. Admiral Kondouriotis was elected Provisional President of the Greek Republic.

For 14 months the National Assembly debated the clauses of a new Republican constitution, and their task was still incomplete in June 1925, when General Pangalos, a picturesque military adventurer, staged a coup with 28 supporters and made himself master of Athens; the Premier Michalakopoulos resigned in his favour. Pangalos was a queer ruler; he hanged officials for peculation, in virtue of an *ex post facto* law; he sought to regulate the length of women's skirts; he gave out over-generous contracts to foreign firms; he settled a frontier dispute with Albania, but tried to plunge Greece into war with Bulgaria (the League of Nations stepped in and stopped him); and he endeavoured to settle the 'Free Zone' dispute with Yugoslavia on terms advantageous to the latter. In January 1926 he openly assumed dictatorship and had himself elected President of the Republic by means of a popular election at which he was the only candidate.

The Pangalos régime lasted a year, and was then over-thrown in 1926 by a coup staged by General Kondylis. But the new master was at this time a republican; he put down a rising of the Pangalist Republican Guards, and held free elections on the basis of Proportional Representation. In these the Venizelist coalition was successful, and Kondylis then handed over the reins of power to the politicians.

In the new Parliament the three Venizelist parties obtained 138 votes, and the two Anti-Venizelist or Royalist Parties of Tsaldaris and Metaxas respectively 63 and 49, or 112 in all. In order to assuage the existing party bitterness, a coalition was formed under a much respected neutral personage, Mr. Zaimis. From December 1926 until June 1928 a succession of coalitions under Zaimis ruled Greece, with considerable success, and made some progress with the post-war reconstruction, so long delayed by factional disputes.

Meanwhile, Mr. Venizelos recovered his health and married a wealthy lady. Early in 1928 he returned from Crete and re-entered political life. He was too big a man for Greek politics, and his first action was to treat his successor in the leadership of the Liberal Party, Kaphandaris, as a mere locum tenens, and to resume the leadership himself. In June 1928 the Zaimis Cabinet resigned, and Venizelos formed a government. He held elections under the old majority system which had proved his undoing in 1920, and this time obtained an overwhelming majority. He was thus assured of a four-year spell of power.

The Republican constitution provided for a Senate, and this had not been appointed when Venizelos came into power. Venizelos obtained the election of 72 out of the 92 elected Senators, which gave him a majority over his elected opponents and the non-elected Senators together. This Venizelist Senate remained in existence after Venizelos' fall, and gave him an advantage in the years when he no longer had a majority in the Chamber.

Venizelos' last long period of power was marked by a series of brilliant diplomatic triumphs. He first made a Pact of Friendship with Italy, shelving the question of the Dodecanese. Anxious not to be left out in the cold, the Yugoslavs purchased a similar Pact by coming to a settlement of the 'Free Zone' dispute on terms less favourable than those which Pangalos had negotiated and which the Greek Assembly had refused to ratify. The Yugoslav question having been settled, Venizelos entered into a Pact of Friendship with Greece's old enemy, Turkey; now that neither of these states governed any appreciable number of the other's co-nationals, there remained nothing to prevent their co-operation. Greece's diplomatic situation was much strengthened by these arrangements, which were developed by Venizelos' successors into the Balkan Pact.

The economic crisis unseated Venizelos. The long series of wars, and the need to borrow heavily for reconstruction and refugee settlement, placed upon Greece a heavy burden of debt; and when international trade was catastrophically diminished it became impossible to meet the service of the foreign loans. Venizelos passed the Premiership to his Left-Wing supporter Papanastasiou, who did not inspire the confidence of the foreign bondholders, and was accordingly unable to obtain favourable terms from them. An election being now imminent, Venizelos took the Premiership again, and passed a Proportional Representation Bill, with a view to minimising his anticipated defeat.

The election of 1932 left the two groups in the Chamber very nearly equal. Tsaldaris, leader of the royalists, obtained two more seats than the Venizelists. An arrangement was come to by which Tsaldaris took office, promising not to raise the question of the régime—he was ostensibly a royalist, but his wife much preferred to be First Lady of the Republic, a position to which President Zaimis' wife did not aspire. Venizelos dissolved the Venizelist Military League, which was contemplating supporting him by force, and agreed not to overthrow the government in Parliament, for the duration of their agreement.

The Tsaldaris 'tolerated' government lasted from September till January, when it fell on the impossible financial situation, and Venizelos took office to hold new elections in March 1933. This time, the Venizelist parties did not do so well, and Tsaldaris was able to form a royalist administration.

THE TRIUMPH OF ROYALISM

The electoral defeat of Venizelos was marked by an attempted coup on the part of the Venizelist General Plastiras, who seized Athens and patrolled it with tanks and armoured cars. Venizelos refused to join this movement and co-operated with Tsaldaris and President Zaimis to put it down. General Plastiras handed over to General Othonaios and walked home. Before anyone thought of arresting him, he fled the country.

Kondylis and Metaxas, both in the new Tsaldaris Cabinet, wanted Venizelos and Plastiras impeached for treason. Venizelos spoke in the Senate in his own defence but was howled down. Tsaldaris, who was not vindictive, carried an Amnesty Bill, and adjourned the Chamber for two months. Meanwhile, in June, a remarkable attempt was made upon Venizelos' life, when a car full of assassins pursued that of the statesman along a main road right into Athens, blazing away all the time with machine-guns. Madame Venizelos was wounded but Venizelos was unhurt. The car used in the attempt was found abandoned next day; it belonged to the brother of the Chief of the Athens Police!

The Tsaldaris administration of 1933–35 was not specially eventful, until it was violently disturbed by a rising in March 1935. The insurgents, who were of the republican persuasion, but not originally instigated by Venizelos, failed to capture the arsenal at Salamis, but obtained possession of the battleship *Averoff* and the cruiser *Helle*, in which they departed to Crete. Had they at once proceeded to Salonika to support the rebellion in Macedonia, it is possible that the rising might have succeeded; but of two Army Corps that were to revolt in that district, the rising of one was cleverly forestalled, and the other fought a somewhat comic opera campaign, made grim by General Kondylis' government bombers, until, unsupported by its fleet, it fell back into Thrace and surrendered, the leaders escaping across the Bulgarian frontier.

The *Averoff* and the *Helle* went to Crete, where they prevailed upon Venizelos to support their rising. This, they calculated, would give them a great psychological advantage; it lent weight to their assertion that they were only trying to forestall the supposed intention of the government to restore the monarchy. In the event, since it was now too late to save the fortunes of the rebellion in Macedonia, all that the rebels did was to discredit the entire Venizelist cause, and to bring upon Greece the restoration of the monarchy that they professed to be resisting. Venizelos and the leaders were conveyed abroad to safety, and the two ships surrendered to the government.

General Kondylis returned in triumph from his victory over the rebels in Macedonia, and became Deputy Prime Minister. He now advocated the immediate restoration of the monarchy. Tsaldaris, on the other hand, did not want a royal restoration to be brought about by a snap election, leaving the royalist-Venizelist feud unhealed. He fought an election, but on the programme of an amiable disposition to proceed to a restoration later, if any great popular demand for it were to emerge. He gained 95 % of the seats in the new Chamber, General Metaxas, who wanted the King to be brought back at once, only securing seven seats.

The rising naturally entailed reprisals upon its perpetrators. Venizelos, Plastiras and Kamenos were condemned to death, but were safely out of the country. Three Venizelist party leaders, Sophoulis, Kaphandaris and Papanastasiou, were tried but acquitted. Several persons were actually executed, and the constitutional guarantee of permanence for the Civil Service was suspended in order that all Venizelist officials might be weeded out.

The new Assembly was elected as a Constituent Assembly, and proceeded to discuss the restoration of the monarchy. A plebiscite was resolved upon, but Tsaldaris, playing for time, and for cooling of passions, put off the date as long as he could, and November 3 was eventually chosen. The republican leaders took heart, and began to organise the electoral campaign against the restoration.

As the republicans began to recover their morale, the out-and-out royalists became more impatient; they saw their opportunity slipping away. On October 10 a group of senior army officers arrested Tsaldaris and informed him that he was no longer Premier; they then waited upon Kondylis and asked him to assume the Premiership. The same afternoon Kondylis proposed in the Assembly the immediate restoration of the monarchy. The supporters of Tsaldaris, still in a majority, but a hopeless majority, walked out, and the resolution was carried. Kondylis was nominated Regent, and on the following day he bade farewell to President Zaimis, and thanked him for his services to Greece.

The plebiscite was duly held; but it was not the honest vote intended by Tsaldaris. Kondylis, who had staked his whole future upon a restoration, and who knew that the

King would not return unless invited by an impressive majority of the Greek people, staged a collossal fake. Enthusiastic royalists vied with one another in voting as many times as they could; some claimed to have recorded sixty votes apiece! Bodies of 'dependable' troops marched from station to station, overawing republican voters and themselves voting for the King. It was a punishable offence to refrain from voting, and a republican would find on arrival at the polling-station that the cards were of two colours, with a transparent envelope in which the 'secret' vote had to be enclosed in the presence of royalist officers. Sometimes the authorities did not even provide any cards of the republican colour. In stations where the voting seemed insufficiently one-sided, the returning officers threw into the urns the plentiful supplies of royalist cards which they held in reserve. The votes counted in favour of the restoration are said to have exceeded the total number of voters! It was officially announced that 98 % of the electors had voted for the restoration. King George, still in London, was convinced of his popularity.

The King was really determined not to return as the puppet of the royalist faction. He resolved that on his return he would pardon and reinstate the whole of the condemned or dismissed Venizelists. For this purpose, he sent strict orders to Kondylis to send him a comprehensive list of all persons who were suffering punishment or deprivation of their posts for their connection or alleged connection with the rising of the previous March. He then set out for Greece, but arrived at Athens to find Kondylis determined to resist the proposed amnesty. For several days a fierce crisis prevailed between the King and the Premier; then King George dismissed his King-Maker, and installed Professor Demerdjis as Prime Minister. He then held free elections for a new parliament.

Upon the fall of Kondylis, King George issued an amnesty of extraordinarily wide scope. Venizelos and Plastiras, in exile and under sentence of death, were pardoned and were free to return to Greece. Colonel Gonatas, who had turned out King Constantine, and was now in solitary confinement for complicity in the March rebellion, was released. Politicians, army officers, civil servants, all were forgiven; only the question of the reinstatement of the dismissed officers had to be postponed, and has never been undertaken for fear of alienating the army.

The King's amnesty produced a complete revolution in Greek politics. Hitherto, there had been royalists and Venizelists. True, there were several separate political parties under each of these headings; true, also, the heads of the largest royalist party, the populists, were not specially keen upon the actual restoration of the monarchy, so long as their party enjoyed a good share of the fruits of office; nevertheless, the ordinary politically-minded Greek—and nearly all Greeks are politically-minded—either believed in the monarchy and hated Venizelos, or else believed in Venizelos and the republic. This classification was entirely upset by the actions of the King at the commencement of his second reign, in the last weeks of 1935. The Venizelists were won for the King; the most ardent royalists were disgruntled and soured.

THE FALL OF DEMOCRACY

The people who were really put out by the King's generosity were those ardent royalists who had banked upon enjoying a privileged position when the King came to his own. Kondylis, for example, was rewarded for the Restoration by receiving the Grand Cross of the Order of the Redeemer; but this was also given to Tsaldaris, who had put on the brake. Mavromichalis, a former Minister, who received an order, returned it in disgust to the King. John Theotokis, leader of the most extreme royalist group, displayed his fury with the anti-royalist King by turning the King's portrait face to the wall at a public gathering. The Venizelists were delighted. If the King was to be completely impartial, the Republic could die unmourned. King George had gone far to realise the idea of a constitutional monarchy which should differ little from a crowned republic, and of a Greece in which the troublesome question of the régime was finally settled, and the King enjoyed the loyalty of all sections of his subjects. His courageous dismissal of Kondylis and the master-stroke of the amnesty laid at last the ghosts of 'The Six', which had so long banefully haunted Greek politics.

The task of reconciliation might have been expected to be facilitated by a remarkable series of deaths, which wiped out in the space of a year almost the whole generation of leading Greek politicians. Ex-President Kondouriotis died just before the Restoration; ex-President Zaimis followed him in the summer. Soon after the January elections General Kondylis had an apoplectic fit and died. Venizelos passed away in Paris within a few weeks. In May there died the populist leader, Tsaldaris, and the temporary Prime Minister Demerdjis. His death unfortunately opened the road to power to General Metaxas. The one man who was all along a convinced adherent of the republican form of government, Papanastasiou, also left the scene.

At the beginning of 1936 the King was faced by the task of restoring parliamentary government. The difficulties—or rather, the slowness of the process—at last daunted him, and made him ready to turn to another solution. To begin with, however, his conduct was scrupulously correct from the democratic point of view. Tsaldaris desired the re-assembly of the old Chamber, in which he had had a majority; but

King George decided that the populist Chamber, elected in the heat of feeling after the March rising, with the Venizelists abstaining, no longer represented the feelings of his reconciled people, and insisted upon holding new elections. These were conducted with scrupulous fairness, under Proportional Representation, and produced, as such elections are prone to do in Greece, approximately a dead heat between the parties of the former royalists and Venezelists. The coalition of royalist groups, including the allied parties of Kondylis and Theotokis, and also Tsaldaris' populists, actually secured one more seat than the assorted liberals, while fifteen communists (an unusually large block, on account of unemployment around Kavalla caused by an American tobacco firm deciding to do its treating of the leaf in the United States) held a sort of balance. The communists supported the monarchy because they saw in it a protection against fascism. Soon after the elections, Kondylis and Theotokis had a violent quarrel, which caused Kondylis to have a fit and die. Their two factions united under the leadership of Theotokis.

At a Crown Council, the King besought the party leaders to compose their differences and supply him with a coalition government which should command a majority in the new Chamber; the 'business' Cabinet of Professor Demerdjis was meanwhile in office. The strongest block in the Chamber was that of the liberals, who, since the death of Venizelos, acknowledged Mr. Sophoulis as their leader. Sophoulis, however, could not form a strong government without the support of one or other of the two big royalist groups— either the populists of Tsaldaris, with 69 seats, or the Kondylis-Theotokis faction, now led by Theotokis, with 63 seats. Venizelos, had he been alive, would no doubt have found a way; but the smaller men debated at great length as to the Premiership and other matters, and it took them till July to present a government to the King. Tsaldaris was now dead, and Sophoulis and Theotokis had managed to come to an arrangement. In view of the prolonged and bitter hostility between these men and their respective followers, the eventual achievement of unity was more remarkable than the length of the negotiations; but the King, annoyed by the rudeness of Theotokis and the haggling of Tsaldaris, the plethora of words and the paucity of action, chose to consider that parliamentary democracy was hopeless, and the proposed government was never put in office.

At the end of April, parliament had been prorogued for the summer, to give the political leaders time to adjust their difficulties. Its place was taken by a representative parliamentary committee. Demerdjis having died, his War Minister, Metaxas, had assumed the Premiership, and the Parliamentary Committee did not withdraw from him its confidence. Well before the expiry of the period for which parliament was prorogued, the party leaders completed their task, and the stage was set for the long-awaited return to parliamentary rule, for which the restored King had been so eager.

The absence of a parliamentary Cabinet, and still more the ordinary causes of industrial unrest, meanwhile gave rise to strikes, in one of which (a one-day general strike in May) there appeared more than a suspicion of political objects. A new general strike was planned for the beginning of August; though the withdrawal, before the date fixed, of the principal trade unions deprived it of the character of 'Direct Action'. These alarms enabled General Metaxas to cry 'wolf'! in regard to communism, and in this way to persuade the King that an active and forceful government was required, in order to save the throne and the social system. He requested the King to invest him with special powers.

Generals have a reputation for considering that committees and compromises are no way to govern the country, and (whether for this reason or from personal ambition), Metaxas now determined that the destinies of Greece should not be entrusted to the elderly and not very energetic Sophoulis and the young, but not specially able, Theotokis. Those who had, with misgiving, watched Metaxas' form during the last few years were the less surprised when, on August 4, Metaxas obtained special powers; parliament and its special committee were suppressed, the political parties abolished by decree, and a strict censorship was instituted. The government took powers to rule by decree, and freedom and democracy were at an end. Dictatorship was once more established in Greece.

METAXAS' 'THIRD CIVILIZATION'

Philosophy of the dictatorship.—In general, the evils of dictatorship are far greater in the moral than in the material field. In the provision of work and sustenance for its people, a dictatorship may be efficient or inefficient; at least, it has special opportunities for swift, decisive and effective action, of which it may avail itself if the men at the top know their job. Apart from mass persecution of Jews (which does not exist at present in Greece), the persons actually mistreated by an authoritarian government are numerically but a small proportion of the whole population; loss to the nation through insufficient consideration and discussion of governmental projects is always probable under dictatorship, but may not outweigh the material gains—again, if the men at the top know their job.

Evils which are spiritual are none the less grievous; for the character of a people, its well-being in the largest sense, is undermined by the lying, spying, personal intrigue, brutality, cult of force, idolatry of the state, and perversion of legalism and justice which are the means by which a dictatorship retains its control.

Curiously enough, it is just in the spiritual field, where dictatorship is at its weakest, that its advocates make the strongest claims. The discipline, the appearance of unity and of national purpose, upon which they are able to insist, seem to dictators to be more important than the freedom, diversity, honesty and essential toleration of free citizens. General Metaxas, with breath-taking candour, forbids the reading or the printing of the Funeral Oration upon the death of Pericles, that monument of Greek political and literary genius. He declares that the best political ideas of ancient Greece were not found in Athens at all, but in Sparta. We are spared the trouble of convicting him of this blasphemy; out of his own mouth he convicts himself.

The political system of Sparta, with all its faults, was no true ancestor of that of Metaxas, for at least it refused to tolerate personal dictatorship, even going to the length, as Mr. Kaphandaris points out, of killing horribly its great general Pausanias because he had projected a bid for personal power. Nevertheless, a comparison not only of the political philosophies of Sparta and Athens, but of their relative efficiency from the point of view of military success and survival value, indicates the total futility of the Spartan Blimpism which inspires such rhapsodies from General Metaxas. In the Peloponesian War, Athens maintained herself successfully for thirty years, and was only at last defeated when Sparta resorted to the treacherous expedient of bringing in the Persians. Even so, Athens recovered, and bequeathed her values to the Macedonian Kingdom, to the Roman Conquerors, and to posterity; while Sparta, home of corruption, brutality and bestial customs, at last perished from her own anarchy.

The third civilisation of Greece is that which has succeeded the liberation from the Turks; it is strongly animated by the spirit of freedom and individualism. Yet General Metaxas claims the title—'The Third Civilisation'—for his own régime, which is the very antithesis of these values.

The faults attributed to the democratic régime—corruption, factionalism, personal careerism—flourish in the Metaxist clique, without the wholesome corrective of fear of scandal and disgrace. Over them, however, is drawn the cloak of religious hypocrisy, ill according with an otherwise blatantly barbarian outlook, unworthy of a people which, despite its weaknesses and its backwardness, is essentially civilised in its sentiments and in its habits.

The dictatorship and its opponents.—General Metaxas' authority rested in the first instance upon the support of the King, and of an army loyal to the King. The King himself had won the allegiance of many former Venizelists, and of all who welcomed his efforts to put an end to the long period of revolts and political reprisals. Thus, Metaxas at first enjoyed the advantage of the royal prestige; his continued authority rests upon the activities of his police, the weariness of party wrangling, and lack of an effective Opposition. Unlike the other Balkan states which are dictatorially governed, Greece is ruled on frankly authoritarian principles. The dictator's police spy out alleged opponents of the régime, who are imprisoned, beaten, tormented and interned. At first the use of the castor-oil bottle was copied from fascist Italy; later, a new device was employed, and prisoners were seated for prolonged periods upon blocks of ice.

The censorship of the press was quickly established in Greece, as under all the current dictatorships. But in Greece the censorship extended its activity not only to the excision of matter distasteful to the authorities, but to the compulsory insertion of items of propaganda, long reports of Metaxas' speeches, and frequent photographs of the dictator.

Soon after the dismissal of parliament and the parliamentary committee, the King received in a farewell audience the leaders of the dissolved parties. He would not see them separately; and (as one of the leaders themselves told me) he showed himself extremely embarrassed at having gone back upon his pledges to democracy. Those who believe in the dictatorship, however, aver that he treated the leaders with contempt, being thoroughly disgusted with their failure to perform their proper function of supplying him with a parliamentary government, until the last minute attempt to maintain their own position.

On the night of the coup, Metaxas arrested all the communist deputies and several of the most competent (and consequently most dangerous) non-communist politicians, among them Sophoulis' assistant, Tsatsos. These men were tried by a packed court and banished to the remoter Aegean Islands, which serve Greece for concentration camps. Tsatsos and some others were released when Metaxas was firmly in the saddle, in deference to Sophoulis, who was at first treated with respect.

At the end of 1936, Sophoulis submitted to the King a long memorandum, arguing the absence of necessity or justification for the abolition of democratic liberty. He was assured that the King had read his memorandum with interest, and there the matter rested. The former Ministers were kept under more or less strict surveillance until a year later, when most of them were arrested and sent to the Aegean Islands. Mr. Michalakopoulos, the Conservative Venizelist, formerly Prime Minister and Foreign Minister, was allowed to return home on account of illness, but only to die. Kaphandaris and Sophoulis remain in exile. Theotokis is confined to the island of Corfu, where his home is situated.

Most of the democratic leaders of republican times have passed from the scene. Their successors live in internment or exile. Many, pining for liberty, placed their hopes in General

Plastiras, who lives in France, and who in the past planned several daring coups against governments to which he was opposed. But the popularity which Plastiras enjoyed with a republican army does not extend to the armed forces which now support the King.

Moreover, the Italian seizure of Albania in April 1939 brought about a cessation of opposition on the part of a number of the Greek exiles, and a group of them in France, including General Plastiras himself, and also the son of Venizelos, announced that the danger to their country led them to sink for the time being their hatred of the dictatorship.

The most important opposition hitherto has come from Mr. Kaphandaris, whose exile resulted from the publication of a reasoned indictment of the dictatorial régime. This document, indeed, affords the principal source of information from the anti-dictatorship point of view, and has to be compared with the dictatorship's own eulogies of its work and of its philosophy. So seriously was this manifesto taken by the government that not only was Kaphandaris sent to the islands, but a false declaration was officially issued, purporting to emanate from the pen of Kaphandaris, in which he was supposed to repudiate all his criticism of the government and to profess support for the ideals of the dictatorship. Kaphandaris and his friends, however, contrived to re-publish their indictment of the régime, with a denial of the authenticity of the recantation issued in his name by the government.

3. SOCIAL AND ECONOMIC POLICY

WHILE condemning the dictatorship for the vices inherent in all authoritarian governments, and especially for the philosophy which this particular régime openly professes, it is necessary to give some account of the work which the dictatorship has set out to achieve, at least, so far as concerns its more important undertakings. Where possible, the government's claims in regard to its achievements are weighed in the light of Mr. Kaphandaris' observations.

FINANCE

During the two and a half years of Metaxas' dictatorship, the expenditure of the Greek state has very greatly increased. The spokesmen of the government have on many occasions referred to the 'financial debauch' of the democratic governments, and the need for reducing the burden of taxation. General Metaxas was an important member of all the governments from 1933 onwards, or, when not actually a Minister, exercised influence upon their policy. Thus, he cannot altogether escape responsibility for the mismanagement and extravagance which he alleges occurred in the years immediately preceding the dictatorship; but since his accession to supreme power the increase has been prodigious, in spite of his public insistence that the most rigorous economies were being carried out. Comparing the budget for 1937–38 with that of two years previously—the last of the democratic régime—expenditure was increased by no less than 37½ %, or well over one-third. In drachmas the increase was 4,563 millions, and of this sum only 2 milliards (less than half) were accounted for by the increased expenditure on armaments.

The three greatest increases are accounted for by rearmament, public works and social insurance. Other large increases are due to the raising of pensions and the salaries of officials, and the increase of the burden of public debt, partly through the payment of a larger proportion of the interest due to foreign bondholders. Increased debt payments account for 146 million drachmas. The government is, of course, entitled to assert that the elaboration of the system of public assistance and social insurance, and the work against disease, are sound objects of expenditure, and, if efficiently carried out, justify increased expenditure. It is not entitled, on the other hand, to claim that it has fulfilled its promise to diminish the burden of taxation.

The government makes much of its claim to have 'restored' the finances. It appears, however, that the budget of 1936–37, the first to be carried out entirely under the control of Metaxas, produced a deficit of 160 millions, the first deficit for some years. The budget for 1937–38 estimated for a deficit of 596·6 millions, but (in spite of additions to the expenditure) the realised deficit was reduced to 175 millions. Further, the dictatorship alleges that the cover for the drachma was diminishing drastically during the period immediately preceding the dictatorship, and would have become entirely exhausted in the course of 1938, had the drain on the gold and foreign exchange holding of the Bank of Greece continued. The former Finance Minister, Kaphandaris, however, challenges the government's claim. According to Mr. Kaphandaris, the cover diminished by 836 million drachmas between October 1935 and July 1936, during most of which period Metaxas was largely in control; and then increased in the first 17 months of the dictatorship by some 781 millions. This increase, he states, should not be taken at its face value. Part of it was only a matter of book-keeping, being due to a revaluation of the gold reserve; this Kaphandaris makes accountable for some 582 millions. A further large increase was due to the unexpected opportunity of exporting war material to both sides in the Spanish Civil War; for this Metaxas cannot claim credit. Since these two circumstances account for much more than the total increase of cover, Mr. Kaphandaris alleges that the measures specifically attributable to the dictatorship would have resulted in a tragic reduction of the drachma cover; and this in spite of exceptionally good harvests, which, had the former financial policy of the Republic been continued, would have resulted in a notable increase. It is notoriously difficult for anyone but a trained financial economist to get at the truth among a welter of figures, assertions and incidental factors; and in this case the government propagandists and Mr. Kaphandaris are both interested parties, the one desiring to enhance, the other to diminish, the credit of the dictatorship; but Mr. Kaphandaris enjoys a very high reputation as a financier, and it is the government which possesses the means to conceal the truth and to create a false impression.

As to the real value of the drachma, both taxes and commodity prices have increased, so that even the increases in salaries have been more than neutralised. The government, covering part of its expenditure by loans, has recognised that these will produce less and less, and that foreign loan markets are closed to it. The celebrated raising of the percentage payable to the foreign bondholders was undertaken for the sake of impressing the great financial Powers; but, according to Mr. Kaphandaris, it neither increased foreign confidence nor avoided contributing to the great increase in national expenditure.

PUBLIC WORKS

It renders no service to the cause of democracy to overstate the case against dictatorship. It is fair to assert that the advantages of authoritarian government are outweighed by the disadvantages; but it is unrealistic to pretend that it has no advantages at all. There are certain spheres of activity in which a dictatorship can 'get things done' by overriding vested interests and antagonistic opinions, and deliberately accepting all the consequences, economic or otherwise, of a given action. One such sphere is that of public works, in which a government enjoying full powers can enforce whatever proposals it thinks fit, and carry them through, extravagantly, perhaps, but effectively and expeditiously.

Greece is a country where there is particular scope for public works. The northern part of the Kingdom was only rescued from the Turks in 1912, and the next ten years gave the Greeks little leisure to make good the neglect of centuries. The work of settling a million and a half refugees from Asia Minor, although assisted by the League of Nations, could not be carried out in a short period, and much remained to be done in the application of modern engineering and science to the land of Greece. The Metaxas government seized its opportunity, and pressed forward with an extensive programme of works, much of which had been initiated by Venizelos but held up by political strife. The following were the chief items:

1. Canalisation of streams, irrigation, communications, land settlement in Macedonia. (In a land of scarce summer rainfall, local irrigation must be mainly based on wells.)
2. Hydraulic works in the plains of Larissa and of Karditza (in Thessaly) and on the River Kephissos, in Boetia. Flood-prevention works, irrigation and drainage in Epirus, Crete and Thessaly.
3. Draining of marshes, regulation of the course of streams, flood prevention works, in Peloponnesus, continental Greece and Corfu.
4. Completion of the system of roads by the construction of new roads. Improvement of the railways and of the harbour at Salonika.

The total cost of all these schemes is estimated at 7,324 million drachmas, and is to be spread over 10 years. It is to be provided as to 4·4 milliards by extraordinary and as to 2·9 milliards by ordinary credits.

These works are responsible for a large part of the increased expenditure so bewailed by Mr. Kaphandaris; but in an insufficiently developed country like Greece there is a strong case to be made out for the undertaking of capital expenditure; stronger, indeed, than the case put forward in this country, and successfully resisted by orthodox financiers of a similar type to Mr. Kaphandaris.

PUBLIC HEALTH AND COMPULSORY HEALTH INSURANCE

Alongside the plan for public works already outlined, must be placed the government's proposals for fighting disease. According to the official figures for 1936, no less than 1·8 million persons were afflicted with disease out of 7 million inhabitants, and the average duration of life was only 34 years, as against 65 in the United States and 55 in Great Britain. Tuberculosis, malaria and syphilis were the worst scourges, together with cancer. Against these terrible afflictions a great governmental campaign was begun in 1937.

The government estimated that there were 13,900 hospital beds, another 17,000 being required. One thousand new beds were provided in 1937, and the campaign continues. Large sums of money are being spent in building new hospitals, enlarging those already existing, and modernising their equipment. The Red Cross and other foundations received large subsidies to enable them to extend their work.

Since there are some 800,000 rural families, and medical requirements are notoriously more difficult to provide in the country than in the towns, a new organisation is to be built up for the provision of facilities in the villages. It was calculated that each family expended upon medical attention some 1,500 drachmas a year in the plains and 800 in the healthier mountain districts. The government decided to substitute a scheme of compulsory insurance, costing each family 500 drachmas in the plains and 300 in the mountains.

These contributions would total about 450 million drachmas, to which the state and the Agricultural Bank were to add a further 150 millions to finance the scheme.

At the beginning of the century, rural health services were totally inadequate. Ten years of war, followed by a vast influx of refugees (among whom, between 1922 and 1924, deaths were three times as numerous as births) raised the problem of health to one of colossal dimensions. The Refugee Commission took various measures, but mortality was still immense as lately as two years ago. The Agricultural Bank was instructed to prepare a scheme for the provision of medical facilities on the basis of compulsory insurance; governmental decrees were then issued with the object of bringing it into force.

The 800,000 rural families are to be organised in 4,000 associations of about 200 families each, small communes combining to form associations. Under the scheme, each local association has certain duties to discharge, and district groups of associations have at their head councils of doctors, chemists and peasants. The district groups in each administrative department have also a departmental council. By means of these bodies the governmental schemes of drainage and irrigation are to be supplemented by local undertakings such as the draining of ponds and small marshes, haunts of the malarial mosquito.

These measures against the causes of disease are the responsibility of the communes; the 600 million drachmas raised by the compulsory contributions of the beneficiaries and the subsidies provided by the state and the Agricultural Bank are spent upon the provision of medical assistance. Doctors, paid salaries of 6,000 drachmas a month, together with free quarters at their dispensaries, cost 288 millions a year. Pharmacists, at 3,000 drachmas and free quarters at their pharmacies, cost another 134 millions. There remain 178 millions for the cost of medicaments. The whole scheme is under the supervision of the Agricultural Bank.

How far the government will actually succeed in implementing these schemes remains to be seen. So far, considerable progress appears to have been made in Athens and the large towns, but little change has as yet been made in the village health services.

THE DICTATORSHIP AND THE WORKERS

The government propaganda department begins an account of the labour policy of the dictatorship with the following remarkable statement:

> No interest, no attention, was formerly given by the governments of 'universal suffrage' to the wage-earners. The workers, abandoned to the greed of the employers, and embittered by the indifference of the state, allowed themselves to be led by adventurers who served ulterior interests. Thus there was created in Greece a workers' movement which threatened every day to overthrow and subvert the social order, although the claims of the workers, purely material, had had nothing to do with communism.

This statement is interesting in view of two other assertions: one, that of Mr. Kaphandaris, that the men now in power were in former times the bitterest opponents of any improvement in the lot of the workers; the other, that of the dictatorship, that the *coup d'état* of 4 August 1936 was necessitated by the danger of communism.

The year 1936 was distinguished in the industrial world by a number of strikes, including a general strike on 13 May, and a threatened general strike at the beginning of August, which furnished the excuse for the installation of the dictatorship. No doubt these strikes were in the main the protest of underpaid workers against their conditions, which the government states were deplorable, since wages were low, hours sometimes as long as 12 or 14 a day, and there was heavy unemployment. Probably, too, as the threat of a reactionary dictatorship grew, a political objective crept into the character of the strikes. For political reasons, the dictatorship was too prone to see revolutionary aims in strikes for better conditions, and to suppress them, sometimes—as in the Salonika tobacco-workers' strike—with bloodshed. The dictatorship claims credit for having put an end to strikes and lock-outs by instituting collective contracts and compulsory arbitration of labour disputes. It is a question how much of reasonable liberty and of the power successfully to resist exploitation was taken from the workers by these measures. The memorandum of Kaphandaris alleges that the main object of this labour legislation was to destroy the genuine trade unions of the workers, and to substitute a machinery imposed from above, thus emasculating the working-class movement.

Certain advantages the government may reasonably claim to have conferred. Seven hundred and fourteen thousand workers were affected by the new collective contracts, and better hours and wages were secured, together with 15 days' paid holidays. It claims that the application of the eight-hours day—in the banks and certain big companies, seven hours—effected a distribution of work, and reduced unemployment by 98,000 persons. Former combatants were found jobs, 3,000 in the Civil Service, 4,500 in the public services and big undertakings, 2,000 elsewhere. Without cavilling at the desire of the government to get the unemployed back to work, it is permissible to wonder whether the placing of 3,000 people in government employment was justified by the needs of the service, or compatible with the strict economy of the national finances of which the government has made a great point.

Under the democratic constitution, a law had been voted

for the provision of social insurance; but its application had been delayed, for political reasons. Metaxas' government has begun to put it into practice in the three big towns, Athens, Piraeus and Salonika, where 350,000 persons are insured against industrial accidents, sickness, disablement and old age. Another 283,000 persons, including professional men, civil servants and soldiers, are to be included in the professional pensions schemes.

The General Confederation of Labour, comprising 846 associations and 820,000 members, in eulogising the government, draws attention to the raising of the wages of 378,000 workers, 226,000 skilled workers and 116,000 salaried employees. Thus, it claims, spending power has increased, and with it the standard of living. Against this must be set the charge of Mr. Kaphandaris that the increase of wages has been generally offset by the increased cost of living, amounting in fact to a lowering of the internal value of the drachma.

REGULATION OF PEASANTS' DEBTS

The post-war period was one of desperate struggle for the Greek peasantry. The absence of young men for nearly 10 consecutive years on military service, the actual devastation of war, the influx of refugees without capital of their own, threw immense numbers of small farmers into the slough of financial indebtedness. Interest rates tended to be high, especially when a farmer, unable to furnish sufficient security to the bank, borrowed from a money-lender or from a more fortunately situated friend. The continuance of hard times resulted in inability to pay interest, which was added to capital. At the time of Metaxas' accession to power there was an immense burden of peasant indebtedness, amounting, it is estimated, to over $9\frac{1}{2}$ milliards of drachmas.

This sum was owed to various creditors in the following amounts (the figures are official):

The Refugee Commission	..	1,150 millions
The Greek State	.. ..	1,250 ,,
'Several corporate bodies'	..	158 ,,
National Bank of Greece	..	165 ,,
Individuals ..	.. ..	4,830 ,,
Agricultural Bank	.. ..	2,084 ,,

General Metaxas' government enacted a drastic regulation of this vast indebtedness. In the first place, the largest class of debts, those to individuals, and two relatively small classes, owed to the National Bank and to the 'several corporate bodies' were dealt with in the following manner:

All payments made after 1 January 1937 were to go to reduction of the capital sum, and all interest overdue at that date was cancelled. The remainder was to carry compound interest at the reduced rate of 3 %, and to be paid off in 12 annual instalments, which were in fact considerably smaller than the annual payments which the farmers had up to then been called upon to pay each year.

Indebtedness ruled to be excessive, that is to say the excess of a man's indebtedness above 60 % of the value of his revenue-producing holding, was cancelled, the loss being borne proportionately by all his creditors.

A premium was placed upon prompt settlement by the granting of a remission of 30 % of any total indebtedness or half of total indebtedness paid off by the end of September 1938, and of 25 % if it were paid off within a period of one further year.

Secondly, a somewhat similar arrangement, but with amortisation in 25 instead of 12 years, was made in respect of farmers' debts to the state. This regulation covered only part of the indebtedness to the state mentioned in the category of debts to the state. However, an earlier regulation had already affected indebtedness to the state by reducing the interest rate from 8 to 6 %, and by empowering debtors to pay in certain bonds. These bonds were credited for debt redemption at their face value, when in fact they had so depreciated that their market value fluctuated between 50 and 60 % of their face value. A similar earlier scaling down had also been applied to the debts to the Refugee Commission, which were not covered by General Metaxas' measure. The largest class of debts excluded altogether from the scheme was the 2 milliards owed to the Agricultural Bank. Very approximately, therefore, it would appear that some 60 % of the existing indebtedness was regulated by Metaxas; some 20 % was not now regulated, but had already been reduced; and about 20 % remained unregulated—that is to say, the debts due to the Agricultural Bank.

Debts which had already been regulated in a manner not less favourable to the farmers than the new scheme, debts incurred as a result of an offence, and debts totalling less than 1,500 drachmas were excluded from the scheme. But all debts whatever were subjected to the provision that interest upon them was reduced to a maximum of 8 %, unless it were already at a lower figure.

To give a fair picture of the effects of the scheme, it is reasonable to quote an opponent of the government, Mr. Kaphandaris. The famous financier denies that the relief was in fact beneficial to the peasants. He states that the establishment of the claim to relief was in any case attended with exasperating formalities. The most important part of peasant indebtedness, according to him, was the money owed to the Agricultural Bank and to the Refugee Commission, borrowed in the first instance for the purpose of installing the refugee upon his new holding and tiding him over the first few years; this was omitted from the scheme. On the other hand, the indebtedness with which Metaxas dealt was that incurred by way of loans from one peasant to another, or by borrowing from relations. The reduction of these debts took money from the pockets of one set of peasants—the lenders, who had equal need of it—to relieve another; and it dried up the springs of current lending, to the great embarrassment of the peasants at large. There is probably much substance in this argument, although it may be a little overstated. Hopeless indebtedness is usually an evil, and when it has accumulated through exceptional circumstances it may occasionally be necessary for a state to resort to drastic measures to reduce it. If it be true that the benefit to the relieved peasant was largely off-sct by increased taxes and the increased cost of living, that is an additional reason for the measure.

EXTERNAL TRADE

The Greek government claims that the restrictive measures taken for monetary reasons have in no way hindered trade. Greece was, of course, greatly assisted in 1937 by extremely good harvests. Credit is further claimed for measures taken to increase exports, and to stimulate industrial production. Imports rose from 2,602,726 metric tons, costing 11,962,620,000 drachmas in 1936, to 2,731,056 metric tons, costing 15,204,363,000 drachmas in 1937, and exports from 986,177 tons, valued at 7,378,877,000 drachmas to 1,376,664 tons, valued at 9,555,293,000 drachmas, in the same period.

The adverse balance of trade, in millions of drachmas, was thus 4,584 in 1936 and 5,649 in 1937. Part of this adverse balance is due to the increased price of cereals, of which Greece does not produce enough for her needs. In two years the cost of importing wheat approximately doubled, without a corresponding increase in the quantity imported. Since this is the principal import, the effect on the trade balance was unavoidable. The government is taking measures to increase the production of wheat; and the area of land under cultivation becomes larger as the irrigation and similar schemes take effect.

Wheat is by far the chief import, followed by coal, cotton, timber and pig iron. The most important export is tobacco, other commodities being grapes, minerals, sultanas and olive oil. Germany has the predominant part in Greek trade, and in 1937 took 30·1 % of her exports (2,863 million drachmas) and supplied 27 % of her imports (4,120 million drachmas). Rumania supplied 1,692 million drachmas worth and Britain 1,667 million. U.S.A. is the second purchaser, taking 1,524 million drachmas worth, and Britain again third with 922 million.

4. FOREIGN POLICY

THE Great War gave a notable stimulus to the sentiment in favour of preserving 'The Balkan Peninsula for the Balkan peoples', in reaction against the system of patronage of small states by Great Powers, which had brought upon the former much unnecessary suffering. At the same time, four out of the six states achieved a position of sufficient territorial satiation and national homogeneity to be able to put aside expansionist ambitions and care only to be left alone to develop their new estate. Greece, in particular, now included all the Greek-inhabited lands except Cyprus, Rhodes and the Dodecanese, and by means of the exchange of populations was assured of a largely homogeneous ethnic character. There remained certain specific problems to be settled, after which Greece need only keep on good terms with her neighbours and turn her attention inwards.

The massacre of Smyrna and the terrible transplantation of fugitives abolished in one drastic stroke the age-long enmity between Greece and Turkey. The settlement by Venizelos in 1928 of the dispute with Yugoslavia over the

control of the Djevdjeli-Salonika railway and the Yugoslav
Free Zone at Salonika ended a long-standing cause of friction
between these two neighbours. By acquiescing in the Italian
possession of Rhodes and the Dodecanese, Venizelos achieved
friendly relations with the neighbouring Great Power. With
Albania relations were sometimes difficult on account of the
minorities of some 30,000 persons on each side of their
common frontier, and from time to time disputes about
minority schools, or about the Greek tendency to treat
Moslem Albanians as Turks and ship them off to Turkey,
had to be taken to Geneva. Only with Bulgaria, however,
did there remain an outstanding cause of serious disagree-
ment, in respect of that kingdom's claim to an Aegean
outlet.

In the distribution of former Turkish territory resulting
from the Balkan Wars of 1912 and 1913, Bulgaria received
a strip of western Thrace, giving her a territorial corridor to
the Aegean. At the end of the Great War Bulgaria was forced
to surrender this corridor to the Allied Powers, who undertook to assure her 'Economic Outlets' to the Aegean. It was
not clearly specified whether this access was to take the form
of a strip of territory or of special rail facilities between
Bulgaria and one of the Greek ports, in which she would
have a Free Zone, somewhat on the lines of the Yugoslav
Free Zone in Salonika. The former interpretation was and
still is maintained by the Bulgarians, the latter by Greece,
to whom the Allies handed the whole Aegean seaboard of
Macedonia and western Thrace, as far as the River Maritza,
which forms the frontier of Turkey.

The Allied Powers made proposals for meeting the
Bulgarian claim, in the Lausanne Conference of 1923, but
Bulgaria refused the arrangement as inadequate, and accordingly got nothing. Successive Greek governments attempted
to induce Bulgaria to accept in settlement of her claim a

Free Zone in any Aegean port that she might choose, with a League Commission to supervise the management of the railway link between the port and the frontier. Bulgaria, however, steadfastly refused to accept less than a strip of territory in full sovereignty. It is not improbable that the diplomatic genius of Venizelos might at last have solved this problem, had his last spell of power been of somewhat longer duration. However, the growth of the Rome-Berlin Axis and the rape of Albania in April 1939 found Bulgaria's claim still unsatisfied, and this situation is one of the factors influencing Bulgaria's decision, whether, in the generally apprehended war, she will throw in her lot with the Balkan allies or with the pair of aggressive but revisionist Powers.

Athens was the scene of the first of the unofficial Balkan Conferences, which did much to appease the mutual hostilities of the Balkan peoples. This remarkable movement led to the assembling, in one Balkan capital after another, of leading representatives of all phases of Balkan life. The discovery of common interests produced an unexpected degree of co-operation, and the conferences resembled a League of Nations in miniature. Like the League of Nations, the conferences were most successful in their non-political work; but, also like the League, the governments watched carefully the political implications of the discussions. Thus, Bulgaria and Albania, being creditor nations in respect of the problem of minorities, pressed for the discussion of minority questions, and, to show their right-mindedness in this matter, signed a convention between themselves for the regulation of the rights of the minorities—numerically entirely negligible—which each claimed to have in the territory of the other.

One notable political consequence flowed from the Balkan conferences. In May 1934 there was signed at Athens the Balkan Pact between Greece, Turkey, Yugoslavia and

Rumania. This Pact developed into the Balkan Entente, an organised collaboration in foreign policy similar to the Little Entente, of which two of the Balkan Entente Powers were also members. Meetings of the Foreign Ministers are held at regular intervals. The Balkan Entente, as now constituted, forms an alliance of four Balkan states against any state other than a Great Power which may attack one of them.

The members of the Balkan Entente were pledged, *inter alia*, not to contract political treaties with other states except with the consent of their partners. It was thus a matter of general Balkan interest when Bulgaria, tired of a policy of isolation and perpetual friction with all her neighbours, and especially with the sister Slav state of Yugoslavia, at length decided to put the Macedonian question into cold storage and come to terms with Belgrad. In January 1937 there was signed the Bulgar-Yugoslav Pact of Friendship. Turkey had a long-standing Pact of Friendship with Bulgaria; Greece and Rumania could hardly withhold their approval. Nevertheless, much anxiety was occasioned in Greece, lest the Bulgarians, having given up for the moment their quarrel with Yugoslavia, might use their liberty of action to press for a settlement of the question of the Aegean outlet. The Opposition leaders used this development to accuse the dictatorship of ineptitude in its foreign policy, since (according to them) Metaxas had allowed himself to be taken by surprise, instead of ensuring that any pacts with Bulgaria should be made by Greece and Yugoslavia simultaneously. That Metaxas himself was disturbed is evidenced by the fact that his Under-Secretary for Foreign Affairs, with Metaxas' approval, secretly consulted Mr. Sophoulis about the situation.

The promoters of the Balkan Entente had, it appears, hoped that Bulgaria, renouncing her irredentist claims, would join in the Pact of May 1934. Such, at least, was the hope of the non-official members of the Balkan conferences. Bulgaria, however, could not make such a renunciation publicly—no government dared incur the consequent charge of lack of patriotism—even though revisionism was not at that time a live issue. Subsequently, however, the German drive to the south-east, at first in the form of economic penetration, and from March 1938 onwards by means of open territorial expansion, caused general alarm in the Balkans, and disposed Bulgaria to insure herself against an attack upon the independence of all the Balkan nations. Thus, in July 1938, she signed a Pact of Friendship with the whole Balkan Entente as such. This Pact was signed at Salonika, by General Metaxas, on behalf of Greece, Rumania, Turkey and Yugoslavia.

The rape of Austria and the check to Germany's designs upon Czechoslovakia in May brought about the Pact of Salonika, by which Bulgaria's neighbours released her from the restriction upon her armaments imposed by the Treaty of Neuilly, the Great Power signatories concurring. The retreat of the anti-aggressive Powers at Munich altered the situation, and the turn of the year found Bulgaria more in the mood to ask for the return of the Quadrilateral of the South Dobruja from Rumania, and to profit from the general confusion, as Hungary and Poland had done in the partition of Czechoslovakia. Rumania, however, seemed little disposed to yield, especially when the final rape of Czechoslovakia opened up the prospect of British and French help against aggression. In this situation, the Italians seized Albania, profiting by the paralysis of Yugoslav policy while the dangerous Croat question—urgent, in view of the threat from Germany—was still unsettled. At once the wrestle for the support of Bulgaria became intense; the Italian army was now just the other side of Macedonia, in a position to attack Bulgaria's old enemy on her south-western flank, and to join hands with Bulgaria in the province of which Bulgarians considered they had been cheated in the wars of 1912–18. On the other hand, it was rumoured that Rumania had become willing to consider a cession of part of Dobruja; and the offer of British protection to Greece raised possibilities of another Allied Army at Salonika.

The attitude of Bulgaria might well prove decisive as to the character (though probably not the outcome) of a war waged in the Balkans. But what is to be the attitude of Greece herself in the event of a general European war? The Greek people retains a high degree of pro-British feeling, based upon assistance rendered during the War of Independence, a common maritime outlook, and a common love of democracy, apart from close relations in the spheres of commerce, finance and culture. Lord Byron, in dying for Greek independence, rendered an inestimable service to his own country. On the other hand, the effective head of the Greek state is an ardent Germanophil, who received his military education at Potsdam, and, as if to confirm his sentiments, received a peculiarly tactless rebuff from a British general during the war. In 1914 Metaxas was Chief of Staff to the pro-German King Constantine, and assisted him in preserving Greek neutrality against the wish of practically the whole political world. The present King of the Hellenes had a German mother and a German education, but was at home in London during his twelve years of exile. Another factor, the extent to which Germany accepts the exports and supplies the imports (particularly the materials of rearmament) of Greece might operate in either direction—desire to keep in with a good customer, or alternatively to break an oppressive commercial predominance. In this connection the mission of Sir Frederick Leith-Ross takes on a particular importance. Metaxas has several times remarked: "Greece is not pro-German; it is a question of finding a market for her tobacco."

So long as the British and French navies maintain their control of the Mediterranean—and there is no evidence that the Italians could do worse than inflict casualties by submarine and aerial warfare—it is impracticable for Greece, even if she wished, to fight upon the side of the Axis Powers. Were Metaxas to attempt to bring her in, there would be civil war or revolution. Venizelos split the country and set up a rebel government at Salonika, under the protection of foreign troops, only to put an end to neutrality; intervention on the wrong side would destroy any government.

Meanwhile, Italy (tyrant of the Greek-inhabited Dodecanese) has placed herself upon Greece's north-western frontier. Corfu, bombarded by Mussolini in 1923, is threatened by Italian guns in Albania. Greece's partners in the Balkan Entente, Yugoslavia and Rumania, are threatened, the one by Germany, the other by both Germany and Italy. Turkey, the other partner, is at any rate uncompromisingly anti-Nazi; at last Britain and France have offered their protection, and Greece has accepted it with gratitude. It seems a safe calculation that, if a general war comes, Greece will be at least neutral, and probably a British ally. It would seem that Metaxas, having backed the wrong side, has got his money back.

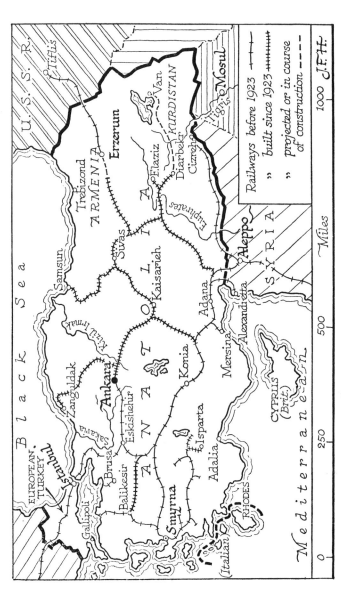

RAILWAY CONSTRUCTION IN TURKEY UNDER THE REPUBLIC

TURKEY

LILO LINKE

NOTE

Figures and statistics about Turkey are often difficult to obtain, and not always reliable. This is usually due not to any desire of the authorities to veil the truth, but to the fact that proper statistics hardly existed in the Ottoman Empire and are now only slowly being built up, with all the errors resulting from inexperience and ignorance. Modernisation on western lines is pushed forward at great speed. The change of standards of measurement, etc., has created bewilderment and confusion. Even in material provided by the government misprints are frequent. For all these reasons any figures mentioned in this chapter have to be treated with caution and can often only be taken as an indication of the general trend of developments.

1. THE TURKISH LAND AND PEOPLE

IN speaking of modern Turkey it is usual to think of the peninsula Asia Minor, also known as Anatolia (Anadolu), and the adjacent highlands to the east. About a thirtieth part of Turkey still lies, however, on European soil—eastern Thrace, with about a thirteenth of the whole Turkish population (7·8 %). Altogether Turkey is three times as large as Great Britain.

Turkey shares her longest frontiers with Syria and USSR, and is further bordered by Iraq, Iran, Bulgaria and Greece. Her sea frontier is nearly a third longer than all her land frontiers taken together. Since the greater part of the country consists of high tableland cut by unnavigable rivers, and of wild mountain ranges, it is not surprising that the density of population is still only 54 per square mile compared with 468 in Great Britain. The past ravages of war and malaria, however, bear a large responsibility for the thinly peopled state of the more fertile parts of the country. The long struggle to maintain Ottoman supremacy over rebellious non-Turkish subjects was a continual drain on Turkish man power until it culminated in the exhausting wars of 1911–23 which finally ended the polyglot Ottoman Empire by creating a nationalist Turkey.

According to the last census, taken in October 1935, Turkey had 16·2 million inhabitants. This figure shows an increase of 18·4 % compared with the result of the first census taken eight years previously (13·6 million). She boasts a birthrate of 23 per 1,000, one of the highest in the world. The authorities admit, however, that thousands of people living in the interior had escaped the first census altogether.

From a study of burial places and archaeological remains, it would appear that the population has changed very little in physical types for more than 4,000 years. The basis of the population in the highlands of Anatolia is very similar to the Alpine type in Europe, and that along the Mediterranean coast resembles the peoples all along the north side of that sea. Numerous migrations have modified this general character in some areas. From the north, round both sides of the Black Sea, have come some 'Nordic' strains which probably included the original invading Hittites and certainly, at a much later date, the Gauls who established the province of Galatia about Ankara (Angora). Semitic influence has been extensive, especially in the south-eastern part of the country, first from the Babylonians and Assyrians and later from the Arabs.

There is little evidence of the size of the Turkish migration which has given the country its name and its language, although it must have been considerable. Belonging originally to one of the Ural-altaic peoples, the Turks seem to have intermarried extensively with their Mongol neighbours in East Central Asia and with the Iranian peoples whose lands they traversed on the way to Anatolia. Arriving there late in the 11th century, the nomad Turkish bands, who had become Moslems during their wanderings, established themselves in its central plain. From there they slowly penetrated the surrounding coastlands, the majority of whose inhabitants were gradually assimilated in language and religion to the conquerors. During the long periods when the country formed part of the Persian, Macedonian, Roman, Byzantine and Ottoman Empires it received elements from their various provinces, particularly from Greece and the Balkans. The exchange of population which has taken place and is taking place with countries in south-eastern Europe is increasing the Balkan elements, as many of the Turks in those countries are descended from native inhabitants who were absorbed by the ruling people under the Ottoman Empire. These, however, do not appear to be very different racially from the present inhabitants of Anatolia.

According to the last census about 85% of the population gave Turkish as their mother tongue. The figures for the various language groups were:

				In thousands
Turks	..	..	..	.. 13,828
Kurds	..	..	..	.. 1,473
Arabs	..	..	..	.. 145
Greeks	..	..	..	.. 109
Circassians	..	..	..	92
Jews (Spanish, Yiddish, etc.)	..			79
Armenians	..	..	..	77

The rest is divided between various insignificant groups. It is significant that only 319,000 (about 2 %) declared themselves as non-Moslem. The biggest sections of this small minority are the Jews (79,000) and the Greek Orthodox

(78,000). The Armenians are split—one group belongs to an independent church, the other to the Catholic Uniates.

The most important of the linguistic minorities is the Kurds, who also inhabit parts of Iran and Iraq. Living on the borders of the old Ottoman and Persian empires, they had always retained considerable independence. The growing authority of the central government following the establishment of the Turkish Republic naturally aroused widespread discontent, and fanned the flames of Mohammedan fanaticism which had been outraged by Kemal's policy of secularisation. Backed by Atatürk's reactionary Turkish opponents, a Kurd insurrection broke out in February 1925; it was crushed within two months with ruthless severity, and all tribal autonomy disappeared.

The Treaty of Lausanne provided extensive protection for minorities, but the relevant clauses soon became inoperative. For the Turkish Constitution recognised everybody born on Turkish soil to be a Turk, irrespective of creed and race, and the government has steadily pursued a policy of Turkification. Whether the Turks will succeed in absorbing the Kurds remains to be seen. The disestablishment of Islam and the westernisation of economic life has bridged many of the differences between the Turks and such Greeks, Armenians and Jews as still remain, chiefly at Istanbul. Provided they wish to be Turkish citizens nothing separates them legally from the rest of the population, and in 1935 two Greeks, one Armenian and one Jew were elected as members of the Grand National Assembly.

About a million and a quarter Turkish-speaking people now remain outside the borders of the Turkish Republic within the former territories of the Ottoman Empire. The vast majority of these are in Europe, where there are still about 800,000 in Bulgaria, 200,000 in the Rumanian Dobruja, 150,000 in Yugoslav Macedonia and 80,000 in Greek

Western Thrace. With the revolt of the subject provinces their Turkish-speaking inhabitants showed a tendency to move within the new Turkish boundaries. This took place to a great extent after the Balkan wars of 1912–13 and has since been much encouraged by the Turkish Government. Seven hundred and seventy-two thousand Turks entered the Republic between 1923–37. These included the 400,000 who left Greece under the exchange of populations following the Lausanne Treaty (see page 276). In recent years Turkey has also concluded treaties with other Balkan states to facilitate the migration of their Turkish minorities. That with Rumania in 1936, for example, arranged for the systematic transference of the Turkish population district by district over a period of five years. Since that date an average of 14,000 Turks has left Rumania yearly. In 1938 a treaty with Yugoslavia aimed at transferring the Turkish minority within six years. The figures for the last four years for which statistics are available (1934–37) show a total immigration of 144,000 persons, chiefly from Rumania and Bulgaria. The majority of the migrants have been settled in Eastern Thrace and Western Anatolia in the territories vacated by the Greeks following Kemal's victory.

This migration is decreasing the proportion the minorities form in the population and is filling some of the empty spaces. The Turkish government ultimately hope to transfer the whole of the Turkish-speaking minorities in the Balkans who have not been assimilated by the states they reside in. In contrast to south-eastern Europe there are very few Turks in the former Ottoman territories in Asia outside Cyprus, where the Turks form 18 % of the population. Since the cession of the Hatay all of the mixed Turkish-Arab borderlands have come inside the Turkish Republic, which has a substantial Arab minority in its south-eastern territories.

There are only three towns with more than 100,000

inhabitants — Istanbul (Constantinople), the old capital (740,000), Izmir (Smyrna) (170,000), and Ankara (Angora), the new capital (125,000). In spite of all government efforts Ankara will for a long time to come remain the smallest of them. The population of Istanbul which was estimated at about 1,125,000 at the outbreak of the Great War, has declined since by about a third, largely owing to the removal of Greeks, Armenians, etc., and to the transfer of the central administration to Ankara.

Only about a quarter of the whole population live in towns or boroughs. The remainder are chiefly peasants and live in villages or on isolated farms.

2. THE FOUNDATION OF MODERN TURKEY

THE END OF THE OTTOMAN EMPIRE

The history of modern Turkey begins about 1876. For over fifty years western ideas had been finding their way into the Ottoman Empire. In 1876 Sultan Abdul Hamid gave his Empire a constitution. Next year it was annulled, but liberal ideas remained very much alive beneath the surface. These were propagated by Turkish exiles in Europe and in Turkey itself by the Young Turks, who organised the Committee of Union and Progress which had widespread support among officers in the army. The Young Turks combined the ideals of 1789 with military aspirations borrowed from the German army. After a year of revolutions and counter-revolutions in 1908–9, the Young Turks overthrew Abdul Hamid, established a constitution, and took over the government.

In a number of ways the Young Turk revolution was a forerunner of the Turkey of Mustafa Kemal. Important reforms were introduced and Turkish national feeling was strengthened. But the mixed populations and creeds of the European, Arab and African sections of the Ottoman Empire made it impossible to create an effective national state. The separation of the Balkan nations from the Ottoman Empire in the 19th century had strengthened Turkish national consciousness. The Italian War, 1911–12, and the Balkan War, 1912–13, stimulated this nationalist feeling still further by depriving Turkey of the last of her African Empire and the greater part of her remaining European possessions.

After these wars Turkey entrusted her reconstruction to German military advisers who severely discouraged all liberal western ideas and worked upon the old Turko-Russian enmity to persuade Turkey to throw in her lot with the Central European Powers in the Great War. At this period the Young Turks attempted to exploit two ideas which were sometimes in conflict one with another: (1) The Pan-Islamic idea by which they hoped to unite all adherents of Islam in the Near East and in India under the Sultan's leadership, particularly against Great Britain, and (2) the Pan-Turanian idea by which they sought to generate a new nationalism covering all Turkish-speaking peoples, including those under Russian rule in Central Asia. In so far as they thought the matter out, a Greater Turkey, including all Turkish-speaking peoples, was to govern the other Moslem peoples of the Near East. The outcome of the war finally swept all these ideas away. For the British overran Palestine and Mesopotamia and in 1918 came the occupation of Constantinople and Straits by British, French and Italian troops, of Cilicia by France, of Konia and Adalia by Italy and of Samsun by the British. Finally on 15 May 1919 the Greeks seized Smyrna.

In August 1920 the peace treaty was signed at Sèvres; it broke up the Ottoman Empire and practically restricted Turkey to Central Asia Minor. The part of Thrace which had remained to Turkey after 1913, and a few islands in the Aegean Sea, were handed over to Greece. Turkey retained Constantinople, which was demilitarised together with the Straits. Syria, Palestine, Arabia and Mesopotamia, henceforth called Iraq, were lost, and even Turkish sovereignty in Anatolia was severely undermined. The northern frontier territory was severed and formed the Armenian Republic, and a Kurd Republic was provided for in the south-east of Anatolia. Britain received a narrow zone of influence on the Turkish–Iraq border and France a wider sphere comprising approximately the triangle Adana–Sivas–Diyarbekir. An Italian zone of influence included the greater part of the coast of south Anatolia and penetrated far into the interior of Anatolia; Greece was given Smyrna and its hinterland to administer. The centuries-old legal, economic and tax privileges of foreigners in Turkey, the Capitulations, were confirmed.

The formation of national states had defeated the Pan-Islamic idea, and the Russian revolution put an end to Pan-Turanian aspirations. Turkey's imminent fate seemed that of becoming a colony, with apparent autonomy but actual exploitation by European Powers. Public opinion was resigned to the worst, and in the general defeatism certain political circles wished for an American mandate, others for a British mandate; a government of the Sultan (which collapsed soon afterwards) even concluded a secret agreement with Britain in 1919, according to which Turkey was to become a British mandated territory.

At the moment when peace was concluded at Sèvres, however, the seeds had already been sown which, in the course of a few years, were to bring about a complete reversal of the political situation and create an independent Turkish national state.

THE WAR OF INDEPENDENCE

The Turko-Greek War.—The history of the Turkish national state begins with the struggle for independence. Four days after the occupation of Smyrna by the Greeks, Mustafa Kemal landed at Samsun, sent by the Sultan's government on a military mission to Anatolia. The Constantinople government, however, was both morally and militarily incapable of resistance. Kemal created the Union for the Defence of the Rights of Anatolia and Rumelia and organised military resistance against Greeks, French and Armenians.

The National Pact of the First National Turkish Congress which Kemal had called at Erzerum (July-August 1919) proclaimed the one and indivisible Turkish fatherland within the national frontiers, rejected the mandate and all forms of protectorate, and recognised only the will and sovereignty of the Turkish people.

In January 1920 members of the Turkish parliament at Constantinople adopted the National Pact and at the same time the first attack by national troops on the French formations was launched. The Allies endeavoured to crush the national movement. In March they again occupied Constantinople and arrested a few leaders of the National Party. But Constantinople was no longer of any importance for the movement. Whilst the Supreme Council of the Allies was drafting the terms of the Treaty of Sèvres (April 1920) a National Assembly met at Angora and elected a provisional government with Mustafa Kemal as leader and military commander. Thus for a few years there were two Turkish governments: that of the Sultan at Constantinople under the control of the Allies, and the independent National government at Angora. True, to begin with, the latter had only a mere handful under it, and these badly armed, half untrained and ready to revolt, but it constituted a dangerous threat to the treaty which was in course of preparation. With the approval of Britain and France, Greek troops entered Thrace in June 1920 and marched from Smyrna and the Sea of Marmora into unoccupied Turkish territory. The signing of the Sèvres treaty by the Constantinople government made no difference; the Angora government refused to acknowledge its validity. In January 1921 the Turkish national troops won their first victory over the Greeks, and it was clear that the Sèvres treaty would have to be revised. A conference in London, in which the chief Allied Powers, the Greeks and both Turkish governments took part (March 1921), was a failure, but a turning point, for the representative of the Constantinople government waived his right to speak in favour of the Angora government representative, whom he referred to as the spokesman of the whole of Turkey. It was significant that after this conference the Allies declared their neutrality as between the Greeks and Turks.

The war proceeded. In July 1921 the Greeks seized Eskischehir, an important railway junction; in August they continued their march eastwards. The Turkish counter-offensive opened in a battle on the River Sakaria at the beginning of September, lasting many weeks. The Turkish army under Kemal, although inferior in numbers and arms, beat the Greeks and forced them to retire to Eskischehir. This was the turning point of the war and the first step towards European recognition of the new Turkey.

A second conference in London, in March 1922, failed like the first. Greece found herself no longer confronted by the irregular Turkish troops of two years before, but by a well-armed, well-trained and well-disciplined army, which was fighting for an idea. At the end of July 1922 the Greek Chief Commissioner at Smyrna proclaimed the 'independence' of Anatolia under Greek occupation. Barely a month later the Turkish general offensive began. At Afium Karah-hissar the Greeks suffered a decisive defeat. On 4 September they were in full retreat and on 9 September the Turks occupied Smyrna. Another section of the Greek army was beaten at Brussa. In 14 days 200,000 Greeks were swept off Turkish soil.

On 11 October 1922 an armistice was signed and a little later Britain and France opened peace negotiations at Lausanne. The armistice not only confirmed the evacuation of Anatolia by the Greeks, but also restored East Thrace to the Turks.

The Armenian question.—Russia and the Ottoman Empire had been constant enemies since the end of the 18th century. For Russia sought to control the entrance from the Black Sea to the Mediterranean through the Straits. To do this effectively she wished to hold Constantinople. This strategic ambition was fired by an accompanying desire to rescue the centre of eastern Christendom from Moslem rule. To promote such an advance southwards Russia did her best to encourage and protect Turkey's Christian minorities.

In the Balkans Turkey's Christian subjects gradually formed independent states which soon desired to stand on their own feet and disliked too much Russian tutelage. The Armenians, however, were unable to acquire independence. For, although partly situated in compact settlements on both sides of the Russo-Turkish border, they were largely scattered amongst Turks, Kurds and Arabs. They were thus powerless to defend themselves, while suspect among their neighbours as tools of Russia.

The intervention of the European Powers proved fatal to the Armenians. After repeated massacres the Young Turks during the war in 1915–16 sought to solve the Armenian question by deportations *en masse* to the Syrian-Mesopotamian desert. As Armenia had long been a troublesome question in European politics, the establishment of an independent Armenian state had been one of the western Powers' war aims.

In 1918 the USSR ceded to Turkey certain Armenian and neighbouring territories. Three independent republics were formed to the north of the new frontier, Georgia, Azerbaijan and an Armenian state which comprised the rest of pre-war Russian Armenia. After the collapse of the Ottoman Empire in October 1918 the old and new Armenian territories of Turkey joined this Armenian Republic.

Republican Turkey's diplomatic relations started with the Armenian question. Its solution terminated the long quarrel between Russia and Turkey. For the two powers were in future to follow a very similar policy over the Straits, and religious differences were no longer to matter. As the Soviet troops reconquered the Caucasian territories Turkey and USSR reached a series of understandings in November 1919 and March and October 1920 which settled all outstanding questions including that of Armenia.

The Turks took Kars in October 1920 and in November concluded an armistice with the Armenians which gave them three-quarters of that part of Armenia which had been Russian in 1914. In December 1920 the Soviet army overran the rest of Armenia, which became a Soviet republic. The Russians and Turks then confirmed the frontiers which had already been fixed.

In March 1921 a Turko-Russian treaty of alliance was concluded in Moscow, in which both partners undertook not to recognise any treaties or international pacts in which either of them had been the object of violence. The Soviet government especially undertook to recognise only those treaties which were accepted by the Turkish national government and abandoned all right to Capitulations. With the object of guaranteeing the freedom of the Straits and the right of free passage, the treaty of alliance called for an international statute to govern the Black Sea and the Straits; a conference of all the coastal states should be given the right to formulate this on condition that sovereignty was not violated.

Russia proved her friendship in these difficult days by supplying Turkey with some of the arms she required. In this way she sought to prevent the western Powers from closing her southern outlets. Turkey had no intention of linking herself solely with Russia; she was pleased, however, to accept help, both diplomatic and military, in her hour of need from an ally whose immediate interests were the same as her own. Turkey had thus closed her back door before winning her victory over the Greeks.

French and Italian evacuation of Anatolia.—Even before the final victory by Kemal over the Greeks, France and Italy had abandoned the benefits given to them by the Treaty of Sèvres. As early as June 1921 the Italian troops left Adalia; soon afterwards the Italian government concluded an agreement with the Angora government by which Italy renounced her claims in Asia Minor, retaining definitely, however, the archipelago in the Aegean Sea (Dodecanese with Rhodes, Leros, Castellorizo) which she had occupied since the Turko-Italian war of 1911. In October 1921 France followed suit with an agreement which determined the frontier between Turkey and the French mandated territory of Syria. The French troops evacuated Cilicia and the supplies of arms and munitions which they left behind were a valuable help for the Turks in the Greek war. The first diplomatic contact of the Angora government with the western Powers had restored Turkish sovereignty in south Anatolia. Besides this direct success, the policy of Turkey had succeeded in splitting the Entente: France had recognised the *de facto* government of Kemal whilst Britain supported both the Sultan's government and the Greeks.

THE TREATY OF LAUSANNE

The peace treaty.—In November 1922 the Peace Conference of Lausanne met. After a breakdown in February 1923 the negotiations were resumed in April and on 24 July 1923 the treaties were signed.

The main stipulations of the peace treaty between Turkey on the one hand and France, Britain, Italy, Greece, Yugoslavia and Rumania on the other were:

(1) *Turkish sovereignty in Anatolia was fully recognised*, the Armenian Republic disappeared, and there was no further talk of a Kurd state. The frontier between Turkey and Syria was already fixed. The frontier between Turkey and Iraq still remained unsettled. This problem, under the name of the Mosul question, occupied and menaced international politics until 1925, when a settlement displeasing to Turkey was made. Constantinople was returned to full Turkish sovereignty, which was now only restricted in the Straits area and on the Greek and Bulgarian frontiers.

(2) *The Capitulations were abolished.* The sovereignty of the Turkish state was thereby completed and the possibility afforded for the reconstruction of Turkish economic life.

(3) *The Ottoman debt to foreign powers* had been safeguarded by an international debt administration which had been set up in 1881, to control to a great extent the finance of the Ottoman Empire. The Lausanne Treaty reduced Turkey's debts and guaranteed her solvency.

(4) *The Millets*, which was the name given to the non-Moslem communities, which enjoyed considerable autonomy in the Ottoman Empire under ecclesiastical rulers and almost formed states within a state, lost their special privileges. It was only by their removal that the creation of a Turkish

TURKEY

state was possible. A treaty relating to the Thracian frontier created a system of demilitarised zones on the Turkish as well as on the Bulgarian and Greek sides of the frontier. A series of commercial treaties completed the work.

(5) *The question of the Straits* led for a time to some tension between Turkey and the USSR. Between 1774 and 1914 Russia had demanded the restriction of the hitherto unlimited sovereignty of the Sultan, the opening of the Straits and free passage in peace and war. As against this, it was a principle of British policy to keep the Straits closed in order to shut Russia out of the Mediterranean. It was only in 1915 that an allied convention assigned to Russia, should victory take place, the Straits and Constantinople. The collapse of Czarist Russia and the establishment of the USSR caused Britain to continue this new policy, but from other motives. The opening of the Straits was one of the aims of the Allies, whilst at the Lausanne Conference the USSR demanded their closure to warships in peace time and war time and full Turkish sovereignty for the fortification and defence of the Straits.

The Straits Convention of Lausanne created an international commission under the presidency of Turkey. The European and Asiatic shores of the Dardanelles and the Bosphorus and the Greek and Turkish islands at the outlet of the Dardanelles and in the Sea of Marmora were demilitarised. A Turkish garrison was allowed to exist at Constantinople. The passage for merchant vessels was made completely free whilst the right of entry to the Black Sea for warships was permitted with certain restrictions. It was a compromise which Turkey accepted under the circumstances. It did not satisfy the USSR, who felt herself menaced by western intervention. She protested against the violation of the Russo-Turkish treaty of 1921 and against the prejudice to Turkish sovereignty in particular.

275

The exchange of populations with Greece.—After the collapse
of the Greek army in Anatolia the Greek and Armenian
inhabitants of the territory formerly occupied by Greece fled
en masse to the west coast. The Turkish government was
determined if possible to get rid of the entire Greek and
Armenian population, whilst the latter endeavoured to avoid
Turkish sovereignty. Dr. Nansen's initiative during the first
Lausanne Conference in January 1923 resulted in an agreement providing for the compulsory exchange of Turkish
subjects of the Greek Orthodox religion and of Greek subjects
professing the religion of Islam, with the exception of the
Mohammedan inhabitants of West Thrace and of the Greeks
who were settled at Constantinople before 30 October 1918.
In the circumstances it was the best and most statesmanlike
solution possible. Considerable hardship was involved, especially for the 1,300,000 Greeks, as against whom there were
only 400,000 Turks to exchange. Greece thus had a difficult
social and economic problem to solve. Although want and
misery have not yet been entirely eradicated among the
repatriated Greeks, the experiment of the exchange of populations was a definite political success. Even before the agreement the majority of Greeks had left Anatolia; the first
problem was, therefore, to remove the Moslems from Greece
and the Greek islands. The Turkish government provided
them with land, if necessary with goods and chattels, and
granted them considerable tax concessions.

By the end of October 1924, 370,000 Mohammedans had
left Greece and almost all the Greeks had left Turkey. The
execution of the provisions of the treaty regarding the
Constantinople Greeks entailed repeated crises, which occasionally jeopardised the whole of the Turko-Greek peace
organisation, but a satisfactory solution was eventually found.
The points of dispute between Turkey and Greece were thus
eliminated in the same way as between Turkey and the

USSR, and the foundations of a second pillar of Turkish foreign policy were laid.

KAMÂL ATATÜRK, FIRST PRESIDENT OF THE TURKISH REPUBLIC

Mustafa Kemal was born in 1880, the only son of a small clerk and later timber merchant at Salonika, which at that time still belonged to Turkey. His parents were of Albanian and Macedonian peasant stock. His father died when he was still a boy. His mother wanted him to be a priest, but he insisted on training as a soldier. After distinguishing himself at the Senior Military School at Monastir, he entered the General Staff College at Constantinople. There he became a member of the secret revolutionary society which wanted to free the Empire from the despotism of Sultan and Mosque, and to modernise the country under a constitutional government.

After a short imprisonment for his political activities, he was transferred by way of punishment to Damascus. After his return to Salonika where he was on the staff of the Third Army, he joined another secret organization, the Committee of Union and Progress. In the revolution of 1908 he took no active part, since he was strongly critical of the Young Turk Party, but assisted in the suppression of the Sultan's counter-revolution.

When Italy attacked Tripoli in 1911, he left the War Office at Constantinople to join the fighting troops in North Africa, and during this campaign and the Balkan wars of 1912–13 he gained further distinction. All the time he had found himself in opposition to Enver Pasha who, also a member of the Committee of Union and Progress, had quickly come to the fore. When Enver became Minister of War, he got Mustafa Kemal out of the way by making him military attaché at Sofia. Mustafa Kemal wanted Turkey to remain neutral in the World War, but after she had joined the Central Powers, Enver promoted him to the rank of general (pasha) and he took up a command under the German, Liman von Sanders, at Gallipoli. The victory over the British and Dominion troops was to a large extent due to his quite outstanding qualities as soldier and organiser.

Later he fought on the Caucasus front and in Syria, where he resigned his commission owing to difficulties with another German general, von Falkenhayn. All his experiences had made of him a fierce Turkish nationalist who resented any foreign interference, on whichever side it might be. After accompanying the Sultan's heir on a visit to the General Headquarters on the Western front, he organized the Aleppo retreat in Syria.

The end of the war brought the breakdown of the Empire. Kemal Pasha realized that the Sultan would not resist the Allies' demands as long as his own life and position were protected. Turkey was threatened not only with the loss of the greater part of her territory but also with the partition of Asia Minor, for many centuries the homeland of the Turks proper. Resistance could only be organised as far away from Constantinople as possible. A mission as army inspector to control unrest that had broken out in the eastern Black Sea regions gave him the excuse to go to Asia Minor. He landed at Samsun four days after the Greeks, with the Allies' permission, had occupied Smyrna. May 19, 1919, the date of his landing, is marked in the history books of Republican Turkey as the birthday of the Turkish national revolution.

From then onward his story is identical with that of Nationalist Turkey. Without him there would have been no War of Independence. He found people tired after nearly eight years of fighting, and ready to give in. Against overwhelming odds, through the strength of his iron will, his patriotism, his ambition, his genius as a soldier and military organiser, he created an army, and in the rôle of generalissimo with dictatorial powers led it to victory in the battle at the Sakaria river in 1921—and that after the Greeks had almost taken Ankara itself.

He was honoured for his victory by the Grand National Assembly who bestowed on him the title of Gazi (Victor in a war against the Infidels). It was by this name that the mass of the people knew him. The Turks, a soldier race, admired him most as their military leader.

It needed another of his victories, a year later, to drive the Greeks out of the country. On 6 September 1922 the Gazi entered Smyrna as 'Liberator of the Fatherland.'

When peace was made with the enemy, another struggle began—the struggle against those of his countrymen who were in opposition to his policy. Kemal wanted to make Turkey a modern state on western European lines and was determined that Sultan and Mosque had to disappear. It was clear that he could never seriously consider accepting for himself the Sultan's crown or the turban of the Caliph. Turkey had to become a republic, with Kemal as president; after all those centuries when Turks had lost their lives to build up and defend their Empire, the time had come when Turkey must concentrate on her internal needs and thereby at last gain her true independence and national sovereignty. This was his line of policy.

In the beginning he had to proceed gradually since he could not risk too strong an opposition to himself and his ideas. He founded the People's Party in order to have a reliable group of men and women to support him. On 29 October 1923, Turkey was at last declared a republic and Mustafa Kemal unanimously elected its president. That was undoubtedly a day of triumph for a proud man, but it marked only the first step towards the realisation of his plans.

In the years that followed there was not a single reform

that did not emanate from him, no subject on which he did not hold and utter very definite views. Soon nothing could happen of which he had not first approved. One by one he silenced his opponents. The Kurdish revolt in 1925 provided the excuse for the setting-up of the so-called Tribunals of Independence, which ruthlessly punished not only anyone directly connected with the revolt and the timely discovered plot against Kemal's life in 1926, but many whose guilt could never be really proved, including some of Kemal's oldest friends and collaborators. A number of important men were hanged, others exiled. (In this connection it is significant that eight men accused of having formed a plot against his life in October 1935 were four months later acquitted for lack of evidence—undoubtedly a sign that the country was being governed under more normal conditions.)

In his triple rôle as President of the Republic, Commander-in-Chief of the Army and head of the People's Party, Kemal became more and more certain of his strength. By 1930 he thought his position firmly enough established to allow a certain amount of criticism. He permitted the constitution of a Liberal Republican Party, under the leadership of his friend, Fethi Okyar, later, until November 1938, Ambassador at the Court of St. James's. Disturbances resulted which were brutally suppressed, and Kemal thought it wiser to revert to the former state of affairs.

Kemal himself always insisted on the description of the Turkish government as truly democratic, but at the same time he maintained that in no circumstances should progress be delayed by useless discussion or by party warfare. Turkey had to make good as quickly as possible the time she had lost during centuries.

In 1934 Kemal Pasha adopted the family name of Atatürk (Father of Turks) and changed the Arabic Kemal to Kamâl. He married shortly after the War of Independence, but divorced his wife less than two years later merely by writing out and signing a deed. His private life has often been criticised, but not even his enemies can deny his genius. He died on 10 November 1938, of cirrhosis of the liver, at the age of 58. Twenty-four hours after the announcement of his death, Ismet Inönü, the retired Prime Minister, was chosen as his successor. The very speed and unanimity of his election were proof of the stability of the régime. It seems safe to say that, as long as Turkey is left undisturbed, Kemalism will continue even without Kemal. Certain changes will be carried out by the new president, but it is unlikely that they will be changes of principle.

3. THE RULERS, THEIR IDEAS AND SOCIAL REFORMS

ISMET INÖNÜ

General Ismet Inönü, formerly known as Ismet Pasha, was born in 1884 at Izmir (Smyrna) as son of a judge and became a professional soldier. During the Great War he held various important commissions. In March 1920 he joined Kemal Pasha and the Nationalist forces at Ankara where the Grand National Assembly elected him Chief of Staff. After successfully beating off enemy attacks in the first battle of Inönü (a name he later adopted as his family name), he was made brigadier-general. When the War of Independence was over, the Gazi sent him as first delegate to the Lausanne Peace Conference, where he stubbornly held out against the Allies' demands. For a time he acted as Foreign Minister, and was in October 1923 made first Prime Minister of the Turkish Republic, an office which he held with one short interruption till his resignation in autumn 1937. Ill health was given as a reason for his retirement, but it is assumed that at last differences of opinion between him and Kamâl Atatürk, chiefly over foreign policy, had come to a head. Ismet has commonly been regarded as a supporter of the Turko-Russian friendship, in spite of his firmness against any communist activities inside Turkey, and of collaboration with the western Powers. In the past he has been rather overshadowed by Atatürk, but there was never any doubt that Ismet Pasha was the one man who could hold his ground beside him. He enjoys great popularity among the mass of the Turkish people, for whose lot he has always shown great concern, both in the army and during his many tours of inspection, which led him even to distant parts of the country. His deafness has made him rather taciturn, but he is an amiable man who takes a great pride in his happy family life. At the age of 54 he is still an excellent horseman, full of energy, alert, and observant. What use he will be able to make of his great abilities depends largely on political developments outside Turkey.

THE NEW CABINET

Certain changes in the Cabinet had to be carried out immediately after Atatürk's death, but it was not till early in 1939 that Ismet Inönü decided on what seems to be the more permanent personnel of the Cabinet. Dr. Refik Saydam, able and successful Minister of Health from the early years of the Republic till 1937, became Prime Minister in the place of Celal Bayar, who in his turn had held the office for little more than a year as Ismet Inönü's successor. Dr. Saydam, a man of 57, is an old friend of Ismet Inönü's.

Faik Öztrak, who hitherto had played no leading part in politics, was made Minister of the Interior and thereby automatically became Secretary-General of the Republican People's Party. Other newcomers to the Cabinet were Fikret Silay (Minister of Justice), Hasan Ali Yücel (Minister of Education), Hüsnü Çakir (Minister of Economics), and

Naci Tinaz (Minister of National Defence). The last mentioned, formerly Commander-in-Chief of the Gendarmerie, is the only professional soldier in the Cabinet. The other men come either from the Civil Service or from the professions.

Sükrü Saraçoglu, who during Atatürk's lifetime had for many years been Minister of Justice, and had deputised for Dr. Tevfik Rüştü Aras during the latter's frequent journeys abroad, became Foreign Minister. Dr. Tevfik Rüştü Aras, Foreign Minister since 1925, well known at Geneva and in many European and Near Eastern capitals, resigned in November and has meanwhile taken up his new post as Ambassador at the Court of St. James's in succession to Fethi Okyar.

The new Cabinet consists of experienced men who are not likely to embark on revolutionary experiments, but who will insist on a steady progress on the accepted lines.

THE CONSTITUTION

The Constitution was voted and published in 1924, although some of its provisions have been amended as the reforms of Kemal have taken effect and public opinion has become accustomed to changes. Thus for example the second article originally contained a statement that the religion of the Turkish state was Islam. On the face of it the constitution, although a written one, seems to be based on the same principles as that of Britain. The National Assembly (the Kamutay) has 'the legislative function and executive power manifest and concentrated in itself'; there is collective responsibility of the Cabinet, whose leader is selected by the President; the judges are protected from all intervention and subject only to the law. At the same time the Constitution lays down that all Turks are born and live free and are equal before the law and guarantees certain 'natural rights', such as inviolability of person, freedom of conscience, thought, speech and press.

The National Assembly is elected every four years by universal suffrage. According to the Constitution it meets annually on November 1, even without being convoked, and must have the Budget placed before it at the beginning of its session. The Assembly elects one of its members to preside over its deliberations and another to be President of the Republic during the Assembly's own term. The right of initiative in legislation belongs to the members of the Assembly and to the Cabinet, and laws when passed must be promulgated by the President within ten days or sent back by him to the Assembly with a statement of his objections. If after reconsideration the Assembly again approves the law the President must promulgate it.

On paper the constitutional power of the President does not appear to be any stronger than in France. In fact, however, his power is very great because he combines in his person not only the Presidency of the Republic but the Presidency of the Grand National Assembly as well as the chief command of the armed forces and the leadership of the Republican People's Party. Despite the maintenance of ministerial responsibility and many of the features of parliamentary government, all possibility of serious conflict between the Kamutay and the government has been eliminated. For the Republican People's Party controls the Kamutay and elects the President to whom it has given so much power.

THE REPUBLICAN PEOPLE'S PARTY

The Republican People's Party (*Cümhuriyet Halk Parfisi*) is the only political party in existence. It was founded by Atatürk in the summer of 1923 by transforming the 'Association for the Defence of the Rights of Anatolia and Rumelia (European Turkey)', which had played an important part

in the War of Independence, from a military organisation
into a political party. Thus Atatürk, victorious hero of the
war, was from the outset in a predominant position. The
Statutes adopted in 1935 named him permanent head of
the party.

The origin of the Party explains the leading rôle which
so many professional soldiers play in the Turkey of today.
Elsewhere the army usually contains one of the most
reactionary parts of the population, but in Turkey it was
for a long time almost the only group which—for reasons
of military efficiency—was allowed closer contact with the
West. Thus it formed the channel through which progressive
ideas entered the country. After the Great War and the War
of Independence, when Greeks, Armenians, etc., had been
eliminated, the army and Turkish civil servants were nearly
all that was left of the bourgeoisie. It is therefore quite
understandable that they came predominantly to the fore.

Many of the leading Turks who in the years of struggle
against Sultan and foreign invaders had been Atatürk's
most active collaborators desired after the War of Independence, when outward victory had been achieved, to set up
a liberal state on western European lines. Soon Atatürk's
line of policy forced them into opposition. Their ranks were
joined by those who wanted a resurrection of the old régime
and by Atatürk's personal enemies. How he silenced opposition and abandoned the idea of a second party has been
described elsewhere

In the early years the People's Party was looked upon as
the vanguard of progress on Kemalist lines. It was an in-
valuable instrument for the supervision of reform, a mouth-
piece whenever the President wanted to address his people.
(His famous six-day speech delivered to the second Party
Congress in 1927 gives the complete and fully documented
history of the Turkish nationalist revolution.) People soon

discovered that membership was practically obligatory if they wanted any position of importance, either as deputies in the Grand National Assembly, or as civil servants, provincial governors (*valis*), mayors, teachers, etc. Only people such as rich landowners could afford to remain aloof. Membership is nominally open to every citizen over 18 years of age 'who habitually speaks Turkish and has assimilated Turkish culture'. All minorities are thereby excluded, but even the Turkish worker or peasant, though generally encouraged to become a member, remains entirely without influence. On the whole the party is an instrument in the hands of the ruling class. It would be wrong, however, to consider it a mere rallying-ground for opportunists. Its members often represent the active, progressive-minded part of the population and work hard for the betterment of conditions.

The educational work is carried out chiefly through the People's Houses (*Halk Evleri*). These were started in pre-Kemalist times as part of the reform movement and in 1932 were taken over by the Party. Their number has now risen from about 13 to more than 200 and is still increasing every year. Eventually every town and village is to have its own *Halk Evi*. With their manifold activities they resemble English adult education settlements and are meant to propagate the cultural, social, and political ideas of the People's Party. In small towns the *Halk Evi* is often the only place where young and old, men and women, well to do and poor, can assemble regardless of Party membership to educate and amuse themselves.

The Party has six main principles, symbolised by six white arrows spreading like sun rays on red ground. It is republican, nationalist, populist (which here roughly means democratic, 'establishment of harmony of interests'), statist (where private enterprise proves insufficient, the state should reserve an active interest, especially in the economic field), secular (complete separation of Mosque and state), and revolutionary (signifying, according to its own explanation, that changes considered necessary need not always be carried out in an evolutionary way).

In 1935 a detailed programme was accepted, and in June 1936 a fresh stage was reached—the union between Party and state. The Minister of the Interior, Sükrü Kaya, became General Secretary of the Party, and the provincial governors (*valis*) automatically took over the presidency of the provincial Party sections. One of the deputies described this step as an expression of the totalitarian character of Kemalism.

Though general elections are held, they cannot be called free, since all candidates are nominated by the Party, or rather by its chief. Only after 1935 were a very small number of 'Independents' admitted to the G.N.A. (Kamutay). In these elections 13 Independents were elected as compared with the 386 members of the People's Party, who included 17 women. Of the 13 Independents, two were representatives of the Greek, one of the Armenian, and one of the Jewish minority. Owing to the increase of population, 422 instead of 399 members were sent to the Kamutay in the general election of March 1939, and the number of women deputies was increased from 17 to 20.

In the circumstances it is impossible to judge the strength of the opposition. The Kurds, a wild mountain people living east of the Euphrates, have periodically revolted, apparently chiefly for religious reasons. It is at least possible that precisely for these reasons the Kurdish revolts were welcomed by a section of the Turkish-speaking population in the east of the country. At any rate to this day the whole east is under a special military régime which can hardly be explained by any threats from across the border.

At the other end of Turkey, Istanbul, with its still numerous non-Turkish population, is heavily hit by the rise of Ankara, and must perhaps be regarded as less fervid in its loyalty to the régime than Anatolia proper. The influence of the remnants of the old régime, particularly the clergy, in Inner Anatolia has dwindled to complete insignificance.

But all these forces of resistance taken together are of no avail whatsoever against the régime. Possible divergences of view within the ruling group are of greater importance. There is still a not inconsiderable section of the Party that holds more liberal ideas than the rest, in regard both to politics and economics. And it looks at present as if this group were having a certain chance of influencing affairs. If the criticism of the government it has been allowed to make in the Kamutay since the last election develops it may profoundly affect constitutional practice.

Little opposition to Kemalist ideas, however, will come from the young. Communism seemed to find support from a few Istanbul students, but since propaganda against the People's Party on whatever grounds is forbidden, they remained completely isolated. On the whole it is safe to say that the young people are enthusiastic supporters of the present régime.

ANKARA

During the War of Independence, Ankara (Angora) was made headquarters of the Nationalist movement. It was then a decayed provincial town of about 75,000 inhabitants where only ruins remained to indicate the rôle it had once played in history. Though the town suffered from a lack of water and was infested with malaria, its position offered great military and political advantages. Right in the centre of Asia Minor, it was far away from Istanbul, which was then dominated by the Allies and the seat of a weak and wavering government. An easily controllable railway line connected the town with the Imperial capital. In October 1923, two weeks before the Republic was formally established, Ankara was made capital of the new Turkey. It was a symbolic gesture, indicating that Turkish interests were from now on concentrated in Asia Minor. And, of course, military and political considerations continued to play their part.

The new capital was set up at the foot of the old town which was built high on the rocks. Human will-power undertook the fight with the arid plain. Nature was defeated. The swamps were drained, the mosquitos destroyed, water led into the town from a distant lake. With a vast expenditure of labour and money the desert was made habitable. A German town planner was called upon to lay out a modern city with a ministerial quarter, dwelling houses, parks, playing fields, and broad tree-lined alleys. A modernised Oriental style of building, with arched doors, little towers, columns and decorations, was soon abandoned in favour of the square block style of 20th-century utility. Building is still continuing at top speed. By the end of 1935 the town numbered 125,000 inhabitants and optimists predict that by 1940 the number will be doubled. Whether they are right will largely depend on the tempo with which the country as a whole develops. At present neither Ankara nor Istanbul give the foreigner a true impression of life in Republican Turkey. The one owes too much to the past, to international trade and European influences; the other is too much a promise for the future to represent the country as a whole. It is one of the many contradictions in Turkey's policy that in spite of its desire to westernise the country, Istanbul, the most westernised Turkish town, has been systematically deprived of its once favoured position at the expense of Ankara.

NATIONALISM

Nationalism has taken the place of religion in modern Turkey, with Atatürk in the place if not of Allah, at least of his prophet. His picture hangs in every classroom, office, shop and coffee-house. His bust in bronze or plaster stands beside a million writing desks; the number of monuments erected to him is legion. Public speakers and journalists continually refer to him as 'Our Great Chief', 'Liberator of the Fatherland', etc. He has even been compared to Christ.

It may seem astonishing that this change has met with comparatively little resistance from the religious side, and the fact cannot be explained to any large extent by the use of force on the part of the government. It must be remembered that 'the vitality[1] which had been the heritage of the Turks from their wild nomadic life was gone. Creativity had been crushed by the weight of Islamic formalism, whose deadening hand had left religion a matter of ritual and precedent, had left law with its sanctions so deeply grounded in the past that progress was wellnigh impossible, and had made literature something Arabicised, foreign to the Turkish spirit, and limited to an exclusive, highly educated circle'.

Thus it had happened that Islam had become more of a political than a religious force, more a means of distinguishing the ruling race from the oppressed Christian 'rayah' than a doctrine of salvation. And with the breakdown of the Ottoman Empire, the political reasons for its maintenance disappeared. After the loss of the greater part of Turkey's European possessions, the destruction of the Armenians, and the exchange of populations between Turkey and the other Balkan states, very few Christians remained under Turkish rule. The Moslem faith therefore lost its meaning as a distinctive attribute of the ruling race.

[1] H. E. Allen, *The Turkish Transformation*.

The Nationalists, eager to modernise the country as the sole means for its survival, realised that the worldly power of Islam stood in their way. Besides, the religion of Mohammed was permeated with Arabic elements. As long as it remained the keystone of Turkish civilisation, it would be impossible to build up a Turkish national culture in a Turkish idiom such as the Kemalists desired. (To this day in India Islam is the greatest obstacle to the full development of Indian nationalism.)

Finally, Islam seemed to be inextricably linked with the idea of the Caliphate. The Sultan was the Caliph of the whole Moslem world, and it would have been difficult to destroy his power and the power of the old régime without thoroughly discrediting him in his religious dignity. The Caliphate was, moreover, likely to entangle Turkey in international obligations from which no secular advantage could be gained for the new state.

It was therefore quite natural that those responsible did not find it too difficult to foster in the place of Islam a sort of family pride in the new country, and so win the co-operation of the mass of the people in putting their house in order. They created a nationalism which found expression inside the country rather than in seeking to expand. That does not mean, of course, that the moment may not come when the Turkish leaders will ask a territorial price from any foreign power that wants to buy their favour, either in case of war or during the preparations for it. Should the quest for oil within the Republic's boundaries prove unsuccessful, the temptation to reach out for neighbouring oilfields will be very great. But it may be safely assumed that for a long time to come they will have no desire to let their nationalism flame up in war.

Once the War of Independence was over, they were only too anxious to live at peace with their neighbours, and they have proved it by the part they have played in the exchange of national minorities with various Balkan states.

The foreigner may often feel inclined to smile when eager Turks try to create the impression that progress in Turkey began only with the foundation of the Republic in 1923. Nothing can be created overnight, and in many ways Republican Turkey is only continuing the work begun in extremely difficult circumstances by the Young Turks and earlier reformers. Yet the foreigner need not withhold his praise. The essential thing is that the work is being carried on, and this in no mere superficial manner to impress the traveller.

In economic policy, Turkey is following in the nationalist footsteps of bigger countries. In her case there is some justification for a policy which in general must be condemned. Only by abolishing the Capitulations, the special rights granted to foreigners under the Ottoman Empire, could Turkey protect herself against the tariff-free influx of foreign goods and begin the development of her own resources.

RELIGION

Moslem laws and customs proved a hindrance to Turkey's modernisation and were therefore pushed aside. In his Six-Day Speech in 1927 Atatürk asked the Congress of the People's Party: 'Has not the Turkish nation for centuries been dragged into endless suffering and into the pestilential swamps of obscurity under this banner, rescue only being possible through great sacrifices?'

The reform work had to proceed gradually. The abolition of the Caliphate has already been described. The religious colleges and tribunals, the Ministry of Islamic Affairs and Pious Foundations were dissolved. The Presidency of Religious Affairs was attached to the Premiership, thereby giving the holder of that office the exclusive right to appoint and dismiss all priests, religious teachers, etc.

After the Kurdish revolt of 1925 all religious houses were closed down, religious sects and orders dissolved, fortune telling of any sort declared illegal. The dervish monasteries (Tekke) were abolished and the countless mausoleums of local saints (Türbe) deprived of official protection. Education was completely secularised, the training of theological students was taken over by the state, but within ten years the number of students dwindled to nil and the government again left the responsibility for religious instruction to private initiative. In 1934 the wearing of religious garments outside places of worship was forbidden.

The hat took the place of the fez, which was declared a sign of ignorance and fanaticism, of hatred of progress and civilisation. The veil was no longer considered obligatory for women, and in the more advanced provinces it was gradually abolished. European clothing was introduced, and dress coat and top hat is the official attire for civilians on ceremonial occasions. With the adoption of the new law codes all religious provisions for everyday life automatically disappeared. But the same new laws also guaranteed the freedom of conscience and religion, in accordance with Article 75 of the constitution. Later, in 1928, the constitution was altered by the removal of the declaration that the Islamic faith was the state religion, and of all other references to any particular religion.

As part of the language reform the Koran has to be used in its Turkish translation. The *muezzin* calling to prayer from the heights of the minaret does so in Turkish. Allah has become Tanri. Today all Kemalist wishes have been fulfilled. Religion is not forbidden, but is deprived of all worldly power and made a matter of purely private concern. We have already tried to explain why so little resistance was shown from the religious side. The young seem to have forgotten, or rather they have never learnt, to follow the call to prayer. Nationalism is their guiding star.

LAW

The Mosque had not only played an important part in education: it had also been a law-giver for the daily life of the people. Its place was now empty and had to be filled by the state. The great legal reforms which made this change date back to 1926. Their thoroughness and scope are un-equalled in history. Modern Turkey showed no scruples in taking what she needed wherever she could find it, and in one sweeping gesture she fetched the Civil Law from Switzer-land, the Penal and part of the Commercial Code from Italy, the rest from Germany. At the same time the whole legal procedure was thoroughly modernised. The Kamutay adopted all the codes *en bloc*—there was no time to be lost in endless debates.

Most important for the life of the ordinary citizen was the adoption of the Swiss Civil Law. It gave all citizens, whatever their race, religion, or their economic position, the same rights and duties. It also laid the legal foundations for the emancipation of women (which is more fully discussed elsewhere).

The greatest difficulties were encountered when the new laws came to be applied. Many of the old judges had to be pensioned off because they found it impossible to adapt themselves to the new system. Young men were hurried into positions of great responsibility. Meanwhile their professional education has been greatly improved. A new Faculty of Law was founded in Ankara where work is carried out on more Turkish lines than those followed at Istanbul University.

For many years, especially after the Kurdish revolt in 1925, special Tribunals of Independence acted as courts martial. Their harsh sentences created widespread resentment, especially since they served chiefly to uphold Atatürk's power, and they were at last dissolved.

In spite of excellent relations with Russia, any active propaganda for communism by Turkish citizens is treated as a criminal offence and punished by imprisonment. Prisons are still extremely primitive. To my knowledge the death penalty is only pronounced for murder.

Innumerable reforms affecting the daily life of the people have been carried out. The majority tend towards a westernisation of the country. Only thus could it be hoped— or so, at least, is the official opinion—to make Turkey an independent, powerful state in the council of nations.

In 1925 the Gregorian calendar and the 24-hour day were introduced; for the change-over from Friday to Sunday as weekly holiday the government waited till 1935, not quite daring to create too much resentment among the mass of the population during the early years of the Republic. Other important reforms were also held back for a few years so that people had a chance to adapt their lives to the new rules and regulations.

A new wave of reforms started in 1934. Old titles—religious, civil and military—were suppressed. New Turkish words were coined for the various military ranks. Today there are no more Pashas, Beys, Efendis. The only prefixes allowed are Bay and Bayan, which have become the Turkish equivalent of Mr. and Miss or Mrs. The government explained that it was undesirable in a democratic state to have any artificial distinctions between people of various classes.

Another law made the adoption of a Turkish family name obligatory. It was at this occasion that Mustafa Kemal Pasha became Kamâl Atatürk. Streets, squares, etc. were also given pure Turkish names. In spring 1938 Turkey was further brought in line with western Europe by a law that forbade haggling in shops and bazaars.

EDUCATION

Under the Ottoman Empire the majority of schools had been attached to the Mosque. Teaching was on the whole primitive and bigoted. The law, which early in 1924 abolished the Caliphate, also secularised education. Religion does not even appear as one of the subjects in the school curriculum. Article 87 of the constitution states that primary education is obligatory and free of charge for every Turk. It has preferably to be acquired in a government school. The private schools still existing, including missionary schools, have to conform to the principles adopted by the state. They are strictly controlled, and many of them have given up the struggle for existence. No new ones are allowed to be built.

Primary schools have five classes, in villages sometimes only three. Pupils can then go on for either three or six-year-courses to primary professional or secondary schools. Work can then be continued in secondary professional schools, which are very modern and quite excellent, or in universities.

The University of Istanbul, founded in 1871, was completely reorganised in 1933. About thirty German (chiefly *emigré*) professors were called to it. The Ankara University is a Republican foundation and is still in process of organisation. It has a purely national character and enjoyed the special protection of Atatürk.

Tuition is free in all government schools, including secondary and professional schools and universities, but generally boarders have to pay for their keep, an important fact since many of the pupils come from distant parts of the country. Most schools are co-educational—equality of sex is one of the main principles of the state. Corporal punishment, publication of school records, the grading of the pupils, or the granting of any special privileges to them on whatever grounds are forbidden.

In the first twelve years of the Republic the total number of schools has only increased from 5,000 to 6,650, whilst the number of pupils has more than doubled. The slow increase is partly due to the fact that old inadequate buildings have been closed down, and to the lack of teachers. In a speech in spring 1935 the General Secretary of the Republican People's Party admitted that only a quarter of the children of school age were as yet receiving some sort of instruction. Since then this proportion will certainly have been increased by the continuous efforts made to improve conditions.

The difficulties with which the government is faced can easily be imagined if one remembers how thinly populated large parts of the country are. With a daily growing expenditure for armaments, no money is available to carry out such plans as sending itinerant teachers into isolated hamlets and villages high up in the mountains or in the plain. But though progress has been slowed down, the day when all children will at least be taught to read and write is in view.

This basic teaching has been immensely simplified by the change-over from the complicated Arabic to the Latin alphabet. In 1928 a law was adopted that forced every citizen under the age of 45 to learn the new alphabet. Illiteracy was not abolished, but was at least considerably reduced. The last available figures, those of 1935, declare that 23 % of the men and 8·2 % of the women are now able to read and write. Atatürk himself, directly responsible for the change of alphabet, assumed the rôle of teacher in various towns and villages. Overnight the whole country was turned into one immense classroom. The story of those months has already assumed the importance of a saga in modern Turkey.

The fact that, by the official abolition of the Arabic

alphabet, very soon only students will be able to read the vast literature of pre-Kemalist times is considered rather an advantage. It gives the government one more means of control over the minds of the people. They are to look forward, not back.

This principle becomes dangerous if one remembers that little or nothing can be printed in Turkey today without official consent. Thus the knowledge of reading and writing may lead thousands of people to the absorption of propaganda, people who as illiterates might at least have preserved a certain independence of mind. Once again progress shows a twofold face.

One of the reasons for secularisation was the desire to base education on science. Frequently, however, the narrow-mindedness of nationalism has taken the place of that of religion. History is used as a means to prove that the Turks were the true originators of civilisation. It has even been maintained that the first intelligible words ever spoken were addressed to the sun in Central Asia, ancient homeland of the Turks. This admiration for the Turkish nomads has been accompanied by a similar glorification of the Hittites and other ancient peoples of Asia Minor who are also now admitted as ancestors. To discover further facts and fantasies about the past, a Society for the Study of the Turkish Language, and another for the Study of Turkish History, have been founded, at the wish of Atatürk and enjoying his active support until his death. The results of these studies are incorporated in the school curricula.

The Language Society has also been charged with the purification of the Turkish language from all foreign words, especially Arabic and Persian. If need be, Turkish words are created. The confusion due to the continuous changes, which were obligatory for journalists, etc., was so great that some time ago the process was slowed down and it was decreed that everybody, whilst endeavouring to speak as pure a Turkish as possible, should express himself in a way by which he could make himself understood.

Subject to these considerable limitations, the Turkish educational system deserves praise. Thousands of young teachers of both sexes work with unselfish enthusiasm even in lonely villages. Pupils are no longer forced to repeat their lessons like parrots, but are made to take interest in their work. Great importance is attached to self-government, savings clubs, school museums built by the pupils themselves, concerts, etc.

A Boy Scout and Girl Guide organisation proudly exists among the pupils of secondary schools, but these organisations, like all the others, are not allowed to affiliate to any international body.

Growing attention is given to physical training both of boys and girls. It follows the most modern methods and signifies more than anything the tremendous change brought about in the life of youth, especially of the girls. Playgrounds and sports fields are laid out in growing numbers.

Adult education is chiefly carried out by the People's Houses (*Halk Evi*), run by the Republican People's Party.

LITERATURE AND ARTS

At the beginning of this century the arts were predominantly under French influence. One of the great representatives of that period, the poet Abdülhak Hâmid, died in 1937 at the age of 86.

For a foreigner the achievements of today are often difficult to judge and should not be compared too strictly with western standards. It is certainly an advantage that the gap once existing between the language and literature of the educated and the mass of the people is slowly being bridged through the efforts of individual writers and poets, who under the Republic have at last found the active support of the government.

On the other hand, the fact remains that arts and literature, like everything else, have to be nationalist in character to find approval. Nazim Hikmet, one of the best of the younger poets, a communist, frequently found himself in prison. He was allowed to publish his non-political poetry, and some of his plays were shown in expurgated form. In 1938 he was shot dead in a railway carriage and the murderers escaped.

Before the war only Istanbul and Izmir had a theatre. The drama had no roots in the Turkish past. With few exceptions actresses were Greek or other foreigners—no Turkish woman was allowed on the stage. The amusements of the common people were shadow plays and concerts in the gardens of the coffee-houses. Now Ankara endeavours to train young Turks as actors and actresses, and the People's Houses encourage amateur theatricals as a means of fostering a national spirit.

Plaintive Oriental music is considered bad taste; a western music, including jazz, has to take its place. The Ankara radio station relays Viennese waltzes and Italian arias. But people are so poor that radio sets are still scarce. Only the bigger towns can boast cinemas. The excellent director of the Istanbul Municipal Theatre is trying hard to build up a Turkish film company in his and his actors' spare time.

Painting and sculpture, which under the Moslem law were forbidden to portray man, Allah's image, are at last free to develop. It is too early yet to expect any show of genius. Here, too, nationalism proves a stumbling-block. It is easier to win praise for a painting of Atatürk at the head of his people than for abstract art. The Government is often the only possible buyer. Even so, every artist has to look for a job to support himself.

The same applies to sculpture. The first monument ever

erected in Turkey (1926) was the one of Atatürk that looks out across the Golden Horn. In time every village may have one. It serves the dual purpose of focusing patriotism on the national hero, and of proving that Allah's wrath will not strike those who break his minor commandments.

In the past the Mosques and the Sultans were the only patrons of the arts. Architecture created jewels of incredible beauty. The crafts flourished. Painted tiles, silverware and carpets won the admiration of the world. The government is now doing all in its power to preserve these treasures and to continue the tradition in schools and factories. Excavations, carried out by foreigners on various historic sites of Asia Minor, are also officially encouraged.

POSITION OF WOMEN

The progress made in this century, especially in the last 15 years, is nowhere more evident than in the life of women. As long as Moslem rules governed the life of the state, men and women were not allowed to meet unless they were closely related, and even then only in their own houses. In the towns a respectable woman of the upper classes appeared in the streets as little as possible and only closely veiled.

Yet harems had begun slowly to disappear before the Great War. Only rich men could afford the four wives allowed to them by Moslem law, and their upkeep in the conventional manner. A few schools for girls were opened and, under European influence, gradually brought about a more enlightened attitude. The war further paved the way to women's activities in various fields. But this could only happen in some of the bigger towns. Among the peasants polygamy continued, partly as a means of securing cheap labour. Women and children were working in the fields whilst husbands idled in the coffee-houses.

Atatürk and the men around him realized that the country

could only advance if it made full use of the forces so long left dormant in women. 'Higher culture will only be attained by the education of future mothers. . . . They must be educated in every field of science. . . . Men and women will walk together in all paths of life', Atatürk declared publicly in 1923.

The change of attitude towards women was declared to be justified by the part they had played during the War of Independence, when many of them had carried munitions and food to the fighting soldiers, and further by the freedom and equality women had enjoyed under the old Turkish civilisation, before the Moslem faith was adopted and Arab influence began to predominate.

The Republican constitution adopted in April 1924 only speaks of 'Turks', without differentiating between men and women, except in the right to vote and eligibility as municipal councillors and deputies. In 1926, through the adoption of the Swiss Civil Code, a further most important step forward was made. The Code made polygamy illegal and made marriage a civil, not a religious ceremony. It gave women equal rights in case of inheritance and admitted them as legal guardians. It protected the wife, especially in case of divorce, which under the Moslem law could be brought about by a mere solemn declaration of the husband. In accordance with the Civil Code the wife can also demand divorce, though it is not easily obtained. Some time before the Code was adopted, Atatürk had divorced his wife by writing out and signing a deed.

In 1930 the Grand National Assembly decided to give women the right to vote and to be candidates in municipal elections. In 1934 they were at last also admitted as electors and candidates to the Grand National Assembly itself. Of the 17 women deputies who joined the Assembly in 1935, all but one were teachers. They all, naturally, belonged to the People's Party.

Thus the Party could declare in its programme of 1935 that it did not make any distinction between men and women. Legal, social, economic and political equality has been obtained. Today women of Turkey live, marry, dress, work and amuse themselves without any other restrictions than those imposed upon them by the often still primitive conditions in the country.

Only in a few backward towns do women still veil their faces. Among the hard-working peasant women, the veil was never customary. The *charshaf*, a sort of cloak covering head and body, but leaving the face free, is still widely used by the poorer and older women, partly because it is cheap, allows any odd garments to be worn underneath and dispenses with the hat.

As for jobs and professions, not a single official bar exists to the activities of women. They can be and are judges, lawyers, doctors, actresses, artists, stenographers, teachers and civil servants. They work in offices, shops and factories, and receive equal wages with men for equal work. These women are as yet an *élite*, but it will not be long now before the mass of girls in small towns and even villages begin to make use of the chances offered them.

The idea of equal duties was carried to its logical conclusion when in September 1937, as a first step towards military service for women, their military education was begun in *lycées* and universities. For the present the upper forms will have one lesson a week. In time they will even be taught to shoot. Among the women whose name and picture appear most frequently in the Turkish press is that of Sabiha Gökcen, a military pilot, adopted daughter of Atatürk's, who accompanied him on an important tour of inspection through the eastern provinces, probably to encourage other women to follow in her steps.

This attitude towards women is one of the important

distinctions between Turkey and the Axis Powers of Germany and Italy, to which she is often compared. In the space of surprisingly few years Turkish women have become the model for all the women of the East, especially those of the Moslem faith, many of whom have only timidly begun their emancipation. It is unlikely that elsewhere it will be carried through with anything like the speed with which it occurred in Turkey.

HYGIENE AND PUBLIC WELFARE

Under the Ottoman Empire the state as such had taken little or no interest in public health. It had been left to the Mosque or the various municipal bodies to found welfare institutions, hospitals, soup kitchens, etc. Under the Republic, a Ministry for Public Health and Welfare was set up at Ankara to centralise and develop work in this field. A sanitary and medical organisation was built up.

The fight against contagious diseases was taken up with the vigour of a military campaign. The chief enemy was malaria, which had always been one of the worst scourges of Turkey. The decline of civilisation in Asia Minor is often attributed to this devastating fever. Innumerable mosquitos found their breeding-ground in the stagnant waters or swamps caused by extensive rains and the formation of the soil-plateaus with inland lakes of all sizes, plains in which the rivers soon lose their speed and idle about in shallow branches and pools. By a special law adopted in 1926 the government placed the fight against malaria at the head of its sanitary programme. In eleven large areas, covering a fifth of the Turkish population, an organised campaign is carried on. Each area has as president a specialist who is directly responsible to the Ministry of Public Health. Each has a special laboratory and several dispensaries, and is divided into various sectors which are under the supervision of 90 doctors and about 300 health agents. The Malaria Institute at Adana, founded in 1928, serves as training centre for all Turkish doctors who are obliged by law to attend a three months' course for the treatment of malaria.

The disease is attacked from three sides. First, by mass examinations in spring and autumn, treatment of all afflicted persons, in most cases free of charge, further free preventive treatment by persons who can be kept under close supervision—school children, soldiers, workmen, etc. Secondly, by draining swamps and stagnant waters in which often the peasants are made to collaborate. Thirdly, by destroying the mosquitos and their larvae. People who disobey the regulations or refuse to carry out instructions are liable to punishment.

The results of these enormous efforts can hardly be exaggerated, and will be relatively greater the longer the campaign is carried on. Whole regions have already been freed of the disease. Thus Ankara, the new capital, once one of the worst affected places, is now completely safe. The effect is also shown in the diminished severity and extension of the epidemics. Optimists predict already the day when malaria will have been completely driven out of Turkey.

Similar campaigns, though on a less extensive scale, have been carried out against trachome (the Egyptian eye disease), which is now so far under control that no fresh cases of blindness have been registered for some time; venereal diseases and tuberculosis. In the case of venereal diseases, treatment is obligatory and can be enforced with the help of the police. Preventive measures were taken against small-pox, cholera and plague. For the needy, treatment of any sort is free of charge. Often compulsion was needed to break down the resistance of the people who considered disease an affliction sent by Allah and therefore inescapable.

The number of general hospitals, maternity homes and

dispensaries is gradually increasing, and their equipment being modernised. The Institute of Hygiene and the great model hospital at Ankara fully justify the pride taken in them by the authorities. Special attention is given to the education of future doctors, health agents, pharmacists, midwives and nurses. Foreign specialists have been appointed to Istanbul University whose medical faculty had a distinguished reputation, and modern institutes placed at their disposal.

Orphanages, nurseries and mental hospitals were founded. In the Party Programme a whole section is dedicated to further steps which will be taken for the protection of public health, especially of mothers and children. Regulations were issued in the interests of the workers who grow more important as the industrialisation of the country is speeded up. No state-controlled insurances of any sort exist as yet. The consumption of dangerous drugs is forbidden. The state holds a monopoly for the sale of opium and controls its production.

Voluntary organisations supplement the official work. The two most important are the Red Crescent (the Turkish Red Cross), and the Association for the Protection of Childhood. The Federation of Turkish Sports Clubs encourages sports —football and wrestling are the most popular—and provides sports grounds and playing fields. Lectures are given on problems of health, etc., even in small villages; films, wall newspapers, posters and pamphlets are used to enlighten the population. The work done would be more effective still if the mass of the population were not so desperately poor.

4. ECONOMIC STRUCTURE

AGRICULTURE

About threequarters of the population still depend for their livelihood on agriculture, the chief basis of the nation's economic life. In no field are official statistics more contra-dictory, but it may be as near the truth as possible to say that roughly one-third is arable land, one-third pasture, and one-third forests, mountains and waste land. Of the arable land less than half is actually under cultivation. This is all the more astonishing if one remembers that Asia Minor was in ancient times known and coveted for its fertility. Wars and neglect brought about the decay. Ruthless deforestation was only one of the symptoms. Today a bare tenth of Turkey is covered by woods.

The climatic contrasts are enormous. Harvesting may have started in one part of the country when elsewhere the peasants have only just sown their seed. Parts of Anatolia, for instance, the western coast bordering the Aegean Sea, are still among the most fertile regions of the world, whilst the bulk of the country is taken up by the vast central plateau which on an average lies 3,000 feet above sea-level and is used only as pasture for sheep and goats. High mountain ranges keep the rain clouds from travelling to the interior. During the long winter, cold winds howl across the snow-covered plain: during the short summer, the sun scorches the soil. None of the big rivers is navigable. They are either swollen by torrential rains or nearly dried up, and cut through uninhabited mountains or lose themselves in the marshes of the plain. Nearly all the great lakes of the interior are salt. These facts explain the great variation in the density of population. There are only 5 souls per sq. mile in the third of Anatolia east of Sivas, whereas the average for the whole country is 54. One can imagine the difficulty of governing such a country.

The majority of Turkish peasants, honest, quiet-living people, are extremely poor since over large areas the soil refuses to yield more than the barest necessities of life. Agricultural methods and instruments are still surprisingly primitive. In 1927, 1·2 million wooden ploughs were counted as compared with 210,000 iron ones, and in the absence of more recent figures it is difficult to say whether any decisive change has taken place since that time. In the early years of the Republic the use of tractors was encouraged by the supply of cheap petrol, but in view of general conditions the attempt failed and was soon abandoned. Oxen and buffaloes are still the prevailing draught animals. There were 7·2 million of them in 1937 (5·2 million in 1930), and only 723,000 (459,000) horses. The same reports mention 1·2 million (856,000) donkeys which are the chief means of transportation and 'maids of all work'. The number of camels is also increasing (from 78,000 in 1930 to 106,000 in 1937), but they are rather discouraged by the government as too oriental. The report on the number of livestock taxed in 1937 for the first time includes 4,000 pigs—another victory over Moslem tradition.

The average size of a farm is 10 acres. There are a few vilayets (provinces) where large estates are run with the help of itinerant labourers, i.e. in the vilayet of Diyarbakir, Turkey's eastern granary, around Aydin in the west where extensive fig plantations prevail, and in the Cilician plain where cotton is grown.

A comparatively large number of peasants do not own the land they till. It is still quite common for them to be tenants of large estate-owners who have little interest in their estates apart from the rent they receive, which may sometimes consist of as much as 50 % of the value of the crops.

No statistics are available concerning the number of peasant-owners and tenants, but in 1937, fourteen years after the foundation of the Republic, members of the government admitted publicly that more than half the peasants were still without land of their own. That proportion is more likely to be under- than over-estimated. These conditions existed in spite of the fact that the Kemalists claim as their chief distinction from the communists their own belief in private property as the foundation of a stable social system, and in spite of all the flattery paid to the peasants as the backbone of that system. Little has been done to put into practice the Party Programme of 1935 which states in article 24:

> It is one of the principal aims of our Party to make each Turkish farmer owner of sufficient land. It is necessary to enact special laws of appropriation in order to distribute land to landless farmers.

From 1930 to 1937—according to official statistics, about 320,000 acres of land, at a total value of 4·6 million ltq., were distributed among peasants, but as far as can be ascertained, this land was not usually handed over to poor peasants, but to those who returned to Turkey from the various Balkan countries with which agreements about an exchange of population had been concluded. It may be argued that these were probably the better farmers who, it was hoped, might favourably influence the more primitive peasants around them. There is also a provision that the state can give hitherto uncultivated land to landless peasants, who must undertake to cultivate it within three years, when it will become their property. No statistics are available to show how far the peasants have made use of this scheme.

All this is disappointing when one remembers that the state is still the biggest landowner. There had always been large tracts of government land, and after the foundation of the Republic the state took over all land that either belonged to or was administered by the Mosque. Yet there are excuses for the state's delay in land-reform. No one can doubt the tremendous possibilities which lie waiting both in Thrace and Anatolia. But the individual peasant cannot properly take advantage of them before far-reaching measures have been carried out by the government, of which proper irrigation schemes are only one, and these measures require both time and money.

Meanwhile the lot of the peasant has been eased, at least on paper. The tithe was abolished by a law of February 1925. A good deal of the peasants' debts to the state was cancelled, their bank debts converted into long-term credits, and the rate of interest, which occasionally had amounted to 50 %, was fixed at about 8·5 % for mortgages and 12 % for ordinary loans. The Agricultural Bank gives loans on mortgages or other securities at a rate of 1 % above the ordinary bank rate, which is at present 4 %. Credits granted by this Bank before 1931 have been converted at a rate of 3 %. On the other hand, though the whole system of taxation has been greatly simplified and regulated by law, the amount the peasant has to pay is still so high that he is nearly broken by the burden. In some regions the peasants have killed off their hens and are keeping wild pheasants instead—till these also come under the taxation laws.

Part of the money the peasants pay flows back to them indirectly. Schools and dispensaries have been built, model poultry houses placed under the supervision of the village headman, and play grounds laid out for the children. They profit from the railways which open up the country, and from other general improvements. A new law forces them to construct a road from their village to the nearest main road which the government or the vilayet have constructed.

With government help, great efforts are being made to improve the livestock. Sheep and goats still outnumber by far any other domestic animal. In 1937, 16·4 million sheep and 12·5 million goats (of which 3·6 million were mohair) were counted, together representing more than two-thirds of the total number of domestic animals (poultry excluded).

The corresponding figures for 1930 are 10·5 million sheep and 11·1 million goats (of which 2·8 million were mohair). Existing government breeding stations have been modernised, and their number increased. They are at the peasants' disposal for advice, and the peasants can also take their better mares, cows, sheep, etc., there to have them served free of charge. Great efforts are being made by these and other means to increase the number of merino sheep, high-quality wool being wanted for export, and even more urgently for the newly-opened state wool factory. The use of the horse is advocated in place of buffaloes, oxen, and donkeys, but the best propaganda will fail if the peasant lacks the money to buy.

As for wheat, the chief agricultural product, the government prides itself that through its policy Turkey since 1931 has changed from an import into an export country. Imports were stopped to encourage the Turkish peasant. In 1938 a special Wheat Board was created with an initial capital of 10 million ltq., which eventually will be increased to 15 million. Its task is to protect and control the price of cereals and to organise the sales abroad. The government will pay subsidies up to 1 million ltq. per year. Surplus wheat will be stored in large modern silos of which, by the autumn of 1938, fourteen were already in existence at various points of the railway lines. Better railway communications have naturally played a great part in a more even distribution of the harvest. At last, sure of a stable income and government assistance, the peasants have only too willingly increased the production. Even in bad years Turkey is now able to supply her own needs, not only of wheat, but of foodstuffs in general, a factor doubly important in case of war. Attention is paid to quality as well as quantity. In the case of wheat as of cotton and similar products the peasants are asked to exchange, free of charge, their inferior seed for first-class supplies from the government seed plantations. The quality and quantity of cotton produced is advancing each year under close government supervision, but it is only recently that cotton has ceased to be merely an article of export. In September 1938, six government factories had to be supplied with home-grown cotton. Rapidly growing state industries have also improved the peasant's lot in other fields. Sugar-beet cultivation, for instance, hardly known in Turkey not very long ago, now offers a safe income; four large sugar factories with an average annual production of about 65,000 tons demand steady supplies. But sugar is still far above world market prices.

Tobacco holds the first place among the agricultural export products (the second most important for home production is cotton, for export, opium). In 1925 the government took the tobacco monopoly out of the hands of a foreign company. Production, sale, and export are free under government control, but the cigarette manufacture in the country is a government monopoly. In 1930, Turkish tobacco production was estimated at 50 million kg., as compared to 50 million kg. produced in Greece and 25 million kg. in Bulgaria.

Many fruit trees originated from the coastal regions of Asia Minor. These regions, however, were badly hit by the return of the Greek minority to Greece after the War of Independence. For they, who had been the most progressive cultivators, set up in competition in their new country. Gradually, however, the Turks are adapting themselves to modern methods. Figs, hazelnuts, olives, and raisins are the chief products of this region, and are prepared for export in their dried state. In time it is hoped also to grow fresh fruit for export and for this purpose standardisation is encouraged.

But all these measures will be of little importance as long as they do not go hand in hand with the general education of the peasants. The government recognised this at an early stage and the already existing old-fashioned agricultural schools were either closed or modernised, and new ones erected in various parts of the country. Students were sent abroad for special studies, foreign experts brought in as instructors. In 1933, a very modern Agricultural Institute was founded at Ankara with German help and under German supervision. In the winter term 1937–38, 700 students were registered, of whom about 30 were girls. They came from all parts of the country, but too many of them were still town bred. After four years of study the students were expected to work, usually as agricultural instructors, for the first six or eight years wherever the government sent them, even in remote parts of the country. In 1937 the government stated that the number of these instructors would be increased to 1,600. It was decided in 1938 to divide this Institute into a number of smaller institutes where greater stress could be laid on practical work and local immediate needs.

A number of model farms were set up of which Atatürk's great farm near Ankara is the most outstanding. The results obtained on the latter are, however, of comparatively little value to the average peasant because it is obvious that it needs unlimited money to make a desert blossom, and the peasants are much too poor.

Experimental stations, and biological and plant pathological institutes were opened. Like all the other institutes they aim at close collaboration with the peasants in the surrounding districts. The peasants can always call for advice and are invited to attend lectures and special classes. Simply-written booklets and papers are sent to them. The People's Houses have a special department that is charged with establishing contact with the peasants and educating them.

Agricultural credit co-operative societies are greatly

encouraged by the government, but are only slowly developing, especially in the more isolated and backward parts. They were started in 1929 in collaboration with the Agricultural Bank, and under a special law were reorganised in 1935. In 1937, 591 co-operative societies existed with about 100,000 members in 3,600 villages, a mere fraction of the total number, with a capital of 4 million ltq. During the same year the Society gave credits amounting to 20·9 million ltq. supplemented by a further 16·4 million ltq. provided by the Agricultural Bank. The Bank accepts agricultural products from the peasants in payment of their debts and has generally been lenient after bad harvests. Co-operative societies for the sale of agricultural products were started in 1937. By the summer of 1938 32 of them, chiefly for the sale of raisins, figs and cotton, had come into existence, with a membership of 15,000. They handled produce to the value of 8 million ltq. during the first year.

Early in 1937, the government published a new and far-reaching agricultural programme. Its chief points were: irrigation systems, on the lines already started in the Adana region, in connection with the large rivers and for the Anatolian plateau, which were to be paid for half by the government and half by the peasants who may give their labour in lieu of money; the establishment of new credit and consumers' co-operatives and the gradual setting up of 1,000 government *combinats* (central training farms) of various sizes, chiefly in central and eastern Anatolia, equipped with sufficient modern machinery to serve the whole surrounding districts. No time limit was fixed for the execution of this programme. So far, little progress seems to have been made towards its realisation. Early in 1939 a great Agricultural Congress, announced and repeatedly delayed for more than a year, met in Ankara and in the main repeated the 1937 programme. To carry intentions into practice, a scheme for a big agricultural bank, the AK Bank (Agrikültur Kalkima, Revival of Agriculture) was launched. This bank will not only give credits, but at the same time distribute seeds and land, send out instructors, encourage a higher standard of agricultural production, etc. It looks as if at last the government were beginning to take matters in hand in a more thorough fashion.

Most forests are owned by the state but were long left undeveloped. In 1937 the forest service was reorganised and a new law was promulgated by which all trees and nurseries were placed under government protection. Peasants, who had often made a modest living by carrying loads of firewood on their primitive ox-carts or donkey's back to distant towns, have been hard hit by this measure, which none the less is essential in the interests of the country as a whole. (The use of charcoal is forbidden, but for the time being coal and coke are still insufficiently provided and badly distributed, and the mass of the population is too poor to buy these and the proper stoves which they require.) Afforestation has begun, though not to any considerable extent as yet. Nurseries have been laid out, two forestry schools opened, students sent abroad, and foreign experts called upon for detailed studies and advice.

No statistics are available about the number of agricultural labourers, chiefly because most of them are still itinerant workers. On the whole they live, like the rest of the population, on a very low level. Often they trek hundreds of miles to the next big estate, usually under the leadership of an elected headman who fixes their wages for them. They are hired by the week, and are apt to cease working the moment they have saved a few coppers. Agricultural wages may rise as the attraction of the new government factories increases and land reform is carried out. There are no insurances of any kind.

In conclusion it can be said that tremendous possibilities lie still waiting both in Thrace and Anatolia. Government officials have stated that the Turkish peasant on an average raises a 70 kg. crop where a Danish or Dutch farmer would raise 150. There is no reason why the area under cultivation should not be doubled in a not too distant time. Efforts so far made all go in the right direction. It can only be hoped that the combined expenditure for industrial development and armaments will not delay or even temporarily stop the carrying out of the agricultural programme.

INDUSTRY

Industrialisation.—The Republican government made industrialisation one of the chief points of its programme, for only in this way could Turkey gain true independence. During the first period, from 1923 to 1933, private undertakings were relied upon to carry out the necessary development. The 'Law for the Encouragement of Industry', May 1926, which granted special advantages, exemptions from taxes, etc., aimed at creating a favourable atmosphere for the free development of private initiative in industry and agriculture. The number of enterprises profiting from this law rose from 342 in 1923 to 1,473 in 1932, but by 1935 it had declined again to 1,161, though the capital value of the various enterprises was said to be higher than ever. Forty-five per cent of the total number were farming, livestock breeding, fishing and hunting enterprises, and 23 % belonged to the textile industry. In spite of all efforts the number of persons (workers, foremen, technical and managing staffs) employed in all the factories and workshops actually benefiting from the law amounted only to 69,000 by the end of 1934, of whom about 16,000 were women. Eighty-three per cent of the necessary raw materials for these factories were during that year supplied by the country itself.

316

In 1933, partly in connection with the world economic crisis, the state decided to intervene directly in the industrial development, and from that time onward dates the second period of industrialisation. The state renounced its attitude of neutral protector and embarked on a policy of state industrialism. Private enterprise was still encouraged but, at the same time a Five-Year Plan was worked out for the establishment of key industries by the state itself. The work was started in 1934. On the whole, government intervention in industry was dictated by the scarcity of the available private capital. Industries of vital importance needing a big capital outlay could generally only be constructed either directly by the state or with state help.

Reasons given for this state intervention were the necessity of changing Turkey into an independent, self-sufficient nation; of producing a weapon against the scarcity of foreign currency; of ensuring for the Turkish workers and farmers a stable home-market, and of protection against foreign exploitation. It was declared that the ultimate aim of the Plan was not the export of the goods manufactured and mined, with the exception perhaps of copper and sulphur, but the development of home consumption. From the very outset stress was laid on the fact that the industrial undertakings should receive their chief supplies from indigenous raw materials and agricultural products.

The following industries, producing consumable goods, were to be established according to the plan:

1. Cotton, hemp, woollen and artificial silk goods.
2. Paper, glass and bottles, porcelain.

Basic industries to be established were those for:

1. The manufacture of iron, coke and the by-products of coal.

2. The production of copper and sulphur.
3. Chemicals (sulphuric acid, chlorides, caustic soda, super-phosphates.

The estimated cost of the Five-Year Plan was 41·5 million ltq. Apart from that the state, *Iş Bankasi* was charged with the erection of a semi-coke (artificial anthracite) plant and a glass works, and with participation in the sulphur refineries, so that the total amount reached nearly 44 million ltq. This amount included the installation and floating capital of the works in question. The chief items were: cotton 18·5 million, iron 10 million, paper 3·8 million, semi-coke 1 million ltq.

To carry out this programme (apart from those tasks allotted to the *Iş Bankasi*) the government created in 1933 the Sümer Bank as a successor to the Industrial and Mining Bank. Its capital was in 1936 raised to 65·5 million ltq. A special law defined its object as the exploitation of the factories taken over from the Industrial and Mining Bank; the administration of state intervention in private industrial enterprises; the preparation of reports and plans of all new state industrial enterprises, which it was to create and manage, except those which were to be erected in virtue of licences granted by special laws; participation in, or support (to the extent of its financial capacity) of those industrial enterprises the creation or the extension of which were considered of profit to the national economy.

By September 1938, the first industrial plan was more or less completed. The greatest advance had been made in the textile industry. The number of spindles had increased from 94,000 in 1932 to 232,000 in 1937, the number of looms from 1,200 to 4,680. About 10,000 workers were employed in the 6 government cotton factories, of which 4 were equipped with German machinery. Together these factories can supply about threequarters of the former average Turkish con-

sumption of cotton thread and cloth. A wool factory, and
an artificial silk factory were opened in February 1938. Like
the cotton mills, sugar factories, etc., these rely on home-
grown raw materials.

In September 1938, a new Five-Year Plan was adopted,
mainly consisting of and extending the Three-Year Mining
Plan of 1937. The coal mines of the great Zonguldak basin
(Black Sea coast) were to be more rationally exploited, and
lignite, copper, chrome, lead, etc., mined on a large and
profitable scale. Before the Great War Turkish coal production had never exceeded 1–2 million tons per year. The 1938
production probably reaches more than 2 million tons and
after the proposed improvements it is hoped gradually to
raise this figure to 5 million tons. Naturally with increased
output the marketing problem will grow ever more urgent,
but the Turks trust in a further extension of trade with
certain European and Near Eastern countries. The Eti Bank,
founded by the government in 1935 with a capital of 20 millions ltq., was charged with the execution of the greater part
of the mining plan, and the carrying out of the electrification
programme.

The new Five-Year Plan further provides for the construction of a new port at Zonguldak, centre of the coal mining
industry, to be linked by rail with the new iron and steel
works at Karabük ; and a second port at Trabzon (Trebizond)
also on the Black Sea, but nearer to Russia—end of the
great trade route via Erzurum from Täbris, Iran; installation of 15 new plants (cotton spinning, jute, tinned food—
meat, fruit, milk—3 sugar factories, etc.) ; linking of European
and Asiatic railway line termini by ferry across the Bosphorus ;
2 large electrical power plants, at Zonguldak and Kütaya ;
production of synthetic petrol and cement; purchase of 28
modern merchant vessels, etc. An amount of 80 millions
ltq. (£13 millions) was provisionally fixed for the execution

of this plan. The greater part of it was provided by a British credit of £10 million.

Railways, roads, bridges.—Under the Ottoman Empire, railways were constructed and run by foreign companies, largely for political motives (Bagdad railway!). After 1923 the construction of railway lines held the foremost place on the list of urgent national enterprises. Foreign help was only temporarily admitted. The construction was financed entirely out of Turkish money. By the end of 1938, nearly 2,000 miles had been built in addition to the 2,540 miles which existed in Anatolia before the foundation of the Republic. The latter were slowly repurchased from their foreign owners and nationalised by the government, apart from the Syrian frontier line Fevsipaşa-Nuseybin (about 313 miles) about which special arrangements were made with the companies and countries concerned. Nearly all the bigger towns are now linked by rail.

Roads and thousands of bridges have been built, existing roads and bridges have been repaired. The most important road is the one leading from Trabzon (Black Sea) via Erzurum to Täbris in Persia. It follows in part the ancient trade route. A branch leads off from Erzurum towards the Russian frontier. The Turks hope with its help to recapture part of the overland traffic which the Russians have diverted to the Trans-Caucasian railway and Batum. In future roads will be built subsidiary to existing Turkish railways and not parallel with them so as to avoid competition. The roads so far constructed have still many defects, partly due to lack of skill, and partly owing to the difficult country and primitive methods of construction. There is no reason, however, to assume that they will not further improve in time.

Labour.—With the growth of industry the training and settlement of workers will become daily of greater importance. According to the general census of 1935, 660,000 men and women, i.e. 8·3 % of the population, were employed as workers or craftsmen. This number is unreliable owing to the peculiarities of the Turkish conditions. Many of the peasants, for instance, accept temporary employment in factories, on the construction of the new railway lines, etc., in order to earn sufficient money to pay their taxes. Only the number of labour days would furnish a reliable figure, but statistics based on these have only recently been started. For the efficient working of coal mines or factories relying on skilled labour, a sufficient number of settled regular workers is absolutely essential. The government has therefore undertaken the construction of 4,000 houses at a cost of 6 million ltq. to settle miners in the Zonguldak basin. Each house will have a small plot of land attached to it where the wife of the miner will work under the instruction and supervision of a government agricultural teacher. Workers' houses have also been built beside the Kayseri cotton combine and will gradually form an integral part of any government plants. The number of dispensaries and first-aid stations attached to coal mines and factories is to be further increased. Clubs, cinemas and People's Houses are opened to make life more attractive.

The proper training of skilled workers, technicians, and engineers has also been tackled to some extent. Some hundreds of foremen and technicians have been sent to Russia and Europe, scholarships have been granted for studies abroad, foreign instructors have been invited to Turkey to supervise work in factories and technical schools till Turks can take their place. On the whole the Turks are quick to learn, but less quick to understand, and it will naturally take some time till any considerable number of them will have adapted themselves to industrial life.

In 1936, the Kamutay (parliament) adopted a Labour Code following European ideas. Apart from the hygienic regulations it is only applicable to industrial establishments with more than ten workers. Labour regulations are based on the general assumption of a private contract between the employer and the individual workers. No rules for collective bargaining, in the proper sense of the word, exist, except provisions for the hiring of itinerant labour gangs on the basis of a bargain with the gang leader. Minimum wages are to be fixed in industrial establishments of public importance. Strikes and lockouts are prohibited. Provisions exist, however, for the settlement of labour disputes, i.e. disputes between at least one-fifth of the workers employed in a factory, and the factory owner; such disputes are referred to the government authorities, unless agreement is reached between workers' delegates specially elected for the purpose, and the employer. The 48-hour week is laid down in principle, but there exist exceptions for special kinds of work, such as bakeries, etc. In agriculture, during harvest time working hours can normally be extended to 11 hours per day. All regulations concerning the working day are liable to exceptions on special request to be granted by the authorities. No trade unions with any international affiliations are permitted. In some areas rudimentary local unions of workers seem to exist, but no national union has so far been formed in any branch of work, and it is doubtful whether any would be tolerated by the government. The fixing of wages and labour conditions in general is still partly an affair the employer can settle at his will, partly one left to the government. The workers themselves have little or nothing to say.

Much remains to be desired with regard to the conditions of agricultural labour, and of that greater section of urban labour which works with very little state protection in establishments with less than ten workers. As to industrial labour proper, its conditions at present are a good deal better than may appear from the legislative provisions described above. It must not be forgotten that, however low the standard of living of the Turkish worker may be as compared to any European level, his lot is without any doubt preferable to that of the average Turkish peasant. And what industrial labour there is, is still almost entirely recruited directly from the countryside.

There is a vague hope existing in Turkey of creating the perfect community in which the harmony of interests will make any social struggle superfluous. But it is too early yet to predict the shape which the social structure will assume. For a considerable time to come the workers, numerically and as a social force, will be much too weak to influence developments. The immediate importance of the Labour Code and all similar regulations is therefore negligible. They are, however, significant in as far as they reveal the government's attitude to problems of labour.

FOREIGN TRADE

Turkey was unable to adopt an independent economic policy until the signing of the Peace Treaty of Lausanne in 1923. One of the most important results of the Treaty was the abolition of the Capitulations—privileges which allowed certain citizens of some of the Great Powers to carry on business throughout the Ottoman Empire whilst they were subject only to the laws of their own country. They were exempted from all tolls and taxes, including customs duties. As a result of the industrial revolution, European manufactured goods were dumped on the Turkish market and soon killed all native industries. Thus Turkey began to rank merely among the producers of raw materials and seemed doomed to become a sort of colony.

After Lausanne, and especially after 1929, when Turkey at last achieved sovereignty over her tariffs, Turkey's policy aimed at the protection of indigenous agriculture and her

growing industries. Many concessions had to be made, however, for the sake of the various clearing agreements. The
tariff revenue was considerably reduced owing to the drastic
cuts in imports necessitated by the country's financial situation, and the endeavour in all circumstances to ensure a
favourable trade balance.

Most important items on the export list are tobacco, dried
fruit (raisins, figs, hazelnuts), livestock and animal products.
On the import list, iron and steel, machinery in general, and
cotton goods rank first, but these items—with the exception
of machinery—will be reduced as the country's industrialisation continues.

Germany ranks far ahead of any other country, both for
exports and imports. Her imports to Turkey are constantly
increasing (35 million ltq. in 1935, 42 million in 1936,
48 million in 1937, 59 million in the first 10 months of 1938).
Turkish exports to Germany jumped from 39 million ltq. in
1935 to no less than 60 million in 1936, thus creating a heavily
adverse balance for Turkey—the usual German manoeuvre
for obliging other countries to take more of her exports. But
in this case the manoeuvre was not wholly successful. Turkey
restricted her exports to Germany to 50 million ltq. in 1937
and to as little as 39 million ltq. in the first 10 months of
1938. Thus it is now Turkey who is heavily in debt to Germany and Germany who must make efforts to recover her
money.

Yet Germany remains by far the most important market
for Turkish goods, especially in view of the trade recession of
1938. Exports to the United States which had risen from
13 million ltq. in 1936 to 19 million ltq. in 1937, declined to
9 million ltq. in the first 10 months of 1938; while exports
to Great Britain stood at only 10 million ltq. in 1937 and
fell as low as 4 million ltq. during the first 10 months of 1938.

But the heavy fall of imports from Germany has given

Great Britain and the United States their chance which they
eagerly exploited. Imports from the United States which
stood at 9 million ltq. in 1936, rose to almost double (17 million ltq.) in 1937 and again reached 14 million ltq. during
the first 10 months of 1938. Imports from Great Britain
which had stood as low as 6 and 7 million ltq. respectively
in 1936 and 1937, jumped to 15 million ltq. during the first
10 months of 1938, owing to the new British credits.

On principle, Turkey wants to 'buy from her customers',
and in 1937 about 90 % of her trade was conducted under
clearing and similar agreements. But Turkey, like most of
the Balkan countries, could not fail to notice in the long run
that barter agreements have their disadvantages. Even if the
Turko-German trade had really balanced, there would still
have remained the impossibility of buying on the cheapest
market, and the lack of free foreign exchange. Thus Turkey,
as shown in the above-mentioned figures, has now started
again to encourage trade with countries which have no
trading restrictions. At the same time, certain modifications
have been introduced in her most recent clearing agreements
with a view to make them less rigid and offer greater scope
to private trading.

NATIONAL FINANCES

A stable currency and a balanced budget are the chief
aims of Turkey's financial policy. From the Ottoman Empire
the Republic inherited, apart from a very few million ltq.
in gold, nothing but debts in the form of uncovered paper
money and her share of the Ottoman Debt. The balance of
trade had been unfavourable for more than 40 years, the
country was impoverished, all important financial enterprises
were in the hands of foreigners. From 1919 to 1929 the value
of Turkish paper money sank from 374 to 1,007 piastres per
pound sterling, and the adverse trade balance had increased

from about 60 million ltq. in 1923 to 101 million ltq. in 1929. The reason for this state of affairs was partly that Turkey, as an agricultural country, had to import all manufactured goods, and partly that her own exports were of a seasonal character, thereby causing considerable fluctuations in the exchange. It is, however, important to notice that even during the worst period of the War of Independence Turkey never resorted to currency inflation. Energetic measures were at last taken to restrict imports and encourage exports, and from 1930 onward the balance of trade has always been in Turkey's favour, in 1937 to the extent of 24 million ltq. (about £4 million). The state intervened to protect and guarantee the value of Turkish money, and in 1930 a Central Bank of Turkey (*Merkez Bankasi*) was founded with a capital of 15 million ltq. It was given the exclusive right of issuing notes and controlling the currency. Turkish money was *de facto* stabilised in relation to gold. At the end of 1934, for instance, it was backed by a gold covering of 14 %. At the end of 1938, the £ sterling was quoted at 575 piastres.

Budget.—The Republican government has always insisted on a balanced budget. It was achieved for the first time in 1925–26, by extremely high taxation on the one hand and curtailed expenditure on the other. The whole system of taxation was entirely altered and modernised, and the tithe, most important of the direct taxes, abolished in 1925. But under different names the total burden has remained the same or has even been increased. In 1932 a special Crisis Tax and an Equilibrium Tax imposed further financial obligations. The comparatively small number of wage-earners and the salary-earning part of the population were hardest hit. A *Times* correspondent reported that in 1932 a salary of 100 ltq. per month (about £17) was taxed to the extent of 20·8 %. More important than direct taxation is indirect taxation which considerably increases the prices of many daily commodities. The third place on the income side of the budget is held by the revenues of government monopolies and tariffs. The most important monopolies are those for tobacco, alcohol and salt.

As to the actual budget figures, the amount rose from 140 million ltq. in 1924 to 248 million ltq. (about £ 41·5 million) for the financial year 1938–39, the highest figure reached so far. To a large extent the increase was due to steadily growing expenditure on armaments. Of the last budget £14·5 million, i.e. about one-third, come under the heading of national defence, for which previously extra-budgetary credits of about £20 million had been voted. £1·2 million are destined for the navy, chiefly to be spent on submarines and the improvement of the naval bases. Other important items are the creation of new civilian air routes, extension of the railways and roads, and the development of industry and agriculture. No new taxation was introduced to meet the increase, since it was hoped that existing taxes, etc., would yield a higher income owing to improved conditions. There were even promises of a gradual reduction of taxation during the next few years, but whether these can be fulfilled remains more than doubtful in the present circumstances.

Ottoman Debt.—The Ottoman Empire had suffered greatly from the fact that it had borrowed indiscriminately at extremely high rates of interest and on most unfavourable terms. Not only were the country's most substantial revenues used to guarantee loans raised abroad, but foreigners had also been entrusted with the practical control of Turkey's finances. On the eve of the Great War, the Ottoman public debt stood at 158·6 million gold ltq. In the budget of 1914–15, the foreign debt annuities absorbed more than one-third of the total budget estimates (in comparison, 1·6 % was reserved for public works, and the same for education). The

Treaty of Lausanne at last gave Turkey sovereignty over her finances (apart from the control over tariffs which she gained in 1929). At the same time the total amount of the Ottoman Debt was fixed at 131 million gold ltq., of which 85 million were allotted to Turkey. Turkey defaulted, however, and twice—in 1928 and 1933—new concessions were made. In 1933 the debt was reduced to 8 million gold ltq. at 7·5 %, the annuity to 0·7 million, and the total amount of all Turkish debts was fixed at 17 million gold ltq. Owing to lack of foreign currency, etc., the agreement was once again broken by Turkey, so that in 1938 still further concessions on both sides were made. Whether Turkey will fulfil her obligations to the 'Council of the Repartitioned Public Debt of the Former Ottoman Empire' which is now administering the debt remains to be seen.

Loan policy.—After the experiences of the Ottoman Empire, the Republic was naturally reluctant to contract large loans abroad, quite apart from the fact that foreign money was difficult to obtain on favourable terms. No private Turkish capital was available to finance industrial and other enterprise on a large enough scale, and the state had therefore to take over this task and provide the greater part of the necessary money out of the ordinary budget. Railway construction, for instance, was largely financed in this way— during the first 12 years 282·3 million ltq. were provided for this purpose out of budget revenue. Foreign private business enterprise, collaborating in the industrial development, granted short-term credits, but they proved to be very expensive, and Turkey found herself faced with great difficulties when the results of the world economic crisis made themselves felt. But with the gradual stabilisation of the internal situation it became possible to call upon long-term internal loans to provide the necessary working capital, especially for the continuation of the railway construction.

Germany and Soviet Russia helped on the basis of special arrangements. Russia, for instance, chiefly for political reasons, set up and delivered the machinery for the great cotton combine in Kayseri on a 20-year interest-free credit of £1·6 million. The American-Turkish Investment Corporation granted the only foreign loan (£10 million) in the ordinary sense.

At the same time Turkey adopted the policy of gradually buying out most of the foreign companies which still held vital controlling interests in Turkish railways, coal mines, telephones, etc. Only a few of these now remain. The Turkish policy was dictated not only by Turkey's nationalism, but by economic necessities, and in the interest of far-reaching reorganisation.

Towards the end of 1937 it was felt that matters needed energetic speeding-up, and with the replacement of Prime Minister Ismet Inönü by Celal Bayar, who had been Minister of Economics, a certain change of policy took place, and it was decided to finance the great Three-Year Mining Plan, and later the second Five-Year Plan, chiefly by foreign government credits. Negotiations were started with Great Britain, and on 27 May 1938, the British parliament granted two 10-year credits to the total amount of £16 million, i.e. £10 million to enable Turkey to develop her national equipment and resources by the purchase of goods and machinery manufactured in Great Britain, and a further £6 million for the purchase of military supplies in Great Britain. Delivery has to be completed by the end of 1940.

The negotiations were difficult because the service of the credits was to be covered by delivery of Turkish goods, and Great Britain had so far offered only a very restricted market. In spite of improvements in recent years, Turko-British trade in 1937 only reached the amount of £1·6 million each way, a mere 50 % of what it had been in 1927 when

Turkish trade had not yet been so completely restricted by clearing agreements, etc. It was finally decided to pay the service of the new credits out of the proceeds of the mineral output of the mines which were to be developed under the Five-Year Plan. A new office, the Anglo-Turkish Commodities Ltd., was set up in London to organise the sale of Turkish metals, mineral ores and concentrates, coal, wheat, timber, etc. At the same time Turkey agreed to eliminate as far as possible the difficulties which had arisen out of the Anglo-Turkish Clearing Agreement. Some time previously, in 1936, a special £3 million credit had already been granted for the erection of the Karabük steel works by the firm of Brassert, London, guaranteed by the British Export Credits Guarantee Department, which also assumed responsibility for the new £10 million credit.

It is obvious that the transaction was of an essentially political character. The *Financial News* said on 30 May 1938: 'It is in keeping with British tradition to grant financial assistance to potential allies'. And the *Financial Times*: 'If activities of this kind bear a suspicious resemblance to those followed by the Great Powers before 1914, the necessities of the times must be blamed'. But hopes of stemming the German economic and political advance all along the Balkans by this timely support of Turkey were to a certain extent disappointed. Barely six months after the British credits had been granted, it became known that the Turkish visit of the German Minister of Economics, Walter Funk, immediately after the Czechoslovak crisis, had resulted in a German credit to Turkey of 150 Million RM (about £12·6 million). It was pointed out that the loan was merely the outcome of the new Turko-German Trade Agreement signed in Berlin last July, and that Germany during recent years had in any case received nearly half of Turkey's total export, but even so British apprehension seems not altogether unjustified. As far as Turkey is concerned, it is not surprising that she takes whatever she can get.

5. FOREIGN POLICY

ASIA MINOR is the bridge between European and western Asiatic culture; and the Arabian Caliphs strove constantly to control the key points of the roads from Europe to central and eastern Asia. The Ottoman Empire realised this ambition for centuries by the possession of Constantinople, Cairo, Damascus and Bagdad.

The new frontiers of Turkey, after the Treaty of Lausanne, did not alter her position as a bridge between Europe and Asia: Constantinople and Thrace connected Turkey with Europe, whilst the problems and frontiers of Anatolia bound her to the political sphere of western Asia. The growth of national states and the entanglement of the East in the political and economic affairs of Europe excluded the possibility of the restoration of a western Asiatic Empire: sovereignty gave place to a system of alliances.

Kemal did not conduct foreign policy from theory, but according to the dictates of geography and the needs of the time. He therefore declined both an alliance of Moslem states on a religious basis and an alliance of Turkish peoples on a racial basis. Instead of these, two definite systems of political alliance determined his relations with the Balkans and with western Asia, and by participating in both these systems, Turkey emphasised and strengthened her dual position as a European and Asiatic state. The Balkan Pact was concluded with Greece, Yugoslavia and Rumania and the Western Asiatic Pact ensured friendship with Iraq, Iran and Afghanistan. Turkey's influence—if not her dominion—stretches, as in the heyday of the Ottoman Empire, from the Illyrian coast and the frontiers of Hungary to the Persian

Gulf. The Turko-Egyptian friendship extends the Turkish sphere of influence as far as the Red Sea and North Africa.

The westernisation of the East is manifest in the replacement of the Islamic theocracy by national states, characterised by organisation and development along military, technical and industrial lines. Westernisation brought with it political, and also economic partners and adversaries among the European powers. The latter have vital interests in south-east Europe and western Asia; these are strategic in Greece, Syria, Palestine, Egypt, Turkey, and economic in Rumania, Iraq, Iran, Egypt and Turkey. In many cases these countries lie on the route to their colonial possessions. But the new situation created by modern Turkey no longer permits them to use the Near East to further their ends at will.

Western Europe created the League of Nations as an international political organisation. By becoming a member, Turkey had a share in such results as it was able to achieve. She has distinguished herself by scrupulous adherence to her international obligations. At Geneva she settled and confirmed her relations with the western Powers, revised the Treaty of Lausanne (in the matter of the Straits) and extended her sphere of influence (Alexandretta).

Thus, with her peculiar geographical position as a basis and supported by a modern military organisation, Turkey has acquired a status in the diplomatic world which makes her a factor of importance in international politics, reaching far beyond the frontiers of the country.

THE BALKAN PACT

The Treaty of Lausanne and the exchange of populations ended the centuries-old dream of the Greeks of a new Greece on both sides of the Aegean Sea, including Constantinople. Greece and Turkey had settled their national frontiers and their common economic position now called for neighbourly co-operation between the two countries. Psychological barriers were, however, not overcome until the Peace Treaty was put into execution. With the appointment in 1925 of the first Turkish Ambassador to Athens since the war, relations between the two countries began to improve, but it was characteristic that the Greco-Yugoslav treaties in 1926 and the rumour of a Greco-Italian pact in the same year caused considerable anxiety in Turkey.

Throughout the third decade of this century a regional pact of the Balkan states on the pattern of the Locarno Pact had been discussed. At first such projects were merely a reflex of the antagonism between France and Italy, both of which aimed at a Balkan alliance to consolidate their power, but at the close of the 'twenties the idea of such a pact took shape in the Balkan states themselves. It was frustrated in the first place by the relations of Greece and Bulgaria and those of both to their other neighbours. Greco-Yugoslav relations were normalised first. At the beginning of 1929, Turkey and Bulgaria concluded a treaty of neutrality and arbitration, and in 1930 a commercial treaty. The points of variance between them were the existence of minorities in both countries (800,000 Turks in Bulgaria and 11,000 Bulgarians in East Thrace, after about 200,000 Bulgarians had returned). At the end of 1929, negotiations opened between Greece and Turkey which led, in October 1930, to a pact of friendship. This began a new era in the relations between the two countries.

Thus the main questions in dispute in the Balkans were settled, with the exception of those between Greece and Bulgaria, and Bulgaria and Yugoslavia. In the same month in which the Turko-Greek Pact was concluded, the first Balkan Conference met at Athens; the countries represented were Albania, Bulgaria, Greece, Yugoslavia, Rumania and

333

Turkey. They discussed the possibilities, organisation and desirability of a Balkan union, and the measures to be taken for the economic and spiritual rapprochement of the Balkan states. The result was the establishment of a permanent office to deal with the problems raised. Albania's dependence on Italy and Bulgaria's revision claims did not permit of a more extensive union, and it was desired above all not to achieve this end without the inclusion of Bulgaria.

In 1930–31 Turko-Greek friendship was strengthened, and this enabled Turkey to act as mediator at the second Balkan Conference (Ankara, 1931) and, in particular, to improve Greco-Bulgarian relations. In the following year a new era in Turko-Greek relations dawned with the establishment of a postal union.

Formerly, the main obstacle in the way of a Balkan pact had lain in the relations between Yugoslavia and Bulgaria. In 1933 a rapprochement was brought about between the two, and Turkey and Greece endeavoured to effect a closer connection with Bulgaria. A new treaty guaranteed the inviolability of their frontiers, the fullest mutual consultations, and reciprocal representation at international conferences. After the conclusion of the Turkish pact of friendship and non-aggression with Yugoslavia and Rumania the treaties between these three countries and Greece were completed.

There was no further obstacle in the way of a pact between these four states, but it was still felt that a Balkan pact without Bulgaria would be incomplete. Repeated attempts to reach a conclusion were wrecked by Bulgaria's revisionist attitude, and in February 1934, promoted by the danger of Italian expansion, a pact between Greece, Yugoslavia, Rumania and Turkey was concluded, to ensure peace in the Balkans, guarantee frontiers and provide for consultation between the signatories.

All this was accomplished by the free initiative of the

334

Balkan states and without the collaboration of the Great Powers, and it was the first instance of a Balkan union which was not aimed at weakening Turkey. On the contrary, modern Turkey is more than an important factor in the alliance; owing to her position and to the fact that she does not take any great part in central European questions, Turkey is sought as an adviser by the other parties of the alliance.

The desire of Greece to avoid collisions with non-Balkan Powers has led to the restriction of the obligations of the pact (Greek armed assistance for Yugoslavia in the event of war between Yugoslavia and Italy and Turkish help for Rumania in a Rumano-Russian war, will thus not be forthcoming). The power-policy value of the Balkan alliance is thus reduced, but not destroyed, for with the danger to peace from the collapse of collective security and with the new struggle for power between the larger countries, a tendency towards isolation and neutrality has become manifest among the smaller nations (Belgium, Sweden). In the attempts to maintain regional neutrality in the event of a conflict between the Great Powers, or in any attempt to revive a system of collective security, the Balkan Alliance might have an important part to play.

As long as Bulgaria remained aloof from a Balkan union, and her revisionist tendencies made her to a certain extent the tool of Germany and Italy, peace in the Balkans was not assured.

The Bulgar-Yugoslav Pact paved Bulgaria's way to a closer relationship with the Balkan Union (1937). In 1938 Bulgaria concluded with the Greek President of the Balkan Union a pact in which she made a promise of non-aggression against the members of the Union. In return she received the right to military equality. The simultaneous removal of the demilitarised zones on the frontiers of Bulgaria, Greece and

Turkey did away with the last restrictions on Turkish sovereignty and the consolidation of the Balkans again advanced without any sponsoring on the part of the Powers.

THE WESTERN ASIA PACT

Before the war there were three states in western Asia (excluding British colonies and protectorates); after it there were nine (independent states or mandated countries on the way to independence): Afghanistan, Iran, Iraq, Palestine, Saudi Arabia, Syria, Transjordan, Turkey and Yemen. The religion of Islam binds the majority of the population together, and this fact has not helped to promote relations between secular Turkey and the western Asiatic states. It is true that the former took part in the Congress of Islam at Mecca in 1926, but she was strongly opposed to that held at Jerusalem in 1931. Turkey, said its Foreign Minister at that time, will not take part in any home or foreign political system which uses religion as a political instrument, thus leading the nations away from the path of progress.

Turkey's inclination towards an alliance with the other western Asiatic states arose from the situation at the end of the war, when western imperialism threatened the independence of the whole of western Asia. It was at that time that the USSR became the champion of western Asiatic independence, stimulating dormant national consciousness to struggle against imperialism (1921). The USSR not only supported Turkey during the War of Independence; she also aided Iran and Afghanistan to protect themselves against British activities. Under Russian supervision, a comprehensive system of individual treaties came into being at Moscow in 1921, through which the three states severally entered into alliance with one another, except for Turkey with Iran, and with the USSR. Between 1925 and 1928 the treaties were renewed and enlarged, and supplemented by the Turko-Iranian treaty in 1926.

In the meantime the western Asiatic states, all three of which had from the start excluded Bolshevik propaganda and avoided dependence on the USSR, outgrew Russian tutelage. By the middle of the 1920's it was clear that western imperialism no longer menaced western Asia, but with the consolidation of the USSR, expansionist tendencies from that quarter seemed not out of the question. Friendly though cool relations between western Asia and Moscow were preserved.

The states continued the work of clearing up the points of variance. Between Turkey and Iran stood centuries-old frontier disputes, due to the division of Kurdistan between the two countries. The attempted Turkification of the Kurds in eastern Turkey led to fresh disputes which occasionally threatened to bring about a break in diplomatic relations. The 1926 treaty bridged the old quarrels for the first time, and in 1928 there followed a treaty of close economic co-operation, which was strengthened by the extension of the old road from Tabris to Trabzon. In 1932 Turko-Iranian relations were put on a firm and definite footing with the establishment of a frontier arbitral court.

Turko-Afghan relations remained constant, as they were based on the most comprehensive of the western Asiatic treaties. Turkey's success at reconstruction after the war induced King Amanullah to summon Turkish advisers (including a military and a medical mission) to his country towards the middle of the twenties.

Frontier problems also divided Iraq from Turkey and Iran. Up to 1926 the dispute centred in the Mosul area between Turkey and Iraq, but since the frontiers were finally settled, relations between the two countries have been most cordial, and were further improved in 1932 by a Turko-Iraq treaty.

A frontier dispute between Iran and Afghanistan was

337   Y

settled in 1935 through Turkish mediation, as was the Iraq-Iran frontier dispute in 1937.

Thus the points of difference between the western Asia powers were all removed and the solidarity between Turkey, Iran and Afghanistan was shown by their common procedure at the disarmament conference in 1933. In 1935 negotiations began for a Middle-Eastern Pact. The initiative for this was taken by Iran and was in accordance with the statement of the Turkish Premier in October 1936 to the effect that collective security was the only remedy for international disputes, but that it could only work on the basis of regional organisation.

In July 1937 such a Pact was concluded between Afghanistan, Iran, Iraq and Turkey. It guarantees the inviolability of frontiers, provides for reciprocal non-aggression, excludes intervention in internal affairs and provides for consultation in all international questions affecting common interests.

By her alliances with Arabia and Yemen, Iraq forms the bridge between the Middle-East Pact states and Arabia, whilst Turkey and Egypt have had a pact of friendship since 1937.[1] A new diplomatic reality has replaced the Pan-Islamic idea and given western and middle Asia added importance in the international struggle for power.

In this connection the possibility of conflicts, caused by national differences between the Middle East states (as for example that between Turkey and Syria over the Hatay) should not be overlooked.

TURKEY AT THE LEAGUE OF NATIONS

At first Turkey saw in the League of Nations an instrument of victorious western European imperialism. To what extent the change in Russian policy to the League after the Japanese

[1] During the Abyssinian war there was talk of a Turko-Egyptian military agreement. In 1937 Turkey suggested that Egypt should join the League of Nations.

invasion of Manchuria influenced her is hard to say. Barely a year after Japan's attack on China, Turkey became a member (July 1932); in September, with the active support of Greece, she was given a place on the Council.

The Italo-Abyssinian war placed Turkey in the forefront of the political stage. As late as the autumn of 1935 she was exporting coal, corn and cattle to Italy, but in November she accepted Sanctions and the Istanbul port authorities refused to supply Italian ships with oil and coal. In October 1935 Turkey and the other Balkan Pact states declared that they would fulfil their Covenant engagements and support Britain in the event of an attack by Italy. Britain and Turkey were drawn more closely together by a special agreement regarding the use of Turkish ports by the British fleet. The Balkan Union, pursuing a united policy in harmony with the Little Entente (Yugoslavia and Rumania being members of both), attained for the time being a new level of importance. In December 1935 Turkey, with Poland, opposed Laval's efforts to get the Hoare-Laval plan adopted by the League of Nations. In March 1936 Turkey, together with Greece, Yugoslavia and Rumania, and in accordance with her obligations under the Covenant, supported the policy of oil Sanctions, which the French Foreign Minister, Flandin, was endeavouring to prevent. On Italy's inquiring how the Sanctions policy was compatible with the Italo-Turkish pact of friendship of 1928, Turkey replied that Covenant obligations took precedence of all others. Turkey was desirous of setting up international machinery to ensure the independence of every country.

In the spring of 1936, however, the policy of Sanctions and collective security broke down altogether, although as late as May 1936 the Turkish Foreign Minister professed belief in collective security, but added that the greatest vigilance was required for national defence.

Italy's conquest of Abyssinia and the remilitarisation of the Rhineland fundamentally altered power policy relations in Europe. The precedent created by Germany and the entanglement of Britain in the conflict with Italy furnished Turkey with an opportunity of revising the Lausanne Straits convention; Turkish diplomacy again showed itself alert to make use of a given situation. It would have been possible to have altered the terms of the treaty unilaterally after the German example, but adherence to treaties was psychologically more advantageous at the moment and more useful for propaganda purposes, without jeopardising chances of success.

The revision of the Straits convention.—In April 1936, Turkey demanded a revision of the statute governing the Straits. At the Disarmament Conference of 1933 she had ventilated the matter for the first time and she referred to it again at Geneva in the two following years. In 1935 she was supported by the USSR, who considered the Lausanne settlement inadequate in its existing state. Turkey could thus be assured of Soviet support, but Britain and France also favourably received the Turkish demands. Italy's increase of power caused England to welcome a counterweight in the east Mediterranean, even though this was favoured by the USSR. France welcomed the strengthening of Russian influence in the Mediterranean, thus making the Franco-Russian pact more effective.

A conference to consider a new Straits statute was held at Montreux in June and July 1936. Its most important result for Turkey was the full restoration of her sovereignty in the Straits area. She received the unrestricted right to occupy and fortify the Dardanelles and Bosphorus.

The Straits remained open to commercial vessels, and in peace time also to warships of the Black Sea states, without restriction. On the other hand the size, number, armament and period of stay of vessels of other nations were greatly limited, both in the Straits and in the Black Sea. During a war the Straits would be closed to vessels of the Black Sea states, except if, under the Covenant obligations, they were proceeding to the aid of an attacked nation. If Turkey were herself at war, the granting of the right of passage would be left to her discretion.

Soviet Russia had combined the aim of Czarist Straits policy with her own aims of 1923 (freedom of passage and Turkish sovereignty), and attained both. For the first time since the beginning of the struggle for the Straits, Turkey, Britain and Russia were at one. This occurred largely through the opposition of all three states to Italian expansion, but it was only made possible by the real independence of Turkey. Her free right to dispose of the Straits considerably extended her power and significance. The Montreux convention was one of the most important stages in the revision of post-war treaties.

The revision of the Statute of Alexandretta.—The Sanjak (administrative district) of Alexandretta, now called the Hatay, to which belongs the city of Antiakije (Antioch), comprises 4,000 sq. km. That the majority of the population speaks Turkish is undisputed, but the predominance of persons with a feeling of Turkish nationality is doubtful. Alexandretta has a good harbour and one capable of development; it is important as being the starting point for Aleppo and the upper Euphrates valley. By the Franco-Turkish agreement of 1921 the Hatay became a part of France's Syrian mandate. This agreement provided for cultural and linguistic freedom for the population, and a further agreement in 1926 laid down special arrangements for autonomy as regards finance, education and local administration.

In 1936 France concluded with the Syrian Government a treaty for the termination of the mandate and the establishment of Syria's independence. The Hatay was not mentioned. Turkey feared that the independent Syrian state with its Arab majority might oppress the Turkish population of the Hatay. The Foreign Minister put forward a number of demands: national independence for the Hatay and its inclusion in a federation with Syria and Lebanon, the demilitarisation of the zone and the lease of part of the port of Alexandretta to Turkey. The demands were based on the supposed Turkish majority in the Hatay and on unconfirmed reports of oppression. In October 1936 the Turkish government attempted to settle the matter by direct negotiations with France, but failed. Unrest followed in Antiakije, and there were reports of mobilisation and a warlike attitude on the part of Turkey.

France submitted the dispute to the League of Nations. In January 1937 a convention was arrived at, according to which the Hatay became a separate political entity with statute and constitution, independent as regards home affairs, but in a customs and currency union with Syria, which was to manage its foreign affairs. The Hatay had no army, fortifications or conscription; a police force was in charge of law and order. Turkey received full rights to use the port of Alexandretta and together with France guaranteed the territorial integrity of the area. The League of Nations Council, through a French delegate elected by it, supervised the application of the statute and the constitution.

After a compromise regarding the language question— Turkish and Arabic were to be the official languages—and various further incidents (general strike in Alexandretta, clashes in Antiakije, Arab protestations in Damascus), the Turko-French treaty was ratified in June 1937. In November the new constitution of the Hatay came into force.

After that the dispute appeared to be settled, but in May 1938 the Turkish government protested at the League of

Nations against French propaganda in the Hatay; France promised to recognise the Turkish majority and a pact of friendship followed. The President and Prime Minister of Hatay were elected as members of the Turkish Kamutay in March 1939—an indication that Turkey hoped to incorporate the Hatay in the Republic in due course. In the negotiations for a Franco-Turkish agreement the Turks renewed their demand and declared that Axis propagandists claimed that the Turkish people were being invited to fight in favour of a French mandate over a Turkish-speaking area of which Turkey had been deprived. Finally the French government agreed to the cession of the Hatay on 23 July—that is, just a month after the signature of the Agreement.

THE BRITISH AND FRENCH GUARANTEES

The invasion of Albania by Italy and the intensified Nazi activity in the Balkans had a profound effect upon Turkish government opinion. A month after the invasion of Albania, the Prime Minister, in presenting the Pact to the Kamutay, stated that the government had sought to remain neutral but that the recent events had faced them with a situation in which neutrality was impossible. Turkey was not seeking to encircle anyone or to encroach upon any rights, but would try to prevent any further encroachment upon the rights of others. The statement made by Mr. Chamberlain in the House of Commons was that, pending the completion of a definite agreement, in the event of an act of aggression leading to war in the Mediterranean area (the two governments) 'would be prepared to co-operate effectively and to lend each other all the aid and assistance in their power'. Turkey also benefits under the British scheme for allowing export credits to friendly countries.

Six weeks later an agreement upon similar lines was reached between Turkey and France. This again was an

343

interim settlement pending the conclusion of a definitive agreement based on reciprocal guarantees. Some delay was caused in the negotiations by the question of the Hatay, which was, however, finally ceded to Turkey. The Turkish Prime Minister, in announcing the signature of the Agreement, declared that Britain, France and Turkey formed the one and only defence front against the storms which were likely to break in the Balkans, the Mediterranean and the Near East. The leaders of the government have made it clear that Turkey's loyalty to the Balkan Entente is in no way weakened by the system of guarantees and that her friendship with Soviet Russia is firmer than ever. Potemkin was given a very cordial reception on his visit to Ankara in April.

THE FUTURE OF TURKISH POLICY

It is clear that the immediate danger of Nazi and Fascist aggression has thus had a direct influence upon Turkey's foreign policy; it is also held in some quarters that her treatment of the Hatay question has shown a deviation from her former policy. For although her methods were peaceful she supported her claims in the early stages by military power and even by military threats.

Turkish foreign policy has clearly been modified by the immediate danger of Nazi and Fascist aggression. There has for some time been much concern in Syria that Turkey will now be tempted to follow a policy of imperialist expansion. Already there are fears that she has designs on Aleppo and the territory immediately south of the railway to Nusaybin, which are certainly not Turkish in population (see p. 265). If oil is not found in the borings at Van and elsewhere and is struck in northern Syria, this temptation may be irresistible. For the course of international events has placed Turkey in a strong position to make such demands at a time when France and Britain could not easily oppose.

Expansion into such non-Turkish territories might well, however, have serious consequences for Turkey. Mustafa Kemal, when laying the foundations of the new Turkey, clearly renounced all desire to incorporate Arab lands within the Turkish Republic. For he thought that discontented subjects in such territories would weaken rather than strengthen his country. Aggression of this kind would certainly antagonise the growing nationalism of the extensive Arab world. It would also arouse distrust among all Turkey's neighbours and would thus weaken her leadership in the Balkan entente and the West Asia Pact, which she has taken such pains to build up as effective barriers to European imperialism. It is to be hoped that Turkey herself will not thus turn from nationalism to imperialism.

6. CONCLUSIONS

To the superficial observer, Turkey may seem simply to be one more case of a 'totalitarian' régime. There is the single party, the Führer at its head; there is extreme nationalism; a state-planned and controlled economy; the fitting of the cultural and intellectual life into one pattern dictated by the state; and the hostility, or rather, in Turkey's case, the indifference, to religion.

Yet the analogy is deceptive. The origins of the Turkish régime differ profoundly from those of other governments of an apparently similar kind. Kamâl Atatürk was not a demagogue owing his position to a wild wave of mass enthusiasm and mass hatreds. He rose to command as the leader of the army in the fight for his country's independence. He had very little resistance to overcome at home, and very much abroad. As against the outside world, his régime was not one of expansion, but rather of retrenchment. At home it did not seek to arouse unscrupulous hatreds, however nationalist it might be.

The very social facts which underlie the rise of Fascism in other countries were completely absent in Turkey. There existed among the Anatolian Turks neither a bourgeoisie nor a proletariat, nor a class struggle between the peasantry and their landlords. The Turkish régime in the main is not the result of a deadlock in a struggle of hostile forces within the country. It is a natural growth, resulting from the need of swift adaptation on the part of Turkey to modern western standards, which was the most essential condition of her survival.

At present the régime is still completely absorbed in its task of developing the country and educating the people. As against this foremost duty, politics in the narrower meaning of the word play no great part. The forces which might aim at influencing the policy of the government in this or that direction according to their own sectional interests have not yet come to full stature. It is therefore difficult to forecast the course of events, once modern Turkey has outgrown her adolescence.

The fundamental difference between say Germany and Turkey becomes apparent in such questions as this: will state enterprise and state planning or private business get the upper hand in the end? In Germany such a question has a meaning because the two systems are struggling against one another. In Turkey the question has no real reference to the present state of things, because every available source of development whether private or public is being tapped to the utmost, and the cumulative efforts of state and private business always lag behind the achievements desired by both.

State banking and private banking, state industry and private industry, state trade and private trade are growing side by side without interfering with one another to any great extent, though the state naturally keeps in hand those positions which are essential for the control and planning of the whole process of development.

The encouragement of private industry has not had the results originally expected from it, and for this much more than for any other reason the state has now become more active in this sphere. But no attempt has been made to take trade in general out of the hands of private merchants, whose activities are encouraged even in the international field. Here is a class which may well grow with time both to wealth and influence. The amount of state organised agricultural credit, too, is considerably inferior to the amount of credits given by the local moneylenders without even so much as an attempt at state interference beyond a few general rules about maximum rates of interest. It must also be remembered that state interference in the matter of wages is not very significant.

A modern economic life, or an efficient army and administration, however, could not be built up if the state did not carry out a violent struggle against medievalism and did not force people by every method of compulsion to adapt themselves to the conditions of the 20th century. The sphere of state interference is thus very extensive in some directions.

A time may come when the bourgeoisie will start developing a large-scale industry and revolt against too much state interference. The peasant is becoming literate and may refuse to remain in his present wretched state. The workers, growing in numbers and importance, may put forward their own demands. If the administration refuses to respond to the claims which are bound to emerge as a result of its own encouragement, then it is conceivable that a conflict between the state and the various social forces may develop and lead to a more liberal régime, or a more thorough and one-sided dictatorship.

347

But at present there are no signs of this. So far the régime has been very sensitive to the real claims of the various groups, and by meeting them as part of the process of modernising the country, has strengthened rather than weakened its position. In a society where everybody is improving his lot and has room to develop, there is little scope for conflict. As far as can be judged, the régime is aware of the potential dangers of the development of a narrow oligarchy. During the first years of the Republic the higher positions were almost exclusively staffed with men who had played a predominant rôle in the War of Independence, and most of them were therefore drawn from the higher ranks of the army. But in recent years many men who had never been professional soldiers have reached the highest positions in the state. And as every inducement is held out to talented young men and women to embark upon an ambitious career through the universities, the basis of the ruling stratum of society is widening rather than narrowing.

Here, as in other respects, the problem is not to find a suitable job for a talented man, but to find the necessary number of people to cope with the enormous tasks facing the country. Recruitment for higher service and employment is still difficult owing to the poverty and ignorance of the masses; but these conditions are rapidly improving through the very efforts of the government. It is, therefore, perhaps not too daring a prophecy to maintain that for a considerable time to come the régime will continue substantially as it is, and not meet with any very serious opposition.

There exists one more factor which works in the same direction and may well in the end determine the character of modern Turkey. She is, like all other countries, forced to make tremendous efforts because of the international situation. If Turkey is to hold her own against the German drive towards the south-east and to attempt to play an independent part between Germany, the USSR, and the western Powers, she must be extremely well armed, well led, and economically strong. No private initiative could supply the enormous short-term efforts which this task involves. It is probably safe to predict that the international crisis will, in Turkey as elsewhere, strengthen the hand of the state as against the individual and sectional interests. And the effect must be very considerable in a country such as Turkey, with its relatively virgin conditions, where the state is already the paramount power. If Turkey, for a second time, is to be saved by the ruling Kemalist group, there is little doubt that this group will for a long time remain and become increasingly dominant in every walk of life.

It is certainly regrettable that Atatürk died prematurely, but whether even he could have stemmed the advance of the Germanic flood, rapidly moving in Turkey's direction, remains more than doubtful. If European civilisation falls into chaos, Turkey will suffer, too. But since she is still poor, she has little to lose but her hopes. The Turkish peasant, accustomed to war and poverty, will simply carry on as before, dragging along his wooden plough. If the international sky should brighten again, there is no reason why Turkey, with her natural resources, her determination, and her common sense, should not develop quickly and successfully into a modern country, well able to play an important rôle as the connecting link between Europe and Asia.

INDEX

YUGOSLAVIA—(*continued*)
    Economic structure of, 17 ff., 20 ff., 28, 32 ff.
        agrarian reform, 17 ff.
        co-operative farming, 20 f.
        foreign investments, 24 ff.
        foreign trade, 21 ff, 28, 87
        industry, 22 ff., 32
        natural resources, 22, 24 f.
        state enterprise, 23 f., 33 f., 63 f.
    Foreign policy of (*see* Little Entente, Balkan Entente), 53, 58 ff., 73 ff, 149, 152, 226
        external pressure on, 75 ff., 91 f.
        influence of Croat problem on, 74, 256
        inter-Balkan relations, 31, 53, 73–75, 77 ff., 83 f., 197–199, 202, 205, 213, 255, 335
    History of, 13 ff., 27
    Minority problems of (*see* Macedonia), 35 ff., 38, 94, 100, 265
    Religious differences in, 40, 56
    Social conditions in, 31 ff., 37 f., 63